DATE			

IMPROVING ECONOMIC AND SOCIAL COHESION IN THE EUROPEAN COMMUNITY

Proceedings of a conference organised by the Centre for European Policy Studies and sponsored by the Commission of the European Communities, the European Investment Bank, Gestifundo S.A., Portugal, and Sevillana de Electricidad S.A. Spain (22 June and 23 June 1992).

Also by Jørgen Mortensen

FEDERALISM VS. CO-ORDINATION: Macroeconomic Policy in the European Community

THE FUTURE OF PENSIONS IN THE EUROPEAN COMMUNITY (*editor*)

Improving Economic and Social Cohesion in the European Community

Edited by

Jørgen Mortensen

Senior Research Fellow
Head of the Financial Markets Unit
Centre for European Policy Studies
Brussels

St. Martin's Press

First published in Great Britain 1994 by
THE MACMILLAN PRESS LTD
Houndmills, Basingstoke, Hampshire RG21 2XS
and London
Companies and representatives
throughout the world

A catalogue record for this book is available
from the British Library.

ISBN 0–333–60875–5

Printed in Great Britain by
Antony Rowe Ltd
Chippenham, Wiltshire

First published in the United States of America 1994 by
Scholarly and Reference Division,
ST. MARTIN'S PRESS, INC.,
175 Fifth Avenue,
New York, N.Y. 10010

ISBN 0–312–12174–1

Library of Congress Cataloging-in-Publication Data
Improving economic and social cohesion in the European Community /
edited by Jørgen Mortensen.
p.   cm.
Includes index.
ISBN 0–312–12174–1
1. European Economic Community countries—Economic conditions–
–Regional disparities.   2. European Economic Community countries–
–Economic policy.   3. European Economic Community countries—Social
policy.   I. Mortensen, Jørgen.
HC241.2.I443   1994
338.94—dc20   94–1155
                                                          CIP

Contents

List of Contributors

Authors

Moreno Bertoldi is an administrator in Directorate-General XXII, Commission of the European Communities.

Andrea Boltho is Fellow and Tutor in Economics, Magdalen College, Oxford.

Nicos Christodoulakis is Vice-Rector of Athens University of Economics and Business.

Henning Christophersen is Vice-President of the Commission of the European Communities.

José Folgado Blanco is Professor of Applied Economics at the Universidad Autónoma de Madrid.

Philippe Goybet is Head of Division, Directorate-General XXII, Commission of the European Communities.

Eugenio Greppi is Head of Directorate, EC Operations, European Investment Bank, Luxembourg.

Ronnie Hall is Principal Administrator, Directorate-General XVI, Commission of the European Communities.

Alexander Italianer is Deputy Head of Unit (Economic Service), Directorate-General II, Commission of the European Communities.

Kieran Kennedy is Director of the Economic and Social Research Institute, Dublin.

Willem Molle is Director of the Nederlands Economisch Instituut, Rotterdam.

John Morley is Head of Unit (Structural Employment Policies and Labour Market), Directorate-General V, Commission of the European Communities.

Jørgen Mortensen is Senior Research Fellow at CEPS.

Jean Pisani-Ferry is Director of the Centre d'Etudes Prospectives et d'Informations Internationales, Paris.

Horst Reichenbach is Acting Director (Economic Service), Directorate-General II, Commission of the European Communities.

Bernhard Seidel is Head of Department of Public Finance at the Deutsches Institut für Wirtschaftsforschung, Berlin.

P. Bernd Spahn is Professor of Public Finance at the University of Frankfurt-am-Main.

Terry Ward is Director of Alphametrics Ltd.

Panel discussants

Iain Begg is Professor of Applied Economics at the University of Cambridge.

Eneko Landaburu Illarrimendi is Director-General of Directorate-General XVI, Commission of the European Communities.

Gavin McCrone is professor at the University of Glasgow.

Thomas O'Dwyer is Director of Directorate-General XVI, Commission of the European Communities.

Paul van den Bempt is a former Director, Directorate-General II, Commission of the European Communities.

Manfred Wegner is Director of the Institut für Wirtschaftsforschung, Halle.

INTRODUCTORY

1 Introduction

Jørgen Mortensen

The effects of economic integration

As Commission Vice-President Christophersen pointed out in his keynote speech to the CEPS conference which gave rise to this book, economic and social cohesion is not a new concept in the Community's policy-making framework. The Luxembourg and Rome Treaties made it clear that the European Community was not and should not be just an extended free-trade area but a framework for the formulation of common policies and a common legal order.

The elimination of barriers to the movement of goods, services, labour and capital has been a key objective of the Community since its inception. The objective was confirmed through the adoption of the Single Market Programme and the Single Act and again in Maastricht. However, the elimination of barriers has been accompanied all along the route towards European Union by efforts to strengthen solidarity between the member states. These efforts are based on the assumption that a balanced Community policy framework, in addition to policies to enhance efficiency and guarantee monetary and financial stability, must include policies aimed at improving equity through fiscal transfers from the richer to the poorer regions and member states. This was stressed in the MacDougall Report in the mid-1970s, the Padoa-Schioppa Report in 1987 and the Delors Report on EMU in 1989.

Yet the question of how economic integration resulting from the elimination of barriers may influence economic and social disparities within a trading area like the Community is, from a theoretical point of view, unresolved. As pointed out by Willem Molle in his chapter in this volume, the literature on the economics of integration is abundant but rather inconclusive as to the size and, above all, the distribution of welfare gains from trade.

Academic studies in general have concluded that trade liberalisation will have positive effects for both parties. Such effects are assumed, in particular, to result from the scope for productivity gains through specialisation and economies of scale. European Commission studies have also concluded that the elimination of barriers and monetary unification inside the EC would lead to overall welfare gains for the member states as a whole. The "costs of non-Europe" (Cecchini) Report suggested that the removal of the remaining non-tariff barriers to trade in goods and services within the Community could lead to significant efficiency gains and price reductions. Similarly, the move to full economic and monetary union, through the elimination of currency risks and exchange costs, would, according to the "One Market, One Money" studies, bring efficiency gains and cost reductions for consumers and non-financial firms.

In a comprehensive study of the impact of the internal market by industrial sector ("Social Europe"), the Commission has, however, also provided evidence that the gains and losses from the Single Market programme are likely to be unevenly distributed throughout the Community. For the most industrialised countries economic integration is already well advanced and production methods are similar. The same types of goods, but of different brands and qualities, are traded between them. The nature and quality of infrastructure, training levels and access to funding are relatively comparable. Hence, even in some weak sectors of these member states, there are firms which can export successfully and gain through access to a larger market. The more industrialised member states are therefore in a strong position to benefit from a greater market by an expansion of their output of goods and services, already growing fast at home.

The less industrialised member states have strong positions in labour-intensive sectors and a higher degree of specialisation in certain products. They are less involved in intra-sectoral trade and their products are often concentrated in categories where demand is growing slowly if at all. For these countries the elimination of technical barriers may allow an expansion of exports of products in which they are already well established. In order to realise these benefits, however, they must retain their competitiveness and avoid relative increases in their labour costs. Whether the process of integration will also bring an expansion of their production of R&D-intensive goods and services will, on the other hand, depend strongly on the overall framework and the strategy of firms in locating their productive activities. Here the less-industrialised countries are directly in competition with the "centre", where the supply of qualified labour and white-collar manpower is both abundant and sufficiently balanced to cover all categories needed.

Furthermore, as stressed in the chapter by Willem Molle, the process of economic and monetary integration is only part of a more general process of political integration. The "deepening" decided at Maastricht in December 1991 and confirmed at Edinburgh in December 1992, the creation of the European Economic Area, the possible enlargement of the Community, and the direction of co-operation with eastern and central Europe and the former USSR, are all building-blocks for a political framework within which decision-makers, both private and public, will operate and which will be decisive for the location of production and distribution facilities.

In this context it is striking to note that, as underlined by Molle, a large majority of the Community's citizens consider their country's EC membership to be a good thing. However, when it comes to assessing the effects on their personal lives, citizens are much less positive, frequently fearing that EC integration will reduce their income and employment opportunities. The fact that the Maastricht Treaty was rejected by the Danish electorate and accepted with only a narrow margin by the French has been interpreted by many observers as a sign that the public at large is becoming less enthusiastic about political integration and more concerned about immediate economic and social problems. This is confirmed by the wide public support for the inclusion of a "social dimension" in the Community policy framework. That the Danish electorate on 18 May 1993 accepted the Maastricht Treaty with the Edinburgh protocol was generally interpreted as an additional confirmation that the Community in future should pay more attention to the preoccupations of its ordinary citizens.

Whether the support for a social dimension to the EC integration can be taken as support for the redistribution of income involved in "economic and social cohesion" is, however, another matter. It is perhaps natural for citizens to be in favour of the social dimension to the extent that it has immediate benefits for themselves, and no more. No doubt citizens in general will need to be better informed both about the need for Community action with respect to economic and social cohesion, and about the effects of such policies, before widespread public support for such programmes can be counted upon. The difficulties in obtaining agreement on the EC's budgetary framework for the 1990s (the final agreement in Edinburgh provided for a lower level of expenditure than envisaged in the "Delors-II" package) also illustrate the serious political obstacles to the introduction of more substantial transfers between the rich and poor regions of the Community.

This book is aimed at improving public awareness of the problems of economic and social cohesion, of the Community policies to improve it, and the difficulties attending their acceptance.

Explaining regional and social inequalities

It should be stressed at the outset that the Community, compared to other integrated economies, is a highly-divergent trading zone. In fact, despite the relatively high degree of economic integration already achieved, divergence with respect to income and unemployment in the Community is much higher than in the United States. This is forcefully demonstrated in the chapter by

Andrea Boltho, which shows that the disparities with respect to GDP per capita are almost twice as high in the EC as in the USA and, with respect to unemployment, more than twice as high. More important still, labour mobility in the Community is much lower than in the United States, not only between but even within member states. In fact, in the early 1980s labour mobility was broadly two to three times higher in the United States than in West Germany or the UK. Consequently, the Community's labour force is much less willing or able to move from one region to another in reaction to changing employment opportunities and income differentials. Pockets of unemployment are therefore likely to persist longer and be more deeply entrenched in the Community than in an area with a more mobile labour force.

On the basis of these findings, Andrea Boltho concludes that the Community should be careful not to rush into economic union without adopting measures to improve member states' capacity to resist the shocks of integration. This would require not only policies to make wages more sensitive to local demand and supply conditions, but also countervailing fiscal policies to cope with the social consequences of large income differentials.

With the accession in 1981 of Greece and in 1986 of Spain and Portugal, the Community clearly reached a new geographical dimension. However, with these enlargements the overall degree of economic and social disparity and hence the need for such countervailing policies rose considerably. Entry into the Community nevertheless appears to have offered new possibilities for expansion in Spain and Portugal. As shown in the chapter by Ronnie Hall, these two countries have succeeded since 1986 in raising their GDP per head relative to the Community average. Meanwhile Greece, Ceuta and Melilla, Northern Ireland and part of the Italian Mezzogiorno fell further behind. On average, therefore, the regional disparities within the Community were not much reduced during the latter half of the 1980s. Moreover, the incorporation into the Community of the former German Democratic Republic entailed a significant increase in the overall degree of disparity within the EC. GDP per capita in the five new Länder in 1990 was less than 50% of the EC average and falling.

Disparities within the Community, however, are not just a matter of differences in the degree of industrialisation between regions. Part of the Community's social problem is rooted in areas which in the past rose to prominence through the coal and steel industries, but have since met considerable difficulties in adapting to new patterns of production and demand in the post-war European economy. As stressed in the chapter by John Morley and Terry Ward, high rates of unemployment within the Community are often found in these formerly highly-developed areas, now in industrial decline and in need of new ideas and initiatives. The combination of industrial decline and low labour mobility has led to a high level of long-term unemployment there. To deal appropriately with these problems, one must do more than simply pour money into these regions (the so-called "Objective 2" regions); there is, Morley and Ward argue, a need for an injection of creative energies and dynamism which will require enhanced training, even new cultural patterns.

For the Community as a whole, however, the principal "catching-up" problems are to be found in the periphery: Ireland, Greece, Portugal, Spain and the Mezzogiorno. Some of these special cases will be looked at in more detail in the following section.

Aspects of the catching-up process

For the Objective 1 and 2 regions as a whole, the challenge over the coming years is not just one of designing the most appropriate mix of catching-up strategies. In addition to attempting to reduce the income-gap with the rest of the EC, these regions must now prepare in earnest for monetary integration, notably the irrevocable fixing of exchange rates and possibly a single currency within the EC before the end of this century. Access to EMU, however, is conditional upon the fulfilment of the Maastricht criteria requiring conditions of sound public finance and fixing maximum levels of inflation and interest rates.[1] Unless their access to EMU is postponed until much later, the less-developed regions will be expected to carry out the monetary and budgetary stabilisation required for these criteria to be satisfied by the time the third phase of EMU is embarked upon. To achieve fast growth in output and employment while at the same time ensuring low budget deficits and low inflation should certainly be a feasible option for any economy. An accommodating monetary and budgetary policy may perhaps offer certain short-term gains in terms of output but, as demonstrated in research papers by the OECD and the EC Commission, must be expected to bring economic losses in a longer perspective. However, in part because they will have to cope with larger income differentials, the less-developed EC member states may encounter greater difficulties than the more-developed ones in reconciling the various targets of economic policy, notably under EMU conditions.

That economic and monetary integration might have beneficial effects on the less-developed regions of the Community was also underlined in the Delors Report. According to the Report, regions with lower wage levels would have an opportunity to attract modern and rapidly-growing service and manufacturing industries for which the choice of location would not necessarily be determined by transport costs, labour skills or market proximity. Still, the Report said, historical experience suggests that in the absence of countervailing policies, the overall impact on peripheral regions could be negative. EMU would thus increase the need for Community policies in the regional and structural field.

Although the Maastricht Treaty did not introduce a hierarchy into the convergence criteria, the rate of inflation is likely to weigh heavily in the decision as to which of the member states will be allowed into EMU at the beginning of phase three. In member states such as Greece and Portugal, which in 1992 were still recording cost and price increases well above the EC average, particular efforts will be needed over the 1990s to dampen inflationary pressures. For Spain and, notably, Ireland the inflation target appears to be easier to achieve.

Ireland

When Ireland joined the EC at the beginning of 1973, its GDP per capita was only half the average of the nine members of that time. Since then, its relative position has improved by about 10 points. However, as underlined by Kieran Kennedy, this improvement does not take account of the fact that the rise in employment has been much too slow to absorb the natural increase in the labour force, and despite large-scale emigration the rate of unemployment has increased from about 6% in 1973 to about 18% in 1992 - now one of the highest in the EC. There is no certainty, therefore, that Ireland is on a course towards convergence with its richer partners. Moreover, given that its growth performance has been accompanied by a pronounced rise in the rate of unemployment, the key issue for Ireland is not - or at least not only - to raise the rate of growth of GDP but to improve the capacity of the economy to generate a reduction in unemployment. With this in mind, Kennedy outlines four possible growth strategies: a) "Asian-style", with an increase in output of at least 6% for an extended period, b) "American style", with a lower overall growth but a high employment content, (c) "Scandinavian style", with a large non-market sector offering jobs to those who cannot sustain the speed of the market economy, and d) a high(er) rate of Irish emigration, to make the most of the free labour movement within the EC.

Each of these strategies, Kennedy points out, has its advantages and drawbacks. The high-growth strategy would hardly be feasible (because of the scale of the improvement in competitiveness that would be required) unless the rest of the EC also succeeded in improving its growth performance; the high-employment content strategy implies income disparities which may be difficult to accept in the domestic context; the Scandinavian strategy would be subject to financial constraints and therefore hardly be compatible with the continuation of the budgetary stabilisation undertaken by the Irish government since 1987. As far as large-scale emigration is concerned, a solution along these lines would no doubt result in an accelerated "brain drain" and make even more difficult the effort to increase the productivity and efficiency of the remaining population.

In any case, the strategies are not mutually exclusive and the final outcome may well involve a combination of elements of all four. Whatever the combination adopted (or imposed), the Community's Structural Funds will, in Kennedy's opinion, have a key role to play both in ensuring a smoother financing of the investment required to make certain policies operative and in enhancing the effectiveness of the measures adopted.

Greece

In Greece the adjustment problems are aggravated by the large government budget deficit. It is therefore legitimate to ask whether there is any chance at all of Greece being able to join the EMU within a reasonable time-horizon. In the opinion of Nicos Christodoulakis, the answer to this question can still be affirmative. In his chapter he puts forward two arguments in support of his view. First, although the budgetary disequilibrium in Greece is of worrying proportions, other EC member states, when faced with a similar deterioration in their public finances, have been able to implement financial-stabilisation programmes successfully. Second, according to the author, a large consensus exists in Greek public opinion in favour of European integration and the Maastricht Treaty. With efficient political and economic management this consensus can be built upon and transformed into support for national economic rehabilitation.

The author, however, not only takes the view that Greece can satisfy most of the convergence criteria at the beginning of phase three of EMU. In his opinion, Greece should make a credible commitment to an anti-inflation policy by rapidly joining the ERM. The gains from "forcing" inflation down through commitment to a higher degree of exchange-rate stability would, he thinks, largely outweigh the possible losses of autonomy in monetary policy. In addition, contrary to the argument put forward in many textbooks, Christodoulakis shows that a high rate of inflation results in revenue losses for Greek governments, thus aggravating the budget deficit (due to the fact that a large proportion of taxes are paid out of the previous rather than the current year's income). Thus the Greek authorities need not worry that a fall in inflation will aggravate the accumulation of public debt. In fact, he argues, the loss in seigniorage[2] resulting from the fall in inflation will be outweighed by a reduction in the loss of real taxes due to delays in their collection.

Opponents of EMU often argue that the loss of the ability to undertake exchange-rate changes vis-à-vis the other members of an economic and monetary union will reduce an economy's capacity to withstand shocks (sudden changes in external or internal supply conditions). Here again, Christodoulakis considers it an open question whether this loss would have serious consequences for Greece. In fact, he argues, most of the shocks which have occurred in the past or may occur in the future are *common* to all EC member states and therefore do not warrant exchange-rate adjustments *within* the group. In the rare cases when "country-specific" shocks occur, the countries most affected should, in Christodoulakis' opinion, be assisted by a special fund, as is often the case in existing economic and monetary unions.

Spain

When Spain entered the Community in 1986, it was just emerging from 10 years of sluggish output growth, a pronounced decline in employment and an increase in the rate of unemployment - from less than 3% of the labour force in the early 1970s to almost 22% in 1985. The Spanish growth performance during this period was, in fact, one of the poorest in Western Europe and Spanish GDP per capita measured against the average of the present twelve member states fell from 82% in 1975 to 72.5% in 1985.

During the first seven years of its EC membership, Spain made great progress towards reducing the income gap vis-à-vis the Community which had opened up during the previous ten years. As underlined in the chapter by José Folgado Blanco, the rapid Spanish growth was to some extent attributable to the favourable external environment: the fall in oil prices and the expansion in world trade. However, the fact that Spain succeeded in improving on its relative position was largely due to an emerging social consensus, ensuring a long period of stable labour costs, a high rate of investment profitability and a policy favouring a rapid integration of the Spanish economy into the Single Market. During the first years of Spanish EC membership the conditions for the latter process thus appeared to be largely satisfied.

However, according to Folgado Blanco, a conflict between stability and growth seems to have emerged since 1988. In fact, although the Spanish economy has been modernised in many respects, significant rigidities persist in the labour market and in many markets for goods and services. Moreover, the government appears, in his view, to have "lost the will to go on fighting for budgetary austerity". Consequently, monetary policy has had to cope with the task of keeping the expansion of domestic demand in check, with the result that interest rates have been pushed to an exorbitant level. This in turn has increased the cost of capital and held back business investment, endangering the future of the catching-up process.

In Folgado Blanco's opinion (and that of other contributors to this book), the solution to the emerging conflict between growth and stability can only be found if the profitability of business investment and the competitiveness of Spanish industry are ensured. The evolution of labour costs is in this respect a key factor. A macroeconomic policy geared to budgetary and monetary stability is another. Once these basic conditions are fulfilled, the Community's assistance through the Structural Funds and the new Cohesion Fund will constitute a complementary element, allowing the domestic economy to reap the full benefits of access to a wider continental market and be in a better position to face the more competitive climate in the Single Market.

Portugal

Much of the above reasoning concerning the Spanish situation and prospects applies with little or no modification to Portugal. As stressed by Francisco Torres in his oral presentation to the CEPS conference (not included here), the principal task of the Portuguese authorities in the coming years will be to promote structural changes and macroeconomic stability. This will require a reinforcement of market mechanisms so as to bring about a more efficient allocation of resources, and budgetary consolidation so as to reduce interest rates and, hence, the cost of investment. Only if these "regime changes" are implemented will Portugal, according to Torres' assessment, be able to obtain the full benefits of the assistance provided by the EC through the Structural Funds, the Cohesion Fund and EIB loans.

The design and impact of Community policies in favour of economic and social cohesion

From a theoretical standpoint, however, it is far from evident that Community action in favour of the least-developed regions will necessarily take the (present) form of subsidies to specific projects via the EC's budget. In fact, as shown by Bernd Spahn, a great deal of soul-searching is going on among the specialists in "fiscal federalism". This has led to a reconsideration of some of the traditional views on the distribution of tasks between the various levels of government.

With respect to the "allocation function" of government, Spahn argues that there is increasing doubt as to the direction and size of gains from centralisation. In particular, he argues, the scope for reaping returns to scale from centralisation may have been exaggerated in the past and this in turn may have led to considerable welfare losses through excessive centralisation. In addition, the costs of co-ordination in federal government have been overlooked and should be examined more carefully.

Concerning the "distribution function", Spahn stresses that the scope for and design of distributive policies must be seen within the general framework of migration of people and capital and of the incidence of taxation on income and consumption. In fact, citizens often "vote with their feet", the rich migrating from municipalities or regions with high redistributive taxation and the poor migrating to municipalities with a high level of public assistance. National redistributive schemes have most often been implemented with a view to dampening this migration or compensating its effect on the tax base of the local authorities. At the EC level, however, cultural and language barriers restrict migration and therefore also reduce the need for fiscal measures to deal with this particular effect of labour mobility. Where a certain degree of regional redistribution is, nevertheless, deemed necessary, this should not necessarily take the shape of centralised policies such as the present Structural Funds. In fact, according to Spahn, redistribution could conceivably also be effected via horizontal grants (directly from local authority to local authority) or in the form of pure transfers such as the German *Finanzausgleich*.

Last but not least, Bernd Spahn argues that the traditional view that a large central budget is needed to implement the "stabilisation function" has been seriously challenged in recent years. First, there is today less confidence than in the past in the effectiveness of central-government *discretionary* measures with the aim of influencing general economic activity. And although the usefulness of "automatic fiscal stabilisers" is still more widely recognised, such stabilisers could, according to Spahn, be allowed to operate at the local level. Thus they do not constitute a valid argument for the transfer of fiscal powers to a central authority. Spahn nevertheless sees scope for stabilisation policies aimed at absorbing "asymmetrical shocks", as proposed in the chapter by Italianer and Pisani-Ferry.

The assignment of policies to various levels of government, however, must take account not only of the assessment of the efficiency of allocation, redistribution and stabilisation functions but also (as already suggested) by the efficiency of the "assignment of taxes". In fact, the assignment of functions does not necessarily correspond to the most efficient assignment of taxes, which may well involve a need for vertical grants between levels of government (upwards or downwards depending upon circumstances). According to Spahn a certain number of taxes could usefully be collected at the EC level and the revenue then handed over to national or local authorities without necessarily serving to finance "common policies". This would be the case for a "carbon tax", for corporate cashflow taxation and the taxation of portfolio capital. In these cases he sees considerable scope for expanding the EC's role in the *collection* of taxes without a commensurate expansion of "ordinary" expenditure via the EC's budget (this of course would not exclude the possibility of fiscal transfers from the EC to member states or local (regional) authorities being designed with due regard for objectives concerning the redistribution of income).

As indicated above, there are today serious doubts as to the efficiency of using public budgets actively with the aim of smoothing out cyclical fluctuations in demand and output. This, in turn, also weakens the argument in favour of a large centralised EC budget. However, in case economic fluctuations are not of a cyclical nature but instead attributable to external or internal shocks, there could still be room for automatic or discretionary "stabilisation mechanisms" aimed at spreading the burden of adjustment over a larger trading zone. Whether or not this stabilisation function should be assigned to the EC budget or remain within the national budgets is, however, another question, the answer to which will depend to some extent on the exchange-rate regime in force.

The chapter by Italianer and Pisani-Ferry shows, first, that the need for (and warranted size of) stabilisation mechanisms at the level of the EC is smaller than sometimes believed. Secondly, it shows that in existing monetary unions the mechanisms are generally attributable to elements in the national budgets which are unlikely to be transferred to the EC budget in the foreseeable future (social expenditure and social security premiums). Thirdly (and here their argumentation joins that of Bernd Spahn), it shows that stabilisation policies aimed at smoothing the effects of asymmetrical shocks (those that hit one or a few regions) need not arise from a centralised EC budget but could be achieved through interregional transfers.

The quantitative analysis and the simulations undertaken by Italianer and Pisani-Ferry nevertheless show that an EC regional stabilisation mechanism providing approximately the same degree of smoothing-out as obtained through the federal budget of the United States would be feasible. In fact, a full stabilisation mechanism would only cost about 0.2% of the Community's GDP and a partial stabilisation mechanism even less.

In practice, however, both the definition of a shock and the more detailed design of the stabilisation mechanism would raise considerable conceptual problems. The authors have assumed that the size of shocks can be measured by the change in the rate of unemployment over and above the change in the EC average and that the stabilisation mechanism would be directly linked to the growth of GDP. This approach, although simple at a first glance, nevertheless leaves aside the possibility that the rise in unemployment may be due to excessively high increases in labour costs and/or labour-market rigidities. Taking such aspects into account would further reduce the warranted size of Community stabilisation mechanisms even under EMU to a tiny share of GDP.

The view expressed above, both by Spahn and by Italianer and Pisani-Ferry, that the Community's budget does not have to be large to be efficient, is also strongly subscribed to by Horst Reichenbach. In fact, according to Reichenbach, (i) existing federations should not be used mechanistically as models for the Community; (ii) more emphasis should be placed on the dangers and costs of centralisation than was contained in the MacDougall report;[3] (iii) the arguments for assigning expenditure functions to the EC's budget should be carefully examined with a view to determining in each case the costs and benefits of centralising the functions; and (iv) the justification for the assignment on efficiency grounds differs from that for the assignment on distributional gounds.

On efficiency grounds EC expenditure corresponding to about 0.1 to 0.2% of Community GDP would, according to Reichenbach, suffice to strengthen the economic efficiency of the completed internal market. Moreover, he sees no convincing argument for assuming that more would be needed in the third stage of economic and monetary union. Leaving aside market intervention, he sees an economic rationale for Community spending on environmental protection, Europe-wide infrastructure, research and development and, to a lesser extent, higher education.

With respect to the expenditure assignment on equity grounds, Reichenbach takes as his point of departure the Commission's 1992 proposals involving an increase in the budget appropriations to structural operations (the Structural Funds and the Cohesion Fund) to 0.47% of Community GDP in the period up to 1997. Although the Commission's plan was scaled down somewhat at the Edinburgh summit in December 1992, the total expenditure under this item would still involve transfers to the less-developed regions which are substantially higher (in proportion to their GDP) than the amounts disbursed to Western Europe by the Marshall Fund in the immediate post-war years.[4] The structural operations are thus already significant components of the policies to promote interregional equity and their importance will grow even further in the coming years.

As underlined by Reichenbach, however, it is not enough just to pour money into the less-industrialised regions. In fact, the desired reduction of regional disparities can only be attained if Community assistance improves the growth potential of the regions concerned. For this to be the case, the operations of the Funds must be subject to ex-ante evaluations and permanent monitoring. Moreover, there could be a case for positive economic conditionality. The Cohesion Fund will make transfers available when member states embark on a path of budget discipline. For the Structural Funds, incorporation into the Community Support Framework of commitments to concrete policy measures aimed at improving supply-side performances would be useful supplements to the existing additionality requirement.

While the Community's Structural Funds clearly help to reduce regional income differentials within the Community, other parts of Community expenditure in fact tend to aggravate such differentials. As shown in the chapter by Bernhard Seidel, the CAP guarantee payments for sugar, cereals, milk, oilseeds and beef (accounting for a total of 70% of this expenditure) in general favour the richer regions of the Community. Only in tobacco, olive oil, sheep- and goat-meat and - to a lesser extent - wine, fruit and vegetables (accounting for less than 20% of expenditure) are the poorer regions of the Community favoured to any extent. According to Seidel, therefore, if the Community is to achieve its aims of economic and social cohesion, a stronger concentration of funds on backward regions appears necessary. In particular, this would require cutting back guaranteed price levels under the CAP and greater stress on regional differentiation in agricultural policy, as envisaged in the CAP reform now under way.

The methodology and preliminary results of an assessment of the Structural Funds' impact on regional income differentials and the growth potential of the backward regions are dealt with in the chapter by Philippe Goybet and Moreno Bertoldi. According to these two authors, the Structural Funds do indeed make a significant contribution to promoting economic activity in the areas concerned. Furthermore, they have a high potential efficiency which, if exploited, can improve the regions' relative growth performance in the longer run. However, due to insufficient microeconomic data, it is impossible to tell whether the Funds' potential is fully exploited or not. But at least the reform of the Funds (undertaken in 1988/89) has helped significantly to improve the efficiency of their planning, management and financing procedures.

Like Horst Reichenbach, however, Goybet and Bertoldi raise some questions concerning the interaction between the Structural Funds and macroeconomic conditions in general. But while Reichenbach suggests making the attribution of the Funds conditional on the fulfilment of criteria with respect to convergence and supply-side policies, Goybet and Bertoldi are concerned with a potential conflict between objectives. In fact, they wonder whether there is not a contradiction between the need for budgetary discipline on the one hand and the principle of "additionality"[5] on the other. With some satisfaction, they note that the new Cohesion Fund is not subject to the additionality rule, thus allowing the beneficiaries to adopt stringent budgetary policies without being forced to weaken or reduce national development expenditure. The Cohesion Fund, once in operation, should therefore help the less-developed regions to realise their growth potential more fully and yet satisfy the convergence criteria fixed in the Maastricht Treaty.

Although the grants and transfers effected via the Community budget are essential elements in the efforts to improve economic and social cohesion, a significant part of national investment is financed through borrowing. The European Investment Bank here has a key role to play, both as a source of funds and as a catalyst for other resources and a link to financial markets in general. As stressed by Eugenio Greppi, the EIB has accumulated a stock of experience which is useful for the assessment of new projects and may thereby serve as a guide both to regional authorities seeking funds and to financial institutions participating in financial engineering in the regions concerned. The EIB, thus, to a significant extent, if only for the projects benefiting from EIB loans, contributes to the ex-ante evaluation of development plans called for by other authors in this book.

However, as stressed forcefully by Eneko Landaburu Illarramendi (Director-General of Regional Policy) in the course of the concluding panel discussion at the CEPS conference, the action of the Structural Funds should not be assessed solely in economic terms but seen as necessary building blocks in the political union. Nevertheless, the economic efficiency of the Funds remains an important aspect and during the coming years the Community will be faced with the challenges of expanding the budget attributions of the Structural Funds while seeking to enhance their efficiency as much as possible. Mr. Illarramendi called in this context for clearer and more precise justification of the use of funds and the objectives pursued, and for a focus of efforts on fields where a high degree of efficiency can be expected and proved. He also expressed the wish that the representatives of regional and national authority would personally become more involved in formulating development policies. Although increased involvement would cause additional problems of co-ordination, the end results would be likely to be positive through an enhanced perception of the scope and aims of interregional cooperation.

The need for a closer involvement of regional authorities was also underlined by Thomas O'Dwyer (Director-General, Co-ordination of Structural Funds). He saw this involvement not just as a means to respect the principle of subsidiarity but more generally as a way to improve the efficiency of the action of the Funds. A closer contact with local groups and decision-makers could in particular, in his view, help to increase the effectiveness of measures aimed at combating unemployment.

Finally, the success of policies in favour of economic and social cohesion is not and cannot be determined by the amount of public funds being pumped into the regions concerned. In the end, the degree of success or failure will depend upon the capacity of such programmes to mobilise the creative and dynamic forces in the economy around new ideas and new initiatives. The firm is the place where these forces express themselves and it therefore has a key role to play as a partner in the promotion of economic and social cohesion. Thus, as underlined by José Antonio Aguirre and by Joâo Oliviera Rendeiro (in contributions not included here), it is only through the harmonisation and interaction of public and private action that the creation of wealth and employment can be guaranteed and economic and social cohesion in the Community enhanced.

NOTES

1. According to the Maastricht Treaty Protocols, governments may not have an "excessive" deficit. This is decided by reference to whether the general government budget deficit exceeds 3% of GDP and whether the ratio of public debt to GDP exceeds 60% without sufficiently declining; the rate of inflation, as observed over a period of one year prior to the examination, should not exceed by more than one and a half points that of the three best-performing member states; a member state must have respected the normal fluctuation margin of the ERM without severe tensions for at least two years; and the nominal long-term interest rate must, over a period of one year, not exceed that of the three best-performing member states by more than two percentage points.

2. The gains accruing to the state or the central bank through the issuing of non-interest-bearing money or "near-money".

3. The report on "The Role of Public Finance in European Integration" published in 1975, which argued that only when Community spending had been raised to some 8-10% of EC GDP could the EC's budget fulfil its allocative, redistributive and stabilising functions.

4. The Marshall Plan involved grants from the United States to Western Europe amounting to about 1% of US GDP over a four-year period, 1948-51, or a cumulative 4%. The annual transfers over the EC's budget are smaller but extend over a longer period.

5. The rule that Community funds must be matched by approximate equivalent amounts of national funds.

2 Cohesion policy before and after Maastricht

Henning Christophersen

Economic and social cohesion is one of the most important objectives of the European Community. It lies, in the Commission's view, at the very heart of European integration.

The aim of solidarity with our fellow citizens and the less-favoured regions did not spring up by magic at Maastricht. The Treaty of Rome mentioned it as part of a concern for the harmonious development of Community territory, and the Single European Act consolidated that aspiration, devoting a section to economic and social cohesion.

The theme, moreover, goes much further than the Structural Funds. The Single Act called on the member states to create a favourable economic environment by implementing suitable economic policies for cohesion, and on the Commission to foster it by the application of common policies and the achievement of the internal market.

Despite this, there has been a tendency to expect the reform of the Structural Funds and the increased budget allocations to solve all the difficulties of the less-favoured regions and groups, and this could not be allowed to continue. Accordingly, the Maastricht Treaty further reinforced the commitment to economic and social cohesion, which was confirmed as one of the cornerstones of the Community. This was done by strengthening the articles of the Treaty relating to the subject, by a specific protocol annexed to the Treaty and by provisions for the creation of a Cohesion Fund.

Structural policies: the mid-term review and beyond

According to initial assessments, the reform of the Structural Funds undertaken from 1989 onwards has had positive results. Structural policies have opened the way to greater economic and social cohesion, provided the necessary impetus and enabled significant progress to be made.

The funds available in 1989-91 have been almost totally used up. The prospects for 1992-93 are also favourable. A more detailed examination supports this assessment. In the regions lagging behind in development (Objective 1 of the Structural Funds), efforts to strengthen cohesion focus on providing better access to isolated areas by improving their basic infrastructure; strengthening productive sectors; improving human potential through training programmes; and making the most of agricultural, fishing and other local resources. Work to assess progress shows that these priorities of the Community Support Frameworks suitably reflect the major problems of structural adjustment in these regions.

The financial transfers benefiting the least prosperous regions are very significant - accounting for approximately 3% of GNP in certain member states. Their economic effects are indisputable. Community aid should help to create about 350,000 jobs in these regions over the period 1989-93.

Measures in areas affected by industrial decline (Objective 2) play a vital role and have provided generally satisfactory results. The allocation of resources has been in line with the problems of those regions, aimed primarily at economic diversification and the creation of alternative job opportunities, in order to renew their economic fabric. More stress has therefore been laid on the development of firms and vocational training than on infrastructure alone (as was previously the case), linked with co-financing from the European Regional Development Fund.

The evaluation of measures implemented under Objectives 3 and 4 shows that aid to training has enhanced Community policies to assist the long-term unemployed and to help young people find their first job. These measures still seem inadequate, however, given all the problems on the labour market. Moreover, Community financial resources still account for only a small percentage compared with national public expenditure on practical measures to increase employment (between 3% and 11% depending on the member state).

Operations part-financed under Objective 5a are a significant aspect of Community support for the process of adapting and modernising agriculture. They contribute substantially to new investment in agricultural holdings and in the initial processing and marketing of agricultural products. Aid to investment in agricultural holdings has, however, been adapted to fit in with market-management measures to reduce agricultural surpluses. It has therefore been channelled to a large extent to smaller holdings and those in less-favoured areas. As for rural development measures under Objective 5b, though they are recent and subject to financial limits their successful application has shown up an indisputable need and responded to deep-seated expectations.

In addition to the five objectives of the reformed Structural Funds, German unification has spurred the Community to efforts to facilitate the integration of the five new Länder and East Berlin. Implementation is broadly following the application of the reform in countries covered by Objective 1. Although the number of unemployed is still rising in the former East Germany, its economy has already begun to recover.

Funds available for Community Initiatives have been limited; in several cases the critical mass necessary to achieve the desired objectives has not been reached. But the Initiatives have proven a valuable addition to the Community Support Frameworks, particularly in cases of cross-border co-operation (*INTERREG*) and rural development (*LEADER*), and many have been substantially over-subscribed.

Funding in the framework of cohesion also has positive effects throughout the Community thanks to the flow of trade. Measures under the Community Support Frameworks will bring about an increase in direct imports of products from other member states into the regions concerned. The Commission estimates that for every 100 Ecu spent on investment in Objective 1 regions of Ireland, Portugal, Spain, and Greece, between 16 and 46 Ecu return in the form of imports. Furthermore, analysis has shown that insofar as it encourages investment over consumption, Community aid does not bring about structural or lasting dependence on the wealthiest countries.

Community structural policies create the conditions for a progressive reduction in such intervention. However, to achieve that aim, certain critical thresholds in terms of infrastructure, skills, capital and production technology must be reached, and these are far from being reached in most regions receiving Community aid, as was demonstrated in the mid-term review. The 1988 reform laid down new rules for the way the Structural Funds should operate, introducing the fundamental principles of concentration, planning, partnership and 'additionality'. These principles are sound and have proved their worth. The Funds should therefore continue to operate on the basis of them in the future.

Certain improvements are nevertheless necessary to increase the effectiveness of the Community's structural policies. We need to further simplify decision-making procedures, to improve integration between structural instruments, and to strengthen the complementarity between Community and national measures. The Community-member state partnership must be developed and enhanced in conjunction with trades unions and employers and the regional and local authorities. Thorough monitoring, systematic evaluation and greater flexibility, including the modulation of interest rates to meet real needs, are also on the agenda in line with the Maastricht protocol on cohesion.

Lastly, an improvement in financial channels between the Community and the recipients, which is currently the subject of an in-depth examination by the Commission staff and the member states, is indispensable if the effectiveness of Community action is to be enhanced.

Cohesion policy after Maastricht

The completion of the internal market has been flanked by a vast gesture of solidarity within the Community. Through the Structural Funds the Community has transferred a volume of resources to the poor areas of the Community - in particular to Greece, Spain, Portugal and Ireland - which over the period 1987-1993 alone will dwarf the Marshall Plan. This solidarity will be continued and reinforced in the future.

The poorer member states and regions of the Community need support as they seek to move closer to the Community's average standard of living and prepare for participation in Economic and Monetary Union. In this context the new Cohesion Fund planned at Maastricht merits particular attention. The Structural Funds have been, and will continue to be, the main Community instrument for narrowing the gap between the richer and the poorer regions of the Community. The Cohesion Fund is much more than a mere addition to this instrument. It constitutes a first attempt to establish a budget-transfer mechanism related to economic performance within the multilateral surveillance system of economic convergence, specifically targeting member states rather than regions.

Assistance from the Fund will be precisely targeted on those areas of the weaker member states' economies which give rise to significant structural handicaps and delay the integration process. Through investment in transport networks and projects to assist these member states to live up to the Community's high environmental standards, the Fund could well become a key instrument in the process of achieving cohesion.

But economic and social cohesion must also be seen in the light of the future role of Europe and the Community to which the Maastricht Treaty aspires. A concerted effort is needed in research and technological development to reinforce the competitiveness of all our industries and assure a continued European presence in the closest-fought world markets. The new tasks of the Structural Funds are part of the response to this challenge.

It would be a tragic irony if we were to succeed in removing our internal frontiers, complete the single market, build Economic and Monetary Union and reduce gaps in our living standards, only to be left behind by our American and Japanese rivals for lack of ability to compete in the most advanced and profitable markets. That would jeopardise our efforts to achieve cohesion - indeed put that objective back years. More money would then have to be spent on foreign affairs and on our moral and political commitments towards our closest neighbours. In the Commission's estimation this last item would more than double in the years up to 1997.

The Maastricht Treaty will strengthen co-operation in the field of foreign and security policy. This element was added to the Treaty text by the intergovernmental conference at a time when the Berlin Wall was crumbling and post-war Europe as we knew it was ceasing to exist. German unification, the dismantling of the Soviet Union and civil war in Yugoslavia have completely changed the picture of Cold-War Europe to which we were used. The Warsaw Pact and COMECON have disappeared.

In this situation, where Europe is undergoing major changes and where the European Community and NATO are the only solid and efficient forms of co-operation which remain, it is of the utmost importance that the Community be able to speak with one voice. This is hinted at in the Maastricht Treaty, though nothing is settled yet. The member states have already scheduled an intergovernmental conference starting in 1996 to deal with these matters.

Meanwhile EFTA countries knock on our door. The single market with all its economic benefits will be extended to them by way of the European Economic Area Agreement. But for some - Austria, Sweden, Switzerland, Finland and possibly Norway - the EEA Agreement is not enough. They want more. They want influence, which can only be obtained as a full member of the Union. This means full participation in all aspects of all Community policies.

Application for membership can mean only one thing: application for membership of the Union. This is specifically recognised in the Treaty of Maastricht. Until the new Treaty is ratified there can be no opening of negotiations on enlargement of the Community.

It is clear that all these elements go hand-in-hand. Europe must take decisive steps to confirm its internal solidarity and live up to the many expectations placed on it by ourselves, our neighbours and the world.

3 European integration: economic analysis and social reality

Willem Molle

1. Introduction

In 1952, at the opening of the intergovernmental conference on the establishment of the European Coal and Steel Community, Jean Monnet spoke the historic words: "Nous sommes là pour accomplir une oeuvre commune, non pour négocier des avantages mais pour rechercher notre avantage dans l'avantage commun". In his view this common advantage was the safeguarding of peace through the mutual economic dependence of the members of a strong supranational institution. In practical policy-making the attention has shifted from common advantages to member-country advantages. This is only logical as the cohesion of the EC is based on a fair distribution of cost and benefits.

In the course of time some have limited the meaning of the advantages and disadvantages (or costs and benefits) of the EC to its member countries to the mere receipts from and payments to the common budget. Others have broadened the notion of costs and benefits to include the safeguarding of democratic forms of government, economic and social cohesion, and a host of other worthy aims, indicated in article 3b of the Maastricht Treaty. In this chapter I shall try to give a picture of the distribution of economic costs and benefits of the integration that has taken place in the European Community, steering a middle course between the two extreme views cited. I shall focus on the element underlying the whole discussion, that is the contribution of integration to economic welfare. I shall make a distinction between the results of market integration (the so-called four freedoms) and policy integration, using the empirical economic studies that have been made.

Empirical economic studies showing what net economic benefits integration brings to the constituent parts of the EC may convince an academic audience. Other pieces of evidence, however, that are part of *social reality* are needed to convince the general public. Indeed, the economic restructuring of a particular sector of activity may be perceived as a benefit by an economist, while signifying a loss of employment to the specific groups engaged in that activity. The former sees the long-term benefits of integration, the latter the short-term adaptation costs. In the final section of this chapter I shall therefore attempt to close the gap between empirical economics and social reality.

2. Welfare gains

2.1 Markets

Effects

Economic integration proceeds in the first instance by the elimination of barriers to the free movement of products and production factors between member countries. The EC, in the forty years of its existence, has gone through several stages and has recently attained the almost complete integration of its markets. Throughout this period economists have tried to come to grips with the methodological challenge of estimating the effects of market integration on welfare levels.

The theory of economic integration (Molle 1990, chs. 2-7) shows how the elimination of barriers to the movement of goods, services and production factors can bring greater efficiency and hence greater welfare. It also indicates the factors that determine the distribution of this increased welfare over the various countries involved, and within these countries over categories of income earner. However, it has not been easy to translate these theoretical notions into operational approaches (Molle 1990, chs. 8-10). I shall describe here in chronological order the progress along this road and the findings of different studies into the effects of market integration in the EC.

Static macro effects

One of the first to analyse the problem of the effects of integration of goods markets on trade, production and income was Verdoorn (1952). In his path-breaking study he found that free trade in Europe would have a positive, albeit rather limited effect on the region's GDP.

In the 1970's some economists (e.g. Balassa 1975) followed an approach indicated by Viner to analyse the static effects of the setting-up of the Common Market. Similar studies have been made of the static effects of the enlargement of the EC to include the UK (Balassa 1975, Miller and Spencer 1977) and Spain (Viaene 1982). However, the main conclusion of these studies - that there was a positive net effect on welfare in all partner countries - was not very significant because the static approach did not include the supposedly more important dynamic effects of the liberalisation of goods, services, labour and capital movements.

Microeconomics

Another type of study, focusing on microeconomic aspects, suggested that the dynamic effects of the liberalisation of goods markets were very significant. These effects result from the structural adaptation of firms to new competitive conditions, through product specialisation, the introduction of new technology, the exploitation of economies of scale and the reorganisation of production and distribution facilities. The advantage of market integration to EC firms was demonstrated by their enhanced competitiveness on both international and domestic markets. However, it is difficult to assess the results of these studies in terms of total increased welfare.

An interesting aspect of some such studies is that the increased welfare seems to have been rather well distributed over the Community countries. The study by Owen (1983) of the EC white goods industry showed how Italian firms have been able to exploit their innovation advantages due to the access they have gained to the markets of other member countries.

Studies of foreign direct investment shed light on the advantages of integration in both goods and capital markets. The attraction of the integrated EC market to outside investors is illustrative in this respect. The rate of growth of US direct investment in the UK, for instance, was equal to that of the EC in the period 1950-58. It dropped to about half that of the EC in the period 1958-73, during which the UK was not yet a member of the Community. The rates became equal again after the UK's accession to the EC (Whichart 1981).

As for Greece, Spain and Portugal, these countries' incoming direct investment from the EC and beyond has increased very quickly since their accession. This investment, triggered by European integration, has helped their catching-up by the renewal of their production structures, creating a number of dynamic effects (see for Portugal Buckley and Artisien 1987, and for Greece Petrochilos 1989).

Combinations with macroeconomics

In the 1980's some analysts tried to overcome the disadvantages of the microeconomic approach by one taking more account of macroeconomic aspects. Márquez Méndez (1986), for instance, was able to quantify a number of macroeconomic effects better than those who had followed the Vinerian analysis before him. However, there were drawbacks to this method as well, among them doubts about the accuracy of individual country results - and accuracy on that score is essential for studying cohesion effects.

In order to overcome the disadvantages of all these approaches, analysts of the effects of the completion of the internal market have followed a combination of macro and micro approaches. The series of studies into the "cost of non-Europe" (Emerson 1988) indicated that the effects of this package of integration measures could be estimated at one percentage point extra growth per year. This result has been questioned, however, on the grounds that the method followed was a rather inadequate way to measure the most important dynamic effects.

General equilibrium analysis

Recently improvements have been made by applying general equilibrium analysis (Smith and Venables 1988) and introducing expectations of economic actors into the models (Baldwin and Lyons 1991), leading to an upward correction of growth effects. An application of general equilibrium modelling (Gasiorek et al., 1992) to the effects of trade liberalisation in the 1992 programme shows not only that the net effects are positive, but also that they tend to be distributed in a way which favours cohesion. Indeed, the welfare gains that result from the model are largest where labour is cheap and industrial concentration high (in particular in Spain, Portugal, Greece and Ireland, which display welfare gains of around 2% of GDP).

General equilibrium models have also proven their utility in calculating the effects of enlarging the Community. For instance, the trade effects of the integration of the EFTA countries through the new European Economic Area (which boils down to the integration of EFTA into the trade system of the EC) are very positive for all trading areas in the world (Haaland and Norman 1992). The magnitude of the effects, however, differs according to partners and sectors. As far as differentiation by country is concerned, one observes that the effects are highest for EFTA, average for the EC, and small for other countries. With respect to particular sectors, the model shows that EFTA trade would have stood to lose very heavily, owing to the increased competitiveness of EC industry, if EFTA had not chosen to enter the EEA scheme.

Conclusion

This review shows that it has taken some time for economists to specify and quantify satisfactorily the negative and positive effects of market integration. Both the studies for particular industries and those for the economy as a whole show that the net effects of integration are positive for all member countries. This is not, however, the whole story; a study is still needed that clearly indicates how far the growth rate of each member state has been dependent on integration of both product and production-factor markets.

Fortunately, politicians have not waited to take the necessary decisions on further integration until economists were ready with their homework on its effects. On the basis of the economists' provisionally positive results and the practical experience of the business community, they have taken important decisions on further integration and the liberalisation of the movement of goods, services and production factors between EC countries.

2.2 Policy

In the mixed economies of the Western world, governments have essential tasks to fulfil, including creating the conditions for an efficiently-functioning economy and an equitable income distribution. Market integration on the Community level must therefore be followed by policy integration on the same level.

In the past forty years Europe has gone through a number of stages of policy integration. Recently the process has accelerated, as can be deduced by the casual observer from such simple indicators as the growth in the number of civil servants at the European Commission. But has this increased integration also given us more wealth? Let us briefly look at a few fields of policy-making and return to the basic questions. First, are there positive effects of policy integration? To answer that we have to look for the efficacy of a policy; however, the costs and benefits are not always easy to identify. Second, have these positive effects been maximised?

The higher the quality of economists' input into this policy design, the greater the chances of a positive answer to these questions. A critical examination (Wegner 1989) of the role of economists in the work of the Commission came to a positive conclusion. For its part, the Commission has always sought the views of economists before defining its own position.

Important examples are to be found in the reports that have preceded a further deepening of integration, such as Spaak (1956) and Cecchini (1988) on the Common (and internal) Market and Werner (1970), MacDougall (1977), Padoa-Schioppa (1987), and Delors (1989) on Economic and Monetary Union. Although the persons who gave their names to these reports were politicians, the content of the reports was largely the work of economists.

However, in the final analysis a choice has sometimes been made in which economic considerations have been sacrificed to political necessities. This has had implications for integration. In the next sections I shall briefly analyse how this has affected the major areas of policy-making.

Allocation

The first area that is relevant in this respect is that of allocation policies, aimed at creating the conditions for an efficient functioning of productive activities in the integrated market. This covers, for example, competition policy and the co-ordination of indirect taxation. Assessing the effects of this type of policy is not easy. In a sense the effects are included in the effects of market integration: a partial fulfilment of the conditions set leads to partial market integration.

The next question concerns whether these internal policies are efficiently designed or whether the EC economy is saddled with inadequate structures. Monnet, in his time, brought the contracting parties to accept a structure for the Community that combined strong interdependence between the member states with strong institutions. As he put it: "La Communauté est une méthode pour réunir les peuples, la zone de libre échange est un arrangement commercial." That political statement cut short the debate among economists about the advantages of a broad zone of free trade over a smaller zone of trade and policy integration.

Monnet did, however, leave room for economists to define the most efficient design of the policies governing the functioning of the common market. As President of the High Authority, Monnet was confronted with a major political dilemma on value-added taxes. He brought in Tinbergen to preside over a commission charged with finding a solution. The economic conclusions of its report (1953) were followed in the rules that were subsequently established.

Observers agree that this is not an isolated case, and that the design of internal-market policy has in general followed good economic principles and practices. To start with, the EC has chosen an economic order that puts decisions concerning production, consumption, and investment into private hands. Exceptions to this persisted until recently in manufacturing and services, and created much inefficiency. A number of them have been abolished under the internal market programme or for other economic reasons (Emerson et al., 1988). I may cite here the case of transport, where among others a report by Klaassen was used as evidence in the case judged by the European Court (ECJ 1985). For other sectors studies with a similar message can be cited (see Pelkmans 1986, Pelkmans and Winters 1988). In agriculture, the persistent dominance of sectoral interests (supported by powerful political lobbies), over the general interest (defended by economists), has led to gigantic inefficiencies. Fortunately, here too the beginning of a solution is in sight.

Another relevant policy-area in this respect is competition. Although the EC rules are considered sound, there are some misgivings about the way they are applied. Indeed, the Commission has found it particularly difficult to prevent governments from supporting their national industries with considerable amounts of subsidies (CEC 1991a).

Finally, taxation policy should be mentioned. Harmonisation of value-added and excise taxes (needed for the smooth functioning of goods markets), and of deposit and corporate taxes (needed for the good functioning of capital markets) has gradually developed. Minimum rates have been agreed, to prevent the negative effects of intra-EC tax competition, on the one hand, and leave room for different national priorities on the other. The lack of mobility of labour means that personal income taxes and social security systems have been subject to only a very rudimentary form of harmonisation. The combination of rigour where necessary and flexibility where possible is an efficient way to make policy.

Stabilisation
In a period when economists were hopelessly divided concerning the advantages of monetary union over a system of free-floating exchange rates, while seeking the best route to monetary stability, three statesmen broke the deadlock. Giscard, Schmidt and Jenkins, seconded by economists like Clappier, Schulman and Emerson, proposed the European Monetary System as a means to stabilise exchange rates.

For a while the EMS met with much criticism of its operating procedures and much scepticism as to its chances of ultimate success. Gradually, however, in the light of practical experience, the conviction grew among economists that the System had certain advantages. The attention then shifted to the conditions under which successful operation could be guaranteed (De Grauwe 1989). Recently the advantages have been stressed to the extent of forgetting some inherent weaknesses in the set-up, as witness the following citation: "Now it is unanimously agreed that the EMS has succeeded far beyond the hopes of even its most fervent advocates in fulfilling the essential function of any exchange-rate system, that is to stabilise real exchange rates within the European Community at competitive levels, consonant with desirable capital movements from its more developed to its less developed participating countries" (Triffin 1992). Now, after the monetary upheaval of 1992 the problems of the chosen system are again getting much attention.

The next step on the integration road implies the creation of an Economic and Monetary Union, with a common currency as centrepiece. Does that spell economic misfortune or clear-cut advantages? In the study "One Market, One Money" (CEC, 1990) a combination of micro and macro approaches was followed in order to assess the various effects of monetary and accompanying economic integration. The results of this study suggested considerable net advantages. They are in line with the everyday experience of business in the EC.

One problem that remains is the need for national macroeconomic and budgetary policies to converge in order to sustain the monetary union. Here the debate among economists about the ways to safeguard a consistent set-up of the system while preserving the potential for growth of low-income countries, has not yet resulted in a consensus. The choice enshrined in the Maastricht Treaty may, however, prove to be another case of decisive politicians cutting short an indecisive debate among economists.

Redistribution
The distribution of the welfare that results from the production process is not always socially acceptable or economically efficient. A policy is therefore needed to correct the outcome of the play of market forces and to arrive at a more equitable and efficient distribution of wealth over social groups and countries - or, at least, one which limits the disparities to a level at which groups feel it worthwhile to continue to belong to the EC.

Redistribution policy brings positive effects to economic welfare in two ways. First, because resources that were not, or not fully, used begin to make a greater contribution to the production process. Second, because social stability enhances economic growth. The EC has developed a cohesion policy with, as an instrument, the considerable resources of the Structural Funds. There are many signs of the beneficial effect of EC redistribution policies in less-developed areas of the Community. However, economists find it difficult to measure the contribution which redistribution has made to the growth of each member country, or to more balanced growth in the Community's economy as a whole (Márquez Méndez 1990).

Economic reasoning has suggested the choice of a relatively efficient form for EC redistribution policies. The central element of the system is support given through the Structural Funds to countries and groups to remove structural weaknesses in their productive capacities or local circumstances. However, the implementation of the policy has been open to criticism. As the European Court of Auditors has often remarked, support for individual projects is not always provided in the most efficient way. One must also remember that the EC tended to itself take away much of the positive effect of this redistribution, because the Common Agricultural Policy favours the richer states.

External relations

The integrated external policies with respect to goods, services, labour and capital bring advantages in several ways. For example, they permit the EC to weigh more heavily in international negotiations. However, it is difficult to measure these advantages precisely.

The manner in which the external policies have been designed can be considered relatively efficient. The EC market is relatively open to products from other parts of the world, which improves the international allocation of resources. International competition, moreover, puts pressure on local producers to be as efficient as possible.

However, some shortcomings persist - in particular, the differentiation of protection according to product. EC trade policy in "sensitive" areas such as agriculture and textiles have seriously detrimental effects on welfare in both developed and developing partner countries. Furthermore, the differentiation of protection according to type of trade partner has come in for criticism. The privileges which the EC grants certain countries do not always contribute to more efficient world production, to say the least.

As far as production factors are concerned, the EC market is now completely open to capital, and this seems the most efficient option. The Community's external policy regarding labour is not well defined; but the member states' policies are rather restrictive. That too seems a relatively efficient approach, as migration does not always bring positive net welfare effects to the countries concerned.

Conclusion

The discussion on policy integration leads to the following conclusions. First, economists have shown themselves capable of specifying the advantages (that is the positive net effects) of passing on to higher stages of economic integration. These advantages mainly concern the recovery, by the Community, of the policy-effectiveness lost to member states' governments by the openness of their economies to their partners. However, the quantification of the effectiveness of policy integration is not well advanced. Second, most EC policies are rather well designed to produce the best results with the available resources. There are, however, large segments where considerable inefficiencies persist. Third, the distributional effect of policy measures are difficult to grasp. No clear picture is at this moment available.

The next stages in European integration concern both more deepening (more policy integration) and more widening (e.g. to take in countries from EFTA and Central and Eastern Europe). However, the advantages of further integration in both areas will be less and less clear in economic terms (CEPR 1992). It is difficult to establish a direct link between the changes in the organisation of the economy and of society, on the one hand, and economic growth on the other. The advantages of absorbing the countries of Eastern Europe into the Community, for instance, are hard to assess at the moment for any of those directly involved.

We may therefore conclude that the advantages of economic integration will in future be even more difficult to pinpoint and to explain to a large audience than today. So in future the economic motivation will lose weight and the political motivation for, and justification of, integration will become predominant.

3. Social reality

3.1 Grasping reality

Let us now leave the ivory tower of economic analysis and go out into the streets to see whether the things I have described correspond to some sort of social reality. It is difficult in the context of this chapter to seize the reality of European integration for specific individuals and groups - the diversity of situations is too great. I shall therefore try to draw some general conclusions based on the reactions of men and women in the street to certain aspects of the process of integration, as manifested in the Eurobarometer results.

3.2 The contradictions between the perception of general and personal advantage

The Eurobarometer results (CEC 1992; CEC 1991b) show very clearly that large sections of the Community's population are aware of the advantages their countries derive from EC membership. In all member countries a large, albeit decreasing majority of people took the view that belonging to the EC was a good thing (EC average 60%, down from 70%) and that their own country had benefited from membership (EC average 50%, down from 60%, with the UK at 30%, down from 47%). However, there is quite a discrepancy between this general notion and actual personal situations; only 50% on average (formerly 55%) thought that the EC influenced their own lives positively.

Could the discrepancy between "country" and "personal life" responses be related to the limited success of economists in quantifying overall and distributional effects, making it difficult to translate the general into the specific? This does not seem very likely. Even in the area of market integration, where economists have correctly measured the advantages, the EC citizen is at best only lukewarm. Less than half the respondents to the 1992 survey quoted above thought that the single market was a good thing *for them*. In some countries there were actually only about 35% of positive replies to this question. I am inclined to conclude that the EC citizen is aware of the general long-term advantages, but also sees for him- or herself the short-term adaptation difficulties - above all, the risk of unemployment. However, a majority seem to accept that matters of market policy, and even of monetary policy, should be handled at Community level (more than 55% acceptance for currency matters). This picture needs to be differentiated for particular groups, subjects and countries.

Traditionally, particular groups in society (notably in agriculture and private enterprise) have been keenly aware of the extent to which their interests are influenced by the outcome of the EC decision-making process. Much larger sections of the population have listened rather absent-mindedly to the specialised debates going on in Brussels. The debate over the Maastricht Treaty, however, has woken them up to the fact that their lives and interests too are affected by European integration, because the somewhat blind confidence that many had placed in the EC's work was quickly eroded in 1992.

3.3 *From economic risk to social security*

Is this new concern a symptom of a more general trend, or are there subjects of greater interest to the average EC citizen and considered with more enthusiasm than the effects of market integration? The answer to the latter question seems to be yes. 70% of the Community's population think that its social dimension is a good thing. There is not very much variation between member countries on this point; as a matter of fact there is a clear-cut majority in favour in all countries (CEC 1991b).

The social dimension of European integration is a wide-ranging notion covering different policies. The Social Charter reflects this heterogeneity. It deals with the basic rights of employed persons in such areas as salary, working conditions, social security, union membership, professional training, the equal treatment of men and women, and worker participation at executive level. Many EC directives give substance to these rights. Although numerous EC citizens have used these rules to their individual advantage - sometimes after intervention by the Court of Justice - in the minds of many, integration spells problems in the social field. The major concern seems to be with the sustainability of social security. This worry has been substantiated by specialised studies, regarding both cost and the capacity to pay.

In the first place, competition between firms seems increasingly to take place through the selective use of already-fragmented labour markets and the early scrapping of human capital - in other words the loss of jobs. The very success of the EC, moreover, makes it an oasis of wealth in a desert of poverty, and this has led to heavy immigration pressures (see Molle, de Koning, and Zandvliet, 1992). Immigrants from poorer countries tend to increase the number of EC citizens dependent on transfer incomes, whether directly or indirectly, through pushing-out effects. Both competition and immigration risk increasing the burden as the numbers benefiting from social security grow. Significantly, a majority of EC citizens appear to believe that their own countries are harbouring too many nationals from countries outside the Community, and some 60% think that immigration, whether from Africa, Eastern Europe or elsewhere, should be restricted (CEC 1992).

Secondly, increased competition between national policies erodes the tax base; for example, the possibility of keeping corporate tax at a certain level has been limited by open capital markets. The rigour of the EMS places limits on excess budget spending. Both factors are perceived as increasing the likelihood of cuts in social security.

3.4 The nationalist reflex

The problems facing social security systems could be solved by EC-wide regulation. The Social Charter and the paragraphs on social policy in the Maastricht Treaty can be seen in this light. EC-wide solutions, moreover, have been advocated by representative organisations such as trade unions.

EC citizens in general, however, do not seem to place much confidence in such measures. Some 55% (and in many smaller northern countries, a much larger proportion) prefer national solutions. This is not so surprising if one recalls that social security rights have all been won in a national context and that the form they take is the result of complicated bargaining between different segments of national society. The EC citizen may very well be a rationally-calculating being, from the economic point of view, believing that the cost of results in a national context is less than in a Community one (BIPE, 1992).

Social security is based on solidarity. The results of the survey just mentioned are in line with those of an earlier one (CEC, 1983). While four out of five respondents seem prepared to pay a fiscal contribution to regional aid for their own countries, only one in three feels the same way about aid to regions in other EC countries. That applies to all countries of the Community, with very little difference between them.

3.5 Conclusion

From the foregoing, one must conclude for the past that while the economic consequences of European integration were positive, the quantification of their distribution over countries was deficient. For the future, as the Community moves towards higher stages of integration (deepening) and the acceptance of new members (widening), the political motivation for integration will clearly take precedence over the economic. On the level of the individual citizen the benefits of integration will continue to be only vaguely perceived, and will be overshadowed by the risks he or she will personally incur in adapting to new situations. Here social concerns play a vital role; and as regards the future of social security, more confidence is placed in national than in Community solutions.

References

Balassa, B. (ed.) (1975), *European Economic Integration*, Amsterdam: North-Holland/American Elsevier.

Baldwin, R. and R. Lyons (1991), "External economies and European integration: the potential for self-fulfilling expectations", in *The Economics of EMU, European Economy* Special Edition 1, 56-75.

BIPE (1992), *Prévisions glissantes détaillées: la France dans l'Europe de 1997*, Paris: Synthèse.

Buckley, P. J. and P. Artisien (1987), *North-South Direct Investment in the European Communities*, London: Macmillan Press.

Cecchini, P. et al. (1988), *The European Challenge 1992: The Benefits of a Single Market*, Aldershot: Gower.

Commission of the European Communities (1977), *Report of the Study Group on the Role of Public Finance in European Integration* (G. D. A. MacDougall et al.), Economy and Finance Series 1, General Report, Brussels.

- (1983), *The Europeans and their Regions*, Brussels.

- (1989), *Report on Economic and Monetary Union in the European Community* (Delors Committee), Brussels.

- (1990), "One market, one money: an evaluation of the potential benefits and costs of forming an Economic and Monetary Union", *European Economy* 44.

- (1991a), "Fair competition in the internal market: Community state-aid policy", *European Economy* 48, 7-114.

- (1991b), *Eurobarometer* 35, June, Brussels.

- (1992), *Eurobarometer* 38, December, Brussels.

CEPR (1992), "Is bigger better? The economics of EC enlargement", London.

Emerson, M. et al. (1988), "The economics of 1992: an assessment of the potential economic effects of completing the internal market of the European Community", *European Economy* 35/3, 5-222.

European Coal and Steel Community (1953), *Report on Problems raised by the Different Turnover Tax Systems applied within the Common Market* (Tinbergen, J. et al.), Luxembourg.

European Court of Justice (1985), Judgement of the Court in case 13/83, *European Parliament vs. Council of the European Communities*, 22 May.

Gasiorek, M., A. Smith and A. Venables (1992), "1992, trade and welfare: a general equilibrium model", paper for the CEPR Paris Conference, "Trade Policies and Trade Flows after 1992".

Grauwe, P. De et al. (1989), *De Europese Monetaire Integratie: Vier Visies*, Den Haag: WRR/V66.

Haaland, J. and V. Norman (1992), "Global production effects of European integration", paper for the CEPR Paris Conference.

Márquez Méndez, A. J. (1986), *Economic Integration and Growth in Europe*, London: Croom Helm.

- (1990), "Economic cohesion in Europe: the impact of the Delors Plan", *Journal of Common Market Studies* 29, 17-36.

Miller, M. H. and Spencer, J. E. (1977), "The static economic effects of the UK joining the EEC: a general equilibrium approach", *Review of Economic Studies* 44, 71-93.

Molle, W. (1990), *The Economics of European Integration: Theory, Practice, Policy*, Aldershot: Dartmouth.

Molle, W., J. de Koning and C. Zandvliet (1992), "Can foreign aid reduce East-West migration in Europe?", Geneva: ILO.

Monnet, J. (1976), *Mémoires*, Paris: Fayard.

Owen, N. (1983), *Economies of Scale, Competitiveness and Trade Patterns within the European Community*, Oxford: Clarendon Press.

Padoa-Schioppa, T. et al. (1987), *Efficiency, Stability and Equity: A Strategy for the Evolution of the Economic System of the European Community*, Oxford University Press.

Pelkmans, J. (1986), *Completing the Internal Market for Industrial Products*, Brussels: Commission of the EC.

Pelkmans, J. and A. Winters (1988), *Europe's Domestic Market* (Chatham House Paper 43), London: Routledge for Royal Institute of International Affairs.

Petrochilos, G. A. (1989), *Foreign Direct Investment and the Development Process*, Aldershot: Avebury.

Smith, A. and Venables, A. J. (1988), "Completing the internal market in the EC: some industry simulations", *European Economic Review* 32, 1501-25.

Spaak, P.- H. et al. (1956), *Rapport des Chefs de Délégation aux Ministres des Affaires Etrangères* (Comité intergouvernemental créé par la Conférence de Messine), Brussels.

Triffin, R. (1992), "IMS: International Monetary System or Scandal?", Florence: European Parliamentary Union/European University Institute, Jean Monnet Papers.

Verdoorn, P. J. (1952), "Welke zijn de achtergronden en vooruitzichten van de economische integratie in Europa en welke gevolgen zou deze integratie hebben, met name voor de welvaart in Nederland?" Overdruk 22, Centraal Planbureau, Den Haag.

Viaene, J.- M. (1982), "A customs union between Spain and the EEC", *European Economic Review* 18, 345-68.

Wegner, M. (1989), "The European Community" in Pechman, J. A. (ed.), *The Role of the Economist in Government: An International Perspective*, New York/London: Harvester/Wheatsheaf, 279-99.

Werner, P. et al. (1970), "Report to the Council, Commission on the realisation by stages of economic and monetary union in the Community", *Bulletin of the EC* 11, supplement.

Whichart, O.G. (1981), "Trends in the US direct investment position abroad, 1950-1979", US Department of Commerce *Survey of Current Business* 61.2, 39-56, Washington, D.C.

Part I

Explaining regional and social inequalities

4

A comparison of regional differentials in the European Community and the United States

Andrea Boltho

Introduction

As has often been noted, the United States and the European Community share a number of common economic features. First and foremost are size and living standards. The population of the United States at the beginning of this decade was about 250 million, as against a European Community figure of some 325 million (270 million if Greece, Portugal and Spain are excluded). Total output, expressed in purchasing-power parities, differed marginally between the $5,400bn of the United States and the EC's $5,100bn, though GDPs per capita, at $21,400 and $15,600 respectively, differed more substantially. Both areas displayed relatively limited openness to foreign trade (once intra-Community exchanges are excluded from the EC data). The share of each in merchandise exports and imports in total output was 17-18%.[1]

The list of similarities is likely to grow as the EC's single market project is completed. Product- and factor-market integration in the EC will then come closer to those of the United States (which has, of course, been a fully-fledged customs union for much longer). And if the Community embraces monetary union by the beginning of the next century, a further major step will have been taken towards the creation of a "United States of Europe". Looking at American experience may thus provide a number of useful pointers to how the Community will evolve and to what policies will be required for achieving as smooth an adjustment as possible towards greater integration.

1. Regional inequality in the United States and the EC

It is well known that in both income and unemployment terms, the United States is spatially much more equal than Western Europe (Boltho, 1989, Eichengreen, 1990). Some indication of the extent of the differences is provided by Table 1, which presents data for 1985, the last year for which complete regional accounts are available for the Community. To strengthen comparability, a virtually identical number of states/regions has been chosen. For the United States, the regional breakdown selects the nine Census regions and the 48 contiguous states of the Union (excluding, therefore, Alaska, Hawaii and the District of Columbia). For the EC, the national breakdown similarly considers nine countries, excluding those economies that have joined the Community most recently and are, therefore, much less integrated than the older members (Greece, Portugal, Spain and the five *Länder* of the erstwhile German Democratic Republic). The regional breakdown looks at 49 of the 51 regions

Table 1
Selected indicators of regional differentials, 1985

	GSP/GDP/GRP per capita	Unemployment rate
	Standard deviation of logs	Standard deviation
US (9 regions)	0.10	1.44
EC (9 countries)	0.18	4.06
US (48 states)	0.15	1.94
EC (49 regions)	0.22	3.10
France (8 regions)	0.19	1.93
West Germany (10 regions)	0.21	2.71
Italy (10 regions)	0.26	2.90
UK (11 regions)	0.10	2.89

Note: US data for Gross State Product are at current prices; EC data for Gross Domestic and Gross Regional Product are at purchasing-power parities.

Sources: Eurostat, Regions - *Statistical Yearbook*, 1986 and 1989; *Survey of Current Business*, December 1991; *Statistical Abstract of the United States* (various issues).

traditionally distinguished in Eurostat data (West Berlin is excluded and the two Italian islands, Sardinia and Sicily, have been combined into one region). Data are also shown for the four major EC economies broken down into a roughly similar number of regions.

As they stand, the figures suggest a much lower dispersion of living standards and joblessness in America than in the EC. This is not surprising. After all, the United States has had a customs union, a monetary union and a federal government for a very long time. The EC, on the other hand, has been an (imperfect) customs union only since 1958 (or 1973 if one includes Denmark, Ireland and the United Kingdom). In the circumstances, it might have been expected that product- and factor-market integration, as well as the workings of fiscal mechanisms designed to redistribute income, would make for a relatively equal North American economy, while the fragmentation of the EC into "nation" states would retard the same process.[2]

It is interesting to note, however, that income inequality seems even lower in the United States than in three of the four larger EC economies shown in the table (and the same result would also hold for Spain). Yet these countries have been unitary states, with common trade, fiscal and monetary policies, for at least a century or longer. The differences are particularly marked if the EC figures are compared not with the American result for the 48 states but with that for the nine regions. The latter is more appropriate for a simple statistical reason - the indicators of inequality are sensitive to the number of regions chosen and, as a rule, rise as this number increases.

Over time, there seems to have been a movement towards convergence between richer and poorer areas in both America and the EC. Recent research suggests, for instance, that over the last century of United States economic history, and over the 35 years from 1950 of European economic history, regions with below-average per capita incomes at the outset have grown somewhat more rapidly than richer regions - a finding that would support neo-classical as opposed to "cumulative causation" mechanisms (Barro and Sala-i-Martin, 1991).

This process of convergence, however, at some 2% per annum, has been slow (*ibid.*). Nor does it seem to have been very linear, at least in the case of the United States. Figure 1 shows how most of the decline in inequality for per capita incomes between the 1920's and the 1980's took place in the first half of the 1940's, a period which saw the breakdown of many of the social barriers limiting non-white mobility (Easterlin, 1971). This was for reasons linked both to the outbreak of World War II, which greatly increased the demand for labour, and to policy changes by the Roosevelt administration in the late 1930's, which, by raising minimum wages, priced many Southern workers out of employment (Eichengreen, 1991). As for the continuing equalisation after the war, this was at least in part due to the greater incidence of social security programmes (Betson and Haveman, 1984).

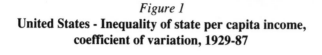

Figure 1
**United States - Inequality of state per capita income,
coefficient of variation, 1929-87**

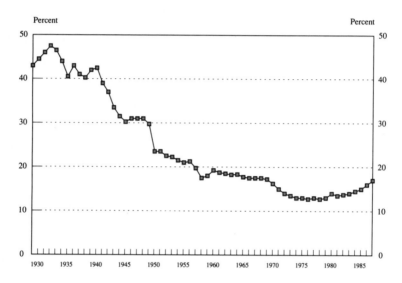

Source: C. C. Coughlin and T. B. Mandelbaum (1989).

More recent trends for Gross Regional (or Gross State) Product are shown in Figure 2. A simple visual inspection suggests that the movement towards lesser income disparities was halted in the United States from the early 1970's onwards and in the EC from the early 1980's.[3] The uneven incidence of supply shocks on natural-resource-dependent states is, no doubt, important in explaining America's experience, at least in the years 1980-82, but later trends may also owe something to the toning-down of the redistributive operations of "fiscal federalism". As for the EC, the factors most responsible were probably lower growth and higher overall unemployment. Here too, however, the reduction in the scope of regional policies, particularly significant in Britain and Italy, may have played a part.[4]

A further notable feature of trends over time is that there seems to be greater variability in the positioning of states or regions in the United States than of regions or countries in the EC. For unemployment, for instance, the location of depressed regions in America varies more over time than in the EC (Eichengreen, 1990). For real per capita GDPs/GRPs, a roughly similar conclusion is suggested by the data of Table 2, which presents, for the 1970's and 80's, two measures of variability - the average standard deviation of yearly percentage changes and the results of some simple rank correlations. For the former indicator, the regions/states of America seem to experience greater

Figure 2
Differentials in regional per capita output
(standard deviation of logs)

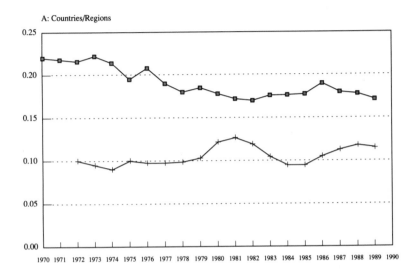

A: Countries/Regions

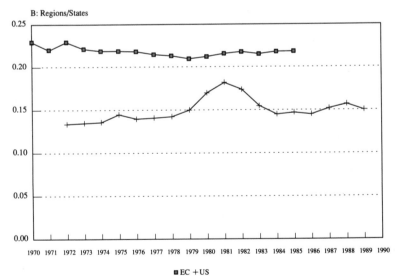

B: Regions/States

■ EC + US

Note: EC country data are in purchasing-power parities; the regional data approximate ppp's through a backward extrapolation from the 1985 benchmark ppp data with the help of current price GRP growth rates deflated by national GDP deflators.
Source: as for Table 2.

fluctuations than their EC equivalents. And a similar impression of lesser stability in the United States is conveyed by the rank correlations: relatively rich states in one year are more likely to be relatively poor a few years hence than is the case for the regions of the EC.[5] Interestingly, however, these broad conclusions no longer seem to hold if attention is concentrated on the regional data for single countries in the EC with the exception of Germany. This supports the view of De Grauwe and Vanhaverbeke that "regions belonging to the same countries in Europe tend to have a more unequal development of their output than nations" (1991, p. 11), just as states in America show greater variability than larger regions.

Table 2
Selected indicators of regional per capita real output variability

	Average of annual standard deviation of regional growth rates	Rank correlations	
		Average of year-to-year correlations	Between first and last year
Nine regions/countries			
US (1972-89)	2.01	0.941	0.817
EC (1972-89)	1.68	0.985	1.000
48 states/49 regions			
US (1972-89)	3.08	0.971	0.734
EC (1970-85)	2.68	0.984	0.778
Individual countries[a]			
France (1970-85)	2.10	0.962	0.810
West Germany (1970-85)	1.19	0.995	0.939
Italy (1970-85)	1.93	0.971	0.915
UK (1970-85)	2.45	0.916	0.682

[a]The number of regions per country is as shown in Table 1.

Source: Eurostat, *Regions - Statistical Yearbook* (various issues); OECD, *National Accounts, 1960-1989*, Vol. 1; *Survey of Current Business*, May 1988 and December 1991; *Statistical Abstract of the United States* (various issues).

2. Issues

The preceding section confirms the well-known proposition that the United States is geographically more equal than the EC. Two major factors could explain this: either a lower incidence of asymmetric (demand or supply) shocks in America than in the EC, and/or America's greater capacity to offset such shocks via appropriate adjustment mechanisms.

Evidence on the first point is mixed. The greater variability of United States output reported above suggests that shocks are more pronounced there than in the EC. Such variability, however, in Eichengreen's view, "reflects both the extent of asymmetrical shocks affecting incomes in different regions differently, and the elasticity of factor flows with respect to regional income differentials" (1991, p. 11).[6] A recent and more thorough investigation, comparing all the EC member countries with eight United States regions over the period 1960-88, concluded that, overall, asymmetric shocks were more prevalent in the EC than in America (Bayoumi and Eichengreen, 1991).

In addition, the speed of adjustment to any given shock in the United States is almost certainly more rapid than it is in the EC. Two major channels of adjustment are possible for American regions or states in the absence of autonomous monetary and fiscal policies: real exchange-rate flexibility and factor mobility. The former has clearly been significantly greater between the nine EC countries chosen here than between the regions of the United States, even in the 1980's when the workings of the European Monetary System limited nominal exchange-rate variability in the Community (Table 3). But the more interesting issue for a future European Monetary Union is whether this variability is higher within America than within a single European Community country. A direct answer to this question has not been given in the literature, but indirect evidence shows that real exchange-rate variability is not absent between the regions of EC countries such as the Netherlands, Spain or the United Kingdom (De Grauwe and Vanhaverbeke, 1991). Table 3 presents the estimates for these countries as well as similar data for the United States. Surprisingly, perhaps, the evidence suggests that the orders of magnitude are very similar for periods stretching over a decade.[7] For shorter time-spans, however, United States variability appears somewhat larger.

For labour mobility, on the other hand, the available evidence unambiguously points to a much greater degree of mobility in America. Inter-country movements in Europe are, of course, limited by obvious linguistic and other social and cultural barriers. But even intra-country mobility seems to be a good deal lower within Europe's unitary states than in the United States - in 1980, for instance, American mobility was broadly two to three times higher than within West Germany, England and Wales, and Sweden (OECD, 1986). Taken together, these various findings may indicate that regional shocks in America are offset in the shorter run by real exchange-rate changes and in the longer run by labour migration. In Europe, adjustments between countries have so far occurred mainly through the former. In a future monetary union,

Table 3
Real exchange-rate variability

	Relative unit labour costs in manufacturing
A. Long-run	
US (9 regions) 1977-87	0.5
EC (9 countries) 1980-90	2.0
US (48 states) 1977-87	0.9
West Germany (11 regions) 1977-87	0.4
Netherlands (4 regions) 1977-88	0.7
B. Medium-term	

		Relative unit labour costs in manufacturing
US (9 regions)	1977-82	0.9
	1982-87	0.5
EC (9 countries)	1980-85	1.9
	1985-90	2.3
US (48 states)	1977-82	1.5
	1982-87	1.4
Spain (16 regions)	1980-85	1.0
UK (11 regions)	1980-85	0.7

Note: Variability is measured as the average of the percentage changes over the period in the regional (or countries') real exchange rates (expressed in absolute terms). The weights for the EC calculation come from Artus and McGuirk (1981); the weights used to compute regional exchange rates are regional output shares.

Source: For the United States and the EC, author's calculations based on data from *Statistical Abstract of the United States* (various issues); OECD, *Historical Statistics, 1960-1990*; IMF, *International Financial Statistics* (1991 Yearbook); for the individual EC countries, De Grauwe and Vanhaverbeke (1991).

however, this channel, let alone labour mobility, would be stunted.

In addition to market-based response mechanisms, a feature that may mitigate the impact of asymmetric shocks on regional incomes is the operation of a federal or national social security system that transfers incomes from rich to poor. Such systems are in widespread use within Europe's unitary states, but also operate in federations like the United States. Where they do *not* operate is at the EC level, as pointed out in the late 1970's by the MacDougall Report (Commission of the European Communities, 1977). Recent research, which largely confirms the findings of that report, suggests that the American Federal tax and transfer system automatically offsets up to 40% of any unfavourable income shock that may hit a state of the union, while a very rough estimate for the Community puts the comparable figure at 0.5% at best (Sachs and Sala-i-Martin, 1991).

The implications of the foregoing for a future European Monetary Union are disturbing. As it is, asymmetric shocks are clearly present both between countries in the EC and between regions within them. Indeed, the shocks may well be larger than their equivalents in the United States. In addition, the EC seems to lack some of the mechanisms that mitigate the impact of such shocks. The potential problems, therefore, may be larger, while the potential solutions may be fewer.

This need not matter, or matter much, if the move toward monetary union were to either diminish the incidence of shocks or strengthen the response mechanisms, or do both. Thus, it has been argued that the process of integration is likely to occur through an intensification of intra-industry trade, which should reduce the likelihood of asymmetric shocks (Commission of the European Communities, 1990). Yet neither American nor EC experience fully supports such optimism. In the United States, for instance, it has been found that the demand (though not the supply) shocks hitting the various regions are as large as, if not larger than, in the EC (Bayoumi and Eichengreen, 1991). The most plausible reason for this "high variability of demand affecting US regions may ... [be] the greater specialisation of industrial production in the US" (*ibid.*, p. 19). And the indirect evidence for EC countries in Table 2 points in the same direction. In other words, integration may have led to increased specialisation rather than the opposite. Pursuing such integration further via economic union could thus bring about a well-known and paradoxical outcome: "The move towards a common currency will lead to the increased specialisation of member countries, hence to greater asymmetric shocks, which constitutes an argument against a common currency" (Blanchard, 1992, p. 152).

Turning to adjustment mechanisms, it could be argued that labour mobility, even if relatively low at present, would increase in a more integrated Europe. While there may be some truth in this, migratory flows can hardly be expected to reach United States levels. In any case, such an adjustment mechanism, in European conditions at least, could well be sub-optimal (MacDougall, 1992). While in large countries such as Canada or the United States the idea of significant population movements from depressed to prosperous areas can be countenanced with reasonable equanimity, in Europe's densely-populated areas, labour mobility is bound to generate rising economic and social costs in the form, for instance, of greater congestion and pollution in some parts of a country and under-utilised social overhead capital in others.

Real exchange-rate flexibility is clearly preferable. If only wages could respond more flexibly to sudden changes - in particular, declines - in the demand for labour, adjustment could be relatively smooth and swift. Yet, as is well known, Europe's labour-market flexibility is very limited (Calmfors and

Driffill, 1988; OECD, 1989). It is true that monetary union may be likened to a "regime change" that could significantly alter wage-setting behaviour in the more inflation-prone countries. The precedent of the EMS is often invoked in this context. Yet the evidence that exchange-rate credibility has permanently modified French and Italian inflation/unemployment trade-offs is weak at best (Giavazzi and Giovannini, 1989).

That leaves fiscal transfers, which could be used as an adjustment mechanism (in the form of regional policies), as an instrument of redistribution, or both (Begg and Mayes, 1991). Here again, however, not much can be hoped for. At present, the bulk of the Community's budget is devoted to a redistribution not from poor to rich but from consumers to producers. Though the Common Agricultural Policy is undergoing a major reform, it does not appear as if its budgetary incidence will decline much. Hence, any new programme of redistribution would require fresh funds. The chances that the major EC net contributors, in particular Germany, will willingly increase their transfers to help the poorer regions of Europe look slim. Germany, for one, is already shouldering the burden of its recent monetary union with the Eastern regions, a burden that is likely to remain substantial for a long time.

3. Conclusion

This very brief review of some selected features of EC and US regional disparities has brought out a number of familiar conclusions. First there is the well-known fact of the smaller incidence of regional income and unemployment differentials in America than in the Community. Some of this is clearly due to the much longer history of American integration, a history that the EC can replicate only gradually, as the single market and economic and monetary union are established. But it should not be forgotten that a good deal of America's regional equality was achieved in a single large jump during World War II, an experience which, for obvious reasons, the EC can hardly imitate. Second, the United States' example suggests that integration, by leading to greater regional specialisation, requires other mechanisms to counter the danger of centrifugal forces - factor mobility, wage flexibility, federal intervention in regional policy and income maintenance.

In today's EC these mechanisms are hardly widespread. Labour mobility is very low (although, given the overcrowding of many of the Community's more prosperous regions, this may not be quite as damaging as commonly thought); real, within-country, exchange-rate flexibility is limited; and equalising transfers from the centre to the regions are virtually non-existent. Before the countries of the Community rush headlong into economic union, therefore, they may be well advised to follow two sets of policies, one market-orientated and the other more interventionist, that could strengthen their cohesion. The deregulation of their labour markets so as to make wages more sensitive to local supply and demand conditions could greatly increase the efficiency of a European common currency area. Countervailing fiscal policies designed to diminish the incidence of large regional income differentials could, equally, greatly strengthen the equity component of a united Europe. Unfortunately, success in either direction, let alone both, seems highly unlikely.

NOTES

1. The 1990 ratio of exports plus imports of goods to GDP was 16.9% in the United States and 17.9% in the EC, once the recorded merchandise import figures of the Community are adjusted downwards by 5% to allow for the c.i.f. component of the customs data.

2. Unless one believes in mechanisms of 'cumulative causation' according to which integration strengthens centrifugal forces and benefits richer areas at the expense of poorer ones (Kaldor, 1970). On the whole, the historical experience suggests that balancing tendencies have been stronger (see below), though policies may well have contributed to this outcome.

3. For the United States this is confirmed by the results of a simple regression between growth rates of per capita Gross State Product from 1972 to 1989 and beginning-of-the-period levels. Although the coefficient linking the two variables has a negative sign, it is statistically insignificant.

4. For some evidence on Italy, see Boltho, 1990.

5. Important changes in rankings have, of course, occurred for all energy-producing regions. Louisiana's per capita output, for instance, fell from 2nd to 32nd place among the 48 states between 1980 and 1987. Conversely, the ranking of the North Netherlands region rose from 34th to 4th place between 1970 and 1981. Otherwise, however, major changes in the EC (with the exception of the United Kingdom) have been relatively rare, while they have not been uncommon in the United States - witness the rise between 1980 and 1987 of Massachusetts from 22nd to 3rd, or of New Hampshire from 37th to 8th position.

6. The use of per capita rather than of total GRPs may weaken this argument somewhat.

7. Real exchange-rate variability need not, however, be a panacea. Thus, in Italy the real exchange rate between South and North has changed, but in a perverse way, with the South suffering from a strong appreciation, particularly in the 1970's and 80's (OECD, 1990).

References

Artus, J. R. and A. K. McGuirk (1981), "A revised version of the multilateral exchange-rate model", *IMF Staff Papers* 28 (2), June, 275-309.

Barro, R. J. and X. Sala-i-Martin (1991), "Convergence across states and regions", *Brookings Papers on Economic Activity* 1, 107-82.

Bayoumi, T. and B. Eichengreen (1992), "Shocking aspects of European monetary unification", in F. Torres and F. Giavazzi (eds.), *The Transition to Economic and Monetary Union in Europe*, Cambridge: Cambridge University Press.

Begg, I. and D. Mayes (1991), "Social and economic cohesion among the regions of Europe in the 1990's", *National Institute Economic Review* 138, November, 63-74.

Betson, D. and R. Haveman (1984), "The role of income transfers in reducing inequality between and within regions", in M. Moon (ed.), *Economic Transfers in the United States, NBER Studies in Income and Wealth* 49, Chicago, IL: University of Chicago Press.

Blanchard, O. J. (1992), "Le rôle de la politique budgétaire dans l'Union économique et monétaire", in Groupe international de politique économique de l'OFCE, *La désinflation compétitive, le mark et les politiques budgétaires en Europe*, Paris: Seuil.

Boltho, A. (1989), "European and United States regional differentials: a note", *Oxford Review of Economic Policy* 5 (2), Summer, 105-15.

- (1990), "The Italian Mezzogiorno: markets or policies?", *Banca Nazionale del Lavoro Quarterly Review* 175, December, 431-39.

Calmfors, L. and J. Driffill (1988), "Centralization of wage bargaining", *Economic Policy* 6, April, 13-61.

Commission of the European Communities (1977), *Report of the Study Group on the Role of Public Finance in European Integration*, Brussels.

- (1990), "One market, one money", *European Economy* 44, October.

Coughlin, C. C. and T. B. Mandelbaum (1989), "Have Federal spending and taxation contributed to the divergence of state per capita incomes in the 1980's?", *Federal Reserve Bank of St. Louis* 71 (4), July-August.

De Grauwe, P. and W. Vanhaverbeke (1991), "Is Europe an optimum currency area? Evidence from regional data", *CEPR Discussion Paper* 555, May.

Easterlin, R. A. (1971), "Regional income trends", in R. W. Fogel and S. L. Engerman (eds.), *The Reinterpretation of American Economic History*, New York: Harper and Row.

Eichengreen, B. (1990), "Currency union", *Economic Policy* 10, April, 117-87.

- (1991), "Is Europe an optimum currency area?", *NBER Working Paper* 3579, January.

Giavazzi, F. and A. Giovannini (1989), *Limiting Exchange-Rate Flexibility: The European Monetary System*, Cambridge, MA: MIT Press.

Kaldor, N. (1970), "The case for regional policy", *Scottish Journal of Political Economy* 17 (3), November, 337-48.

MacDougall, D. (1992), "Economic and Monetary Union and the European Community budget", *National Institute Economic Review* 140, May, 64-68.

OECD (1986), *Flexibility in the Labour Market*, Paris.

- (1989), *Economies in Transition*, Paris.

- (1990), *Economic Surveys: Italy 1989/1990*, Paris.

Sachs, J. and X. Sala-i-Martin (1991), "Fiscal federalism and optimum currency areas: evidence for Europe from the United States", *NBER Working Paper* 3855, October.

5 Regional disparities and Community policy

Ronnie Hall

Introduction[1]

The Community's interest in the regions and their disparities has its origins in the effort to increase economic and social cohesion. This is reflected in Article 130a of the Treaty of Rome amended by the Single Act, which for the first time explicitly incorporated the aim of economic and social cohesion, defined as promoting "the harmonious development of the Community and a reduction in disparities between the various regions and the backwardness of the least-favoured regions". In the Treaty agreed by the European Council in Maastricht in December 1991 this aim was further strengthened, cohesion becoming one of the central "pillars" of the new European Union.

The analysis of the regions of the Community which follows is set in this policy context. It considers the major differences between regions, with particular reference to areas assisted under the reform of the Structural Funds introduced in 1988. For this reason the analysis will largely focus on the recent period, beginning in the mid-1980s. This happens to have been a period of relative stability in the Community in terms of membership, the last enlargement - bringing in Spain and Portugal - having taken place in 1986.

It is useful to begin with a brief reminder of how regions are defined in Community regional policy and how the sub-set of assisted regions has been determined. The identification of the Community's problem regions under the 1988 reforms reflected a typological approach. The weaker regions were classified according to three mutually-exclusive categories and identified according to statistical criteria, as follows:

(a) Regions whose development is lagging behind the rest of the Community (Objective 1). The standard condition of eligibility for Objective 1 was that a region should have a GDP per head of less than 75% of the Community average.[2]

(b) Traditional industrial regions undergoing restructuring (Objective 2).

Eligibility was determined mainly according to quantitative labour-market criteria: unemployment rates, rate of industrial employment, and industrial job losses.[3]

(c) Rural problem areas (Objective 5b). These were determined according to a mixture of quantitative and qualitative criteria, mostly relating to relative dependence on a declining agricultural sector.[4]

Determining the eligibility of regions for each of these Objectives required that the data be available in comparable or harmonised form on a Community-wide basis. The most important data in this respect are GDP figures, expressed per capita and in purchasing-power standards, and labour-market data, principally unemployment rates. These data form the basis of the analysis of regional differences in the Community which follows. In considering the assisted regions the analysis will focus on the Objective 1 and Objective 2 regions which were determined with particular reference to GDP and unemployment criteria respectively. Objective 5b, with its mixture of quantitative and qualitative criteria, is less open to this kind of statistical approach.

The data must, of course, have a spatial frame of reference or regional grid. The Community system of classification of regions - *NUTS* - is by now relatively familiar.[5] This represents an attempt to have a uniform classification of regions across the member states. One important characteristic of this system, however, is that it does not attempt to impose any new structures. Rather, it uses the administrative units which already exist. While every effort is made to maximise comparability at each level of the *NUTS* hierarchy of regions - for example, by grouping administrative units together where these are unusually small - there remain considerable differences in population and surface area. It is also the case that at *NUTS* level II, the region can be a member state, as is the case, for example, for Ireland. This too is indicative of the wide differences between the Community's level II regions in relation to their access to the levers which control economic development policy in all its facets.

From the Community's point of view, regional administrative structures are a matter for the member states: an example of "subsidiarity" in action. More important is for Community regional policies to have a margin of flexibility to work around the regional grid in order to identify those areas most in need of assistance. In the regional policies introduced in 1988, therefore, the areas finally assisted were not necessarily whole *NUTS* units. This was the case for the list of areas eligible as traditional industrial regions in decline (the Objective 2 regions), where only 27 whole *NUTS* level III regions were on the list while a further 104 *NUTS* III regions had parts on the list.

In identifying parts of *NUTS* III regions much use was made of functional spatial units in two countries where these have been defined for national purposes. Thus, "Travel-to-Work" areas in the UK and *Zones d'Emploi* in France (two member states accounting between them for nearly

60% of population coverage under Objective 2) were used extensively to pinpoint areas of need. In view of their usefulness, the Statistical Office of the Commission has since embarked on a project in co-operation with the member states to define similar labour-market areas for the Community as a whole using common definitions. For the present, the analysis of regional disparities must remain within the confines of the *NUTS* system.

Disparities in income per head

A snapshot of average incomes per head for the regions in 1990 - the most recent year for which data are available - confirms the existence of wide disparities (Map 1). The average incomes per head in the bottom 10 regions situated in Greece and Portugal are only one-third of those in the top 10 regions

Graph 1
Trends in regional income disparities[1] in the Community, 1980-90

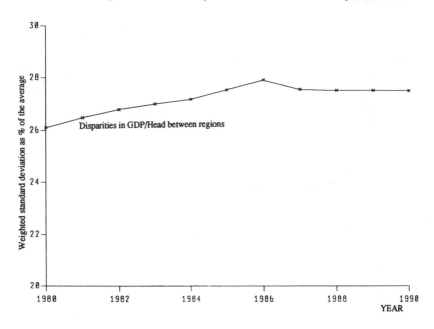

1. Disparities are measured by the weighted standard deviation of regional values for GDP in purchasing power standards. The standard deviation is a statistical measure used variously in this report to measure disparities over time. It is always positive, the higher the value, the greater the degree of dispersion.

In the present context, in order to avoid giving the same weight in the calculation of standard deviation to both large and small regions, it is weighted by the size of the population in each region (or each Member State as appropriate).

The weighted standard deviation is given by $s = \mathcal{S}(Xr-X)^2 Wr/W$ where X is the average GDP per head, Xr is the region's GDP per head and Wr and W are the size of population in the region and

Regional GDP per inhabitant, 1990

MAP 1

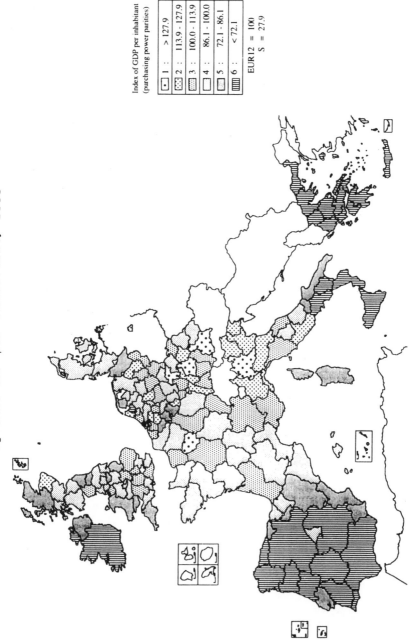

Index of GDP per inhabitant
(purchasing power parities)

1 : > 127.9
2 : 113.9 - 127.9
3 : 100.0 - 113.9
4 : 86.1 - 100.0
5 : 72.1 - 86.1
6 : < 72.1

EUR12 = 100
S = 27.9

Table 1
GDP (in purchasing-power standards)
EC-12 = 100 (excluding ex-GDR)

	1985	1988	1989	1990	88/90 average
Greece	51	49	49	47	48
Spain					
Galicia	55	56	57	58	57
Asturias	73	71	73	74	73
Castilla y León	67	67	69	69	68
Castilla-la-Mancha	57	62	63	64	63
Extremadura	48	47	48	48	48
Comunidad Valenciana	73	74	5	76	75
Andalucía	54	56	56	57	56
Murcia	63	70	71	71	71
Ceuta y Melilla	65	60	61	61	61
Canarias	68	74	75	75	75
Total Objective 1	61	63	64	64	64
France					
Corse	82	81	82	82	82
Départements d'Outre-Mer	-	44 (1986)	-	-	-
Total Objective 1	-	-	-	-	-
Ireland	62	62	65	68	65
Italy					
Campania	70	66	66	66	66
Abruzzi	89	88	88	88	88
Molise	78	79	79	79	79
Puglia	71	73	73	72	73
Basilicata	66	62	62	62	62
Calabria	62	57	57	56	57
Sicilia	69	68	68	68	68
Sardegna	76	75	75	74	75
Total Objective 1	70	69	69	69	69
Portugal	51	54	55	56	55
United Kingdom					
Northern Ireland	78	77	77	74	76
Objective 1 average (excluding French overseas departments)	62	62	62	63	62
Other regions average	110	110	110	110	110

situated in and around the Community's prosperous spine, running through southern England, Benelux and western Germany to northern and central Italy.

In terms of trends over time, the late 1980s witnessed a levelling-off and the beginnings of a reduction in disparities in incomes per head (measured using the weighted standard deviation) following a long period of rising disparities since the 1970s (Graph 1). In a policy context, the performance of the regions defined as Objective 1 under the reform of the Structural Funds is of particular interest. These regions, which are defined in relation to their GDP per head (see list in Table 1), are the priority areas. This is reflected in the fact that with just over 50% of a total population of 140 million assisted by Community policies, they receive nearly 65% of the total financial allocations and 80% of the allocations of the European Regional Development Fund.

Over the second half of the 1980s, the Objective 1 regions broadly maintained their position vis-à-vis the rest of the Community (Table 1). Within this broad trend there were, however, major differences, many regions showing a marked convergence towards the average Community GDP per head while others diverged. In almost all the Spanish Objective 1 regions, Ireland and Portugal, there was a clearly-discernible trend of improvement in GDP per head relative to the Community average. In Ireland,[6] Portugal and two of the Spanish regions this resulted in gains relative to the Community average of five percentage points or more - a considerable feat in such a short time.

By contrast, in Greece, Ceuta and Melilla (Spain), four (or half) of the Italian Objective 1 regions and Northern Ireland, there was a deterioration in GDP per head relative to the Community average between 1985 and 1990. In southern Italy, the poor economic performance of some regions means that disparities within the Mezzogiorno are now greater than those between the Mezzogiorno and the rest of the country.

Finally, the regions which could be said to have experienced little or no change over the period vis-à-vis the rest of the Community are Extremadura (Spain), Corsica (France), and the remaining four Italian Objective 1 regions.

A wide variety of reasons have been put forward to explain the differences in performance of the Objective 1 regions. For example, in the rapidly-growing Spanish regions and in Portugal, there was a trend during the 1980s towards rising export-market shares. This reflects the adjustment of their production structures towards areas where world demand was growing fastest, underpinned by improvements in competitiveness, quality and marketing. Infrastructural inadequacies, however, meant that growth tended to be concentrated in and around the main urban areas.

Greek economic development continued to be handicapped by an inadequate economic infrastructure. In the face of public-sector imbalances, public investment to remedy the deficiencies was held back. The Greek economy remains dependent on traditional industries which are sensitive to the effects of competition in a single European market.

In Northern Ireland, income from employment struggled to keep pace with growth in the population and labour force. This region is characterised by a relatively high dependence on the public sector - a factor of economic stability but not of growth. Similarly in Italy, public-sector transfers to the South have been a major component of aggregate demand but appear to have failed to produce the necessary improvements on the supply side. Rather, these transfers have given rise to problems of dependence in the South which seem to have reduced the potential for indigenous development.

Disparities in unemployment rates

In the Community as a whole, the rate of unemployment stood at 8.7% in 1991, the latest year for which regional data are available. There is, however, considerable variation around the average (Map 2). In the ten worst-affected regions (situated in Spain and southern Italy), the rate of unemployment averaged over 22%, compared to just under 2.5% in the ten least-affected regions (which are mostly German).

Regarding the statistical measure of disparities for the Community as a whole (the weighted standard deviation), the evidence suggests that the rising trend came to an end in the mid-1980s, since when there has been a levelling-off or slight decline (Graph 2). An important factor in this trend has been the performance of many regions in Spain and the UK. In both countries there were

Graph 2
Trends in regional unemployment disparities[1] in the Community, 1970-91

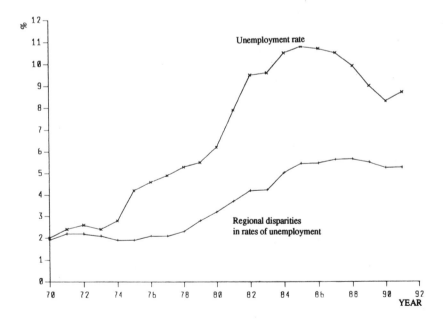

Standard deviation weighted by the regional shares of the labour force.

NB. Data from 1970 to 1982 are based on statistics for registered unemployed; Data from 1983 to 1990 are based on harmonised unemployment statistics. Greece is not included before 1983.

MAP 2
Regional unemployment rates, 1991

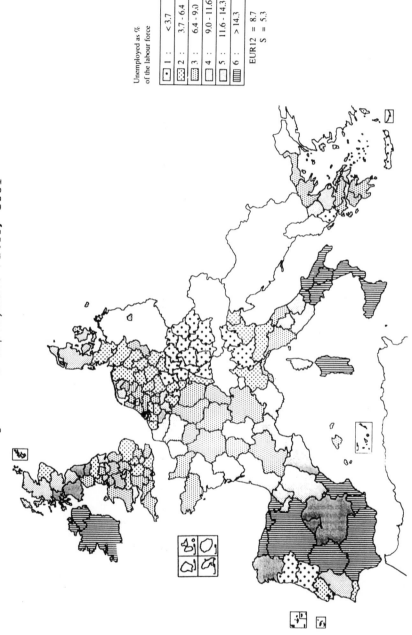

Unemployed as %
of the labour force

1 : < 3.7
2 : 3.7 - 6.4
3 : 6.4 - 9.0
4 : 9.0 - 11.6
5 : 11.6 - 14.3
6 : > 14.3

EUR12 = 8.7
S = 5.3

Table 2
Evolution of unemployment in Objective 1 regions (1985-91)

Regions	85	86	87	88	89	90	91	Difference % points 1985-90
EC-12	10.8	10.7	10.5	9.9	9.0	8.3	8.7	-2.5
Greece	7.8	7.4	7.4	7.7	7.5	7.0	8.1	-0.8
Spain								
Galicia	13.2	13.9	13.4	13.2	12.5	11.9	12.4	-1.2
Asturias	18.8	18.8	19.7	20.2	17.4	17.4	16.2	-1.4
Castilla y León	18.5	18.1	17.6	17.7	17.3	15.6	14.6	-2.9
Castilla-La-Mancha	17.5	15.4	15.1	16.6	14.8	13.3	13.7	-4.1
Extremadura	28.0	28.3	25.9	27.1	26.8	25.5	24.4	-2.5
Comunidad Valenciana	21.1	19.7	20.0	18.3	15.3	14.1	16.0	-7.0
Andalucía	30.7	30.3	31.1	29.2	27.2	26.0	24.8	-4.8
Murcia	21.1	18.4	21.4	17.6	16.1	15.8	16.6	-5.2
Ceuta y Melilla	29.3	28.8	29.8	35.3	31.6	29.8	29.9	+0.5
Canarias	28.0	26.5	25.5	22.5	22.4	23.2	24.5	-4.8
Total Objective 1	23.1	22.4	22.6	21.6	20.0	19.0	19.0	-4.1
France								
Corse	12.0	11.7	11.9	10.6	9.4	9.8	11.1	-2.2
Départements d'Outre-Mer	9.9	10.0	10.4	9.7				
Total Objective 1	10.2	10.3	10.6	9.8				
Ireland	18.1	18.1	18.1	17.5	16.1	14.2	15.7	-3.9
Italy								
Campania	13.9	16.6	21.5	23.0	22.5	19.2	21.0	+5.3
Abruzzi	8.6	11.7	8.6	9.3	10.4	9.9	9.7	+1.3
Molise	8.5	7.1	12.2	12.4	13.2	11.7	15.3	+3.2
Puglia	10.7	14.3	13.2	15.7	14.9	14.0	15.5	+3.3
Basilicata	9.4	21.0	15.9	21.5	20.7	20.8	20.2	+11.4
Calabria	15.6	15.4	17.8	22.6	25.2	21.9	21.9	+6.3
Sicilia	14.0	15.1	16.0	18.6	21.8	21.1	22.1	+7.0
Sardegna	19.0	20.2	16.2	18.4	19.0	18.4	18.7	-0.6
Total Objective 1	13.3	15.7	16.7	19.1	19.9	18.2	19.3	+4.9
Portugal	8.9	8.6	7.0	6.0	5.0	4.2	3.9	-4.7
United Kingdom								
Northern Ireland	17.8	17.7	18.6	17.1	17.3	17.1	16.8	-0.7

MAP 3

Change in regional rates of unemployment, 1'

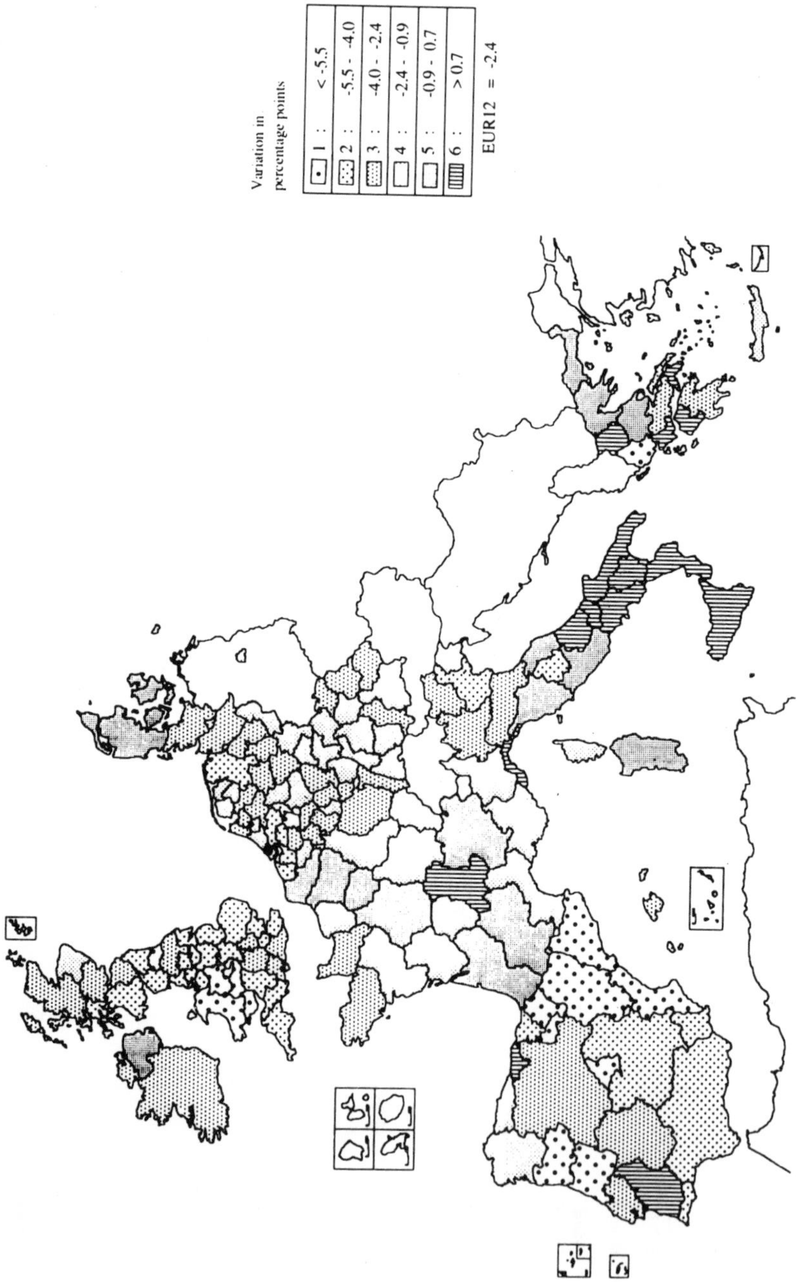

Variation in
percentage points

1 :	< -5.5
2 :	-5.5 - -4.0
3 :	-4.0 - -2.4
4 :	-2.4 - -0.9
5 :	-0.9 - 0.7
6 :	> 0.7

EUR12 = -2.4

regions with unemployment rates in 1990 some five percentage points below their 1985 rates. In 1991 there was something of a reversal, a cyclical rise in the rates being particularly evident in many UK regions. The Italian case is again worthy of consideration for the very clear separation between North and South: rapid falls in unemployment rates in northern regions have been mirrored by often-serious rises in southern regions over the same period. Indeed, the high and rising unemployment rates of southern Italy were a key factor in the failure of unemployment-rate disparities in the Community as a whole to fall during the 1980s, a time of a general rise in employment.

Unemployment in Objective 1 regions
The regions of southern Italy are part of the group of Objective 1 regions, whose performance with regard to unemployment has been generally favourable since the mid-1980s. One general observation is in order at the outset regarding unemployment rates in these regions: they tend to be much higher than the Community average (though this criterion was not incorporated in the conditions for eligibility since it is lack of development which underlies their difficulties). In 1985, few of the Objective 1 regions had unemployment rates below the Community average, while a relatively large number had rates up to 2 or even 3 times the average (Table 2). Consequently, while these regions may achieve improvement in absolute terms, it is more difficult for them to achieve an improvement in relative terms.

Over the period 1985-90, the Objective 1 regions characterised by high rates of unemployment in Spain, Ireland and Northern Ireland in fact saw falls in their unemployment rates beginning in 1988 in absolute terms, although these were not sufficient to bring about improvement relative to the Community average. One exception is Comunidad Valenciana (Spain). This region has seen a marked improvement in both absolute terms and relative to the rest of the Community, beginning in 1987. Portugal has also seen both an absolute and relative improvement although it is generally a country of relatively low unemployment rates.

In Greece, unemployment rates remained broadly constant over the period, with a fall in 1990 (but rising again in 1991). This leaves the Italian Objective 1 regions where the majority, which had relatively high rates of unemployment at the outset, saw a steady increase in the rates up to 1989 with a slight decrease only in 1990 (not, however, sustained in 1991). The figures for southern Italy show clearly the degree to which the Abruzzi region has become dissociated from its neighbours: its rate of unemployment is now about half that of the rest of southern Italy, after having been two-thirds of it in 1985.

Unemployment in Objective 2 regions
These regions, by definition, share the general characteristic of average unemployment rates higher than the Community average, though they tend not to reach the levels of the worst-affected Objective 1 regions (Table 3). Before the 1988 reform of the Structural Funds, the evidence suggests that this group of

Table 3

Evolution of unemployment in Objective 2 regions

(1985-91)

Objective 2 regions[a]	Unemployment rate							Difference % points 1985-90
	85	86	87	88	89	90	91	
EC-12	10.8	10.7	9.9	9.0	8.3	8.7	8.7	-2.5
B	14.9	14.9	14.8	14.0	11.6	10.5	10.7	-4.4
D	10.4	10.0	9.9	9.9	9.2	8.1	7.3	-2.4
E	22.1	22.2	21.3	20.1	15.7	14.2	13.4	-7.9
F	11.9	12.0	12.6	11.7	11.1	10.4	10.4	-1.5
I	10.1	10.7	9.3	9.6	9.1	8.5	8.9	-1.6
NL	13.0	11.7	11.4	12.5	10.7	10.1	9.4	-2.9
UK	15.2	15.2	14.8	12.5	10.7	10.0	11.4	-5.2
Total	14.6	14.6	14.2	13.1	11.3	10.4	10.6	-4.2

[a]*NUTS* III regions with more than 50% of population eligible for Objective 2.

regions - with a population of just over 50 million people in 9 member states - had an average unemployment rate slightly more than 3 percentage points above the Community average. Since then the performance of these regions has been generally encouraging, with unemployment rates tending to fall to a greater extent than the Community average during the period of favourable labour-market conditions in 1985-90. The gap between the Objective 2 regions and the Community average is now of the order of 2 percentage points.

French and Italian Objective 2 regions (which account for approximately 20% and 7% respectively of total Community population coverage under this Objective) represent something of an exception to this trend, recording a smaller fall in unemployment rates than the Community average. In these countries even the favourable macroeconomic circumstances of the late 1980s were not sufficient to stimulate the growth in employment needed for appreciable reductions in unemployment to take place. In Spain, the same favourable national macroeconomic circumstances which produced rapid growth in most of its Objective 1 regions seem to have had similarly profound effects on the labour markets of its Objective 2 regions. Even after significant improvement, however, the latter (17% of total Community coverage under Objective 2) still have higher unemployment rates than most other Objective 2 regions, reflecting the severity of the problem which they faced at the outset. The evidence suggests that, on average performance, the German Objective 2 regions (10% of total Community population coverage under Objective 2) are the only ones to have achieved unemployment rates below those for the Community as a whole by the beginning of the 1990s.

The situation in the former German Democratic Republic

The preceding analyses do not include the new regions of the Community in the former GDR. The explanation is relatively simple, in that data according to western definitions will take time to develop. Moreover, data for East Germany for the period before German unification in October 1990 are of limited interest since they refer to the period before economic transition began, with all that that implies for the system of price formation and the valuation of resources.

First estimates of GDP have, however, been produced for 1991. These suggest, with a margin of error of 10%, that average GDP per head in the new German Länder is about one-third of the Community average. This is considerably lower than in Greece (47% of the Community average in 1990). The data suggest that East Berlin is the most prosperous part of the ex-GDR, with a GDP per head of about half the Community average.

The effects of economic transition are particularly evident in the labour markets of eastern Germany. Since German unification employment has fallen by over 40%, although the effect on measured unemployment has not been in proportion, owing to a number of factors, such as short-time working, public-works schemes, early retirement and a large-scale retraining programme, together with a considerable degree of migration and commuting to western Germany. In January 1992, many people previously defined as on short-time working were registered as unemployed; the rate then jumped to 17.0% from 11.8% the previous month. Major regional variations at the level of the Länder have not yet emerged, with rates of unemployment in January 1992 running from 15.8% in Saxony to 19.0% in Mecklenburg-Vorpommern.

Disparities reconsidered

The focus on the standard economic indicators of disparity - GDP, unemployment, and so on - has a natural corollary in that these same indicators can be considered to represent the extent of the challenge facing regional policy. By the same token, the success of regional policy is judged according to the extent to which these regional disparities are reduced. This is clearly reflected in the debates in the European Parliament and elsewhere about the future of Community efforts to increase economic and social cohesion.

The established approach, however, while having all the virtues of simplicity, is not unproblematic. At one level, there is a problem of time horizons, since the time taken to achieve appreciable reductions in disparities is considerably longer than the normal political cycles through which resource transfers to promote regional development are granted. This is particularly the case for disparities in GDP per head, the principal means by which the Community's weakest regions (i.e. Objective 1) are identified. Simple arithmetic demonstrates that for a region to achieve a 20-point reduction in its

Table 4
Requirements for regional convergence: economic growth

Change in GDP per head EC 12 = 100		Period (years)		
from (A)	to (B)	10	15	20
		Required deviation of regional growth from EC average		
50	70	3.5	2.25	1.75
50	90	6 - 6.5	4 - 4.5	3
70	90	2.5	1.75	1.25

income per head disparity with the rest of the Community, it has to sustain a growth rate of more than 2 percentage points above the average for a period of 15 years. This is well beyond any normal public-expenditure planning period (Table 4).[7]

In addition, there are the peculiarities of the relationship between a given input in terms of regional policy and the outcome in terms of changes in GDP. Regional policies can provide the necessary conditions for more rapid economic growth but they cannot guarantee that these will be sufficient. For example, there seems little doubt that the lack of modern infrastructure in the regions whose development is lagging behind - especially transport, telecommunications and energy networks - is a key factor explaining their situation. But even the most ambitious policy of infrastructural investment cannot guarantee the outcome in terms of raising GDP per head - especially over the short to medium term - except perhaps in the directly Keynesian sense of an injection into aggregate demand. If regional policy, traditionally measured, is perceived to fail in some parts of the Community, this may be due to particular and local socio-cultural factors, which it may not be possible or desirable for policy to change, especially in the short term.

It is for these reasons that an alternative approach might be considered, based on the idea of regional disparities seen in terms of differences in economic opportunities. In this sense, the aims of Community regional policy would be to reduce gaps in opportunities between the regions to ensure that individuals and firms have from the outset the material conditions to allow them to compete effectively and fairly in a single market. As discussed below, moreover, the provision of such conditions is something which lends itself to measurement and, more important, to the establishment of performance targets which can be achieved in a reasonable time. Finally, this approach would put the spotlight on the nature and extent of the deficiences within each of the Community's regions and should concentrate minds on the issue of the appropriate policy response, which should be differentiated according to circumstances.

This differentiation should in particular be reflected in the definition and measurement of the gaps. In certain cases, such gaps could be considered as flowing from existing or proposed EC legislation, and the appropriate performance target to be that of pre-established standards. This could extend to environmentally-related differences, where an appropriate performance target would be the level of investment required for the regions to meet standards relating to, say, water or air quality.

In other cases, the point of reference would be the levels of provision obtaining outside the weaker regions. For certain of these cases, the performance target should be the achievement in full of this level of provision. An example is education and training, where the concept of a citizens' Europe calls for greater attention to the conditions for the realisation of individual human potential. An appropriate aim might be to eliminate the disparity in participation rates in education and training for 15- to 19-year-olds between the Objective 1 regions and the rest of the Community. Studies indicate that about a million extra education and training places are required in these regions for this aim to be fulfilled.

In some other cases, however, achieving the level of provision of the most advanced regions would not be appropriate. For example, in relation to transport, energy and telecommunications it would be sufficient to ensure that infrastructure does not constitute a bottleneck for regional development. The performance target might therefore be the achievement of the capacity to meet current and foreseeable demand. Particular importance would be attached to the completion of so-called Trans-European networks falling within the weaker regions as well as the secondary connections to these networks.

Some research has already been undertaken regarding the levels of investment required over time to close the gaps between the Community's weakest regions - Objective 1 - and the rest in the areas of transport, telecommunications, energy, environmental infrastructure, education and training and aid to productive investment.[8] This research suggests a need for a Community contribution - under co-financing arrangements - of well over 20bn Ecu (at 1992 prices) per year over the period 1994-2000. This amounts to about 0.5% of Community GDP or more than twice the resources allocated to the Objective 1 regions in 1992. But at least, with this kind of approach, the aim of economic and social cohesion can be quantified in terms of the regions' individual needs, and set within the context of a normal period for the planning of public expenditure.

Conclusion

In February 1992 the Commission put forward its proposals for the Community's budget for the period 1994-97 inclusive in the form of the Delors-II package.[9] These proposals represented the Commission's views on the financial implications of achieving the more integrated Europe envisaged in the Maastricht Treaty. For the Objective 1 regions an increase in annual expenditure of two-thirds over 1992 was to be achieved by 1997. This was to be complemented by resource transfers for Greece, Ireland, Spain and Portugal under the new Cohesion Fund agreed at Maastricht, thereby doubling the funds available for those countries' Objective 1 regions. On average the sums available for the latter each year were to be of the order of 15bn Ecu (1992 prices). The estimates mentioned above, however, suggest that even these sums would fail to address the needs of Objective 1 regions within the proposed time-scale.[10]

In the context of a more economically-integrated Community, the continuing absence of basic factors of competitiveness will be particularly serious. The case of the five new Länder is instructive in this regard. In July 1990 they entered into an economic and monetary union with West Germany from a position of greatly inferior economic performance. Since then, the expectations of the citizens of the former GDR have risen considerably while increases in economic capacity have failed to keep pace.

While eastern Germany is very much a special case, a more integrated Community may generate similar expectations among its citizens in low-wage regional economies. There is evidence that this is already the case in Italy, where the decreasing wage-gap between North and South has acted as a disincentive to private investment in the latter.

With the loss of exchange-rate flexibility there could be serious damage to industrial competitiveness in the Community's weaker regions. The only available solution for the longer term is to raise regional competitiveness through an adequately-funded regional policy to remedy the major infrastructural and other deficits mentioned above. At the same time, it has to be recognised that the provision of basic infrastructure is a necessary but not a sufficient condition for accelerated economic growth, and that it is important to avoid regional "growth recessions" where increasing productivity simply releases labour which is not taken up elsewhere in the local economy. This is a reminder of the importance of the existence of a creative economic environment so that the productive base and employment enter a virtuous circle of renewal and expansion. In other words, regional policy should not be simply a lifeless accounting procedure to make sure that a given number of kilometres of road are constructed or telephone lines installed. There must be additional efforts to strike the sparks which ignite regional development and create a dynamic entrepreneurial environment.

As well as measures to put in place essential infrastructure in the weaker regions, the Commission has been attempting to promote creative potential within the scope of the regional policies of the 1988 reform. This is evident in the emphasis on human-resource development and in the partnership arrangements whereby local actors are involved in identifying priorities and managing regional development strategies. It is also evident in the innovative measures and initiatives which have attempted to promote the transfer of ideas and know-how, especially across national frontiers. The Commission is currently evaluating the effects of its policies under the reform of the Structural Funds, where the many success stories - which include parts of otherwise poorly-performing regions - as well as the failures, can provide important lessons for the future. Other research is also considering how the creative energy of regional economies can be stimulated and the Directorate-General for Regional Policy is investigating the factors underlying the process of innovation in terms of the involvement of local resources, the creation of synergies between local actors and factors and link-ups with external dynamics.

The effort to reduce disparities must therefore be pursued simultaneously on two fronts: providing the hardware which will eliminate the physical bottlenecks to development while attempting to stimulate the creative potential of the regions. It is the latter which will be the most difficult, and there is considerable scope for improving our understanding of how these creative processes work.

NOTES

1. The views expressed in this chapter are those of the author and should not be attributed to the Commission of the European Communities.

2. See Regulation (EC) No. 2052/88, Article 8.

3. *Ibid.*, Article 9.

4. See Regulation (EC) No. 4253/88, Article 4.

5. Commission of the European Communities, Statistical Office, Regions: Nomenclature of Territorial Units for Statistics, November 1991.

6. For Ireland, there was an important difference between GNP and GDP: GNP per head was appreciably lower than GDP per head. While trends over time can differ, in the late 1980s both GNP per head and GDP per head were rising relative to the rest of the Community.

7. Commission of the European Communities, COM (90) 609, "The Regions in the 1990s: Fourth Periodic Report on the Socio-Economic Situation and Development of the Regions of the Community". See especially Chapter 4.

8. Commission of the European Communities, COM (92) 84, Community Structural Policies: Assessment and Outlook. See Section 1.2.

9. Commission of the European Communities, COM (92) 2000, "From the Single Act to Maastricht and Beyond: The Means to Match our Ambitions".

10. The Edinburgh summit agreement of December 1992, moreover (which took place after this chapter was written), implies that the overall budget appropriations for the Structural Funds will be increased by rather less than envisaged in the Delors-II package.

6 Cohesion, real incomes and employment opportunities

John Morley and Terry Ward

Introduction[1]

When the benefits of European integration are considered, the main emphasis is generally placed on the aggregate effects. However, it is also important that the unification process serves to narrow disparities in real income and employment opportunities between different parts of the Community, and indeed between different social groups.

There is a need to identify the nature and scale of the challenge confronting the Community in its efforts to ensure that people in different areas have comparable opportunities to find decent jobs, and to assess how far recent experience suggests that the Community is converging in employment and labour-market terms.

The focus on regional differences in employment and labour-market supply conditions is particularly important since, as the process of unification and integration goes forward, the economic relevance of national boundaries will progressively diminish. At the same time, the creation of a single economic space within the Community implies that the regional balance in the demand for, and supply of, labour will increasingly become a matter of general Community policy concern and not just that of the member states concerned. Moreover, rising unemployment and the general deterioration in labour-market conditions across the Community over the past two years should focus attention on the interdependence between structural convergence and the overall rate of economic growth.

The process of European labour-market integration

Up to now, movements of labour, or indeed capital, in response to demand and supply imbalances have largely taken place within national borders. The scale of transnational flows of labour, with notable exceptions, has been relatively small and has decreased rather than increased in recent years. In effect, economic adjustments between member states have occurred more through trade and exchange-rate adjustments than through movements of the factors of production.

This pattern could change as a result of further integration measures and the economic forces which they are designed to release. On the other hand, in terms of the pursuit of greater economic and social cohesion, it is important that a balanced development is achieved, not only between member states, but also between regions. Large movements of labour from one area to another are liable both to widen disparities in economic performance, as the workforce in weaker regions is depleted, and to add to congestion and environmental problems in the stronger regions.

Long-term trends in economic growth and real income in member states need to be reviewed. Particular attention, however, should be paid to the period 1985 to 1989. This is not only because it is the longest period for which reasonably consistent regional data are available, but also because it was a period of sustained growth in output and an especially high rate of employment growth in the Community as a whole.

The impact of high economic growth rates on unemployment and labour-force participation, as between regions, can be studied in order to anticipate what degree of progress might be achieved if such growth rates were to be re-established and sustained. It also serves to indicate whether there has been any long-term convergence or divergence in GDP growth, income per head, employment creation and unemployment between member states of the Community over time.

The main emphasis here, however, is on identifying future employment needs in different parts of the Community, based on their expected growth in working-age population and prevailing levels of unemployment and inactivity.

Convergence in economic performance

Achieving real economic convergence between the different regions and areas of the Community is the process of bringing together their economic and social standards and the reduction of disparities in relative levels of income per head.

Over the past 25 years, the less-developed countries of the Community have tended to show a higher rate of economic growth than the more developed member states. This was particularly so in the ten years between 1965 and 1975, when Spain, Portugal, Greece and Ireland all grew much faster, in terms of GDP, than the rest of the Community, the difference averaging around 1-2% a year. Italy, whose southern regions are among the least developed in the Community but whose northern regions are among the most prosperous, also grew significantly faster than the Community average.

In the following ten years, 1975 to 1985, the experience was more mixed, with Spain growing by only 1.5% a year - a slower rate than any other member state - and growth in Greece and Portugal averaging only 0.5% a year more than the Community average. Ireland was an exception, continuing to grow at 3.7% a year over this period.

Between 1985 and 1990, there was a dramatic improvement in Spain's growth performance, which exceeded the Community average by 1% a year. Portugal also achieved a similarly high growth rate. Ireland fell back a little in relative terms, although its rate of GDP growth was still slightly better than average, while the Greek performance deteriorated considerably, its average growth rate being under 2% a year - over 1% below the Community average. Growth in Italy was around the average.

The relative growth performance of the less-developed countries since 1965 suggests progress in real convergence over this period as a whole. However, account has also to be taken of differences in relative rates of population growth. Since this has been much higher in the less-developed countries than elsewhere in the Community over much of the past 25 years, GDP growth needed to be higher simply to maintain relative real income levels.

In fact, although growth rates in the less-developed countries in the period 1965 to 1975 were more than sufficient to compensate for their higher growth of population, in the following ten years their GDP growth (with the exception of Ireland) fell short of this requirement. The gap in income per head between the more- and less-developed member states, which had narrowed appreciably over the preceding ten years, widened again.

Since 1985, Spain, Portugal and Ireland have again enjoyed growth in GDP per head well above the Community average - by 1% a year more - and the average gap in real income per head between the richer and poorer countries narrowed perceptibly between 1985 and 1990. In Greece, however, growth in output per head was over 1% a year below average.

Despite these improvements, the income gap remains substantial. In 1990, the average level of real income in the four less-developed member states (measured in terms of purchasing-power standards to allow for differences in consumption patterns) was less than 70% of the average level in the seven more developed countries (excluding Italy from the comparison because of the differences between the north and south). This difference is the same as it was 15 years earlier, in 1975.

Fixed investment is important for strengthening productive capacity over the long term, and the less-developed countries have had, on average, a consistently higher level of expenditure in relation to GDP than the rest of the Community. The difference has followed closely the relative rates of GDP growth, widening between 1965 and 1975 when the growth performance of the less-developed countries was superior, narrowing significantly over the next ten years when growth fell and widening again after 1985. This illustrates the role of GDP growth in stimulating the investment required to support and reinforce the growth of output and real income.

Regional trends in income per head

Income per head, of course, varies much more between regions across the Community than between member states. In 1989, the average level of income per head (measured in terms of purchasing-power standards) in all regions of Ireland, Portugal, southern Italy and Greece and almost all regions of Spain was over 20% below the Community average. In contrast, in a number of regions of southern Germany and northern Italy, Greater London, Paris and north-east Scotland (where oil is important) the average level was 20% above.

There was little sign of any narrowing of the gap in income per head over the 1980s as a whole. In the first half of the decade, regions to experience the highest gains included parts of southern Germany, south-east England, Denmark and Paris, where income per head was already relatively high. On the other hand, Northern Ireland, central Portugal and parts of eastern Spain and southern Italy, which had amongst the lowest levels of income per head in the Community, also showed significant gains over this period.

In the second half of the 1980s, between 1985 and 1989, the pattern of relative rates of change was quite different. Most of southern Germany, Denmark and the Paris region, which had high rates of growth in income per head in the earlier five years, all experienced relatively low rates of growth in the latter part of the decade, so tending to narrow the gap between rich and poor regions. At the same time, Northern Ireland, central Portugal and southern Italy, as well as many parts of Greece, also experienced relatively low rates of increase, which worked in the opposite direction.

On the other hand, many parts of Spain, Portugal and Ireland, which had experienced relatively small rises in income per head or even decreases over the first half of the 1980s, all showed above-average growth in the second half, so tending to narrow disparities. For the less-developed regions as a whole (those classified as Objective 1 regions for Structural Fund purposes), the average increase in income per head was slightly greater between 1985 and 1989 than in the rest of the Community (about 0.5% a year more), whereas it had been smaller over the preceding five years (about 0.25% a year less). Nevertheless the average income per head in the less-developed regions was still less than 60% of the level in the other Community regions in 1989.

Wages and labour costs

It is difficult to examine wages and labour costs on a regional basis except for manufacturing industry, because of data problems. At the national level, the average levels of compensation of employees (wages plus non-wage labour costs in the form of social insurance contributions and so on, which is arguably a more comparable measure not only of labour costs but also of wage income than gross wages alone) in 1988 were very similar in most northern member states.

In Ecu terms, the difference in average labour costs per employee between the Netherlands, which had the highest level in the Community, and Denmark, which had the sixth highest level, was only around 8%. This is significantly less than the difference in 1985 (18%) or in 1980 (30%). The average cost of employing someone has therefore become much closer in these countries. Moreover, the rank order of the northern countries in terms of average compensation of employees did not change much over the 1980s, except that Germany moved successively from being fifth to fourth to second over the period.

The rank order of the remaining six countries also remained more or less the same during these years, except that Greece replaced Portugal as the country with the lowest average labour costs in the Community, with a level in 1988 only around one-seventh of that in the six northern countries.

The difference in average labour costs between the six lower-wage countries, and between them and the six high-wage countries, tended to widen over the 1980s. In particular (leaving aside Portugal and Greece where wages were considerably lower than elsewhere) the difference in the average level between Italy, the seventh-ranked country, and Spain, the tenth-ranked, was over 30% in 1988 as against less than 10% in 1980. Conversely the difference between average labour costs in the highest and lowest ranked countries in the Community narrowed from around 5 times to 4 times, between 1980 and 1988.

Measured in terms of purchasing-power standards, which take account of differences in consumption patterns and relative prices between countries, the differences in average labour costs per employee between countries are significantly less than when measured in terms of Ecus. This is because the levels of consumption of different types of goods and services are not the same across countries. Moreover, goods and services tend to have lower prices where they are heavily consumed, equalising to some extent relative real incomes. When measured in these terms, the gap between the highest- and lowest-wage countries is reduced from 4 times to 2 times in 1988.

Comparing average compensation per employee across member states with average real income per head of population shows a similar pattern, with one or two exceptions. One particular exception is the UK. Compared with other member states, it has a significantly higher level of income per head of population relative to its average compensation per employee - which was considerably below the Community average in 1988. The reason is that, relative to other countries, the UK has more of its population in employment and generating income. This compensates for the low level of productivity - and wages - per worker in the UK and raises the real income per head of population. Much the same is true of Denmark, while the reverse applies to Spain and Italy, both of which have low proportions of their populations in employment.

The pattern of average labour costs per employee for the economy as a whole, as between member states, is broadly repeated for individual sectors. However, while the rank order of countries is similar in each case, the scale difference between countries tends to be somewhat greater when each sector is considered individually.

Convergence in employment levels

Despite their success in achieving relatively high rates of economic growth, the less-developed countries' employment growth has been disappointing over the last 25 years. In the period 1965 to 1975, only Spain managed to achieve an increase in employment above the Community average while, over the following ten years, only Greece had any significant expansion in employment at all. In both Spain and Portugal, employment declined between 1975 and 1985 and in Ireland it remained more or less constant.

Since 1985, of the less-developed countries only Spain has achieved a rate of employment growth above the Community average. In Greece and Ireland, growth of employment was under 1% a year, while employment in Portugal fell slightly.[2] Unemployment rates in all the less-developed countries were above those in the rest of the Community over the period 1965 to 1975. However, only in Ireland - where unemployment at the time was 6%, and the highest in the Community - was the difference substantial. In Spain, Portugal and Greece, the rate of unemployment averaged 3-4% over these ten years. In the following ten years, only Greece had an average unemployment rate below the Community average, the rate in Spain and Ireland being close to 12%. Over the period 1985 to 1990, unemployment in Portugal fell below that in most of the rest of the Community, but in Spain and Ireland the rate increased even further above the Community average to reach 18-19%.

Measuring employment needs

The employment needs of particular regions can be measured in terms of two factors - the number of people joining the labour market for the first time, and the numbers at present without a job. The first factor is not difficult to measure in the sense that changes in the population of working age - i.e. those aged between 15 and 64 - are known, and give a reasonable estimate of those potentially available to come onto the labour market. The second is, however, more problematic.

The usual measure of the number of people looking for work is unemployment statistics. However, these statistics include only those who have clearly indicated that they are looking for work. They do not cover all those who might like to be in employment if they could find a job, or who would be encouraged to work if work were available. Even where appropriate adjustments are made to the estimates of the numbers unemployed, a sizeable proportion of people may remain unrecorded. These people, mostly women, are usually regarded as inactive and therefore not part of the labour force. Yet whenever there is any sizeable expansion in the number of jobs on offer, these supposedly inactive people appear to fill a significant proportion of the jobs which become available.

Unemployment figures may not, therefore, be a reliable guide to those who might want to work if more suitable jobs became available, as would happen if closer European integration had the effect on employment widely expected of it. A better indication of this - and therefore of the unused labour force in any locality - is given by the ratio of employment to working-age population. In places where this is low, it seems reasonable to assume that there are relatively high numbers of economically inactive people who would like to work if employment opportunities were created, whether these are revealed in the unemployment figures or not.

The proportion of the working-age population in employment tends to be higher, in general, in the more prosperous and developed northern regions than in the less-developed southern regions. On average, this proportion was 62% in 1989 in the more developed parts of the Community as against only just over 50% in the developing regions (Objective 1). Moreover, since 1985 the proportion has increased more in developed regions than in the less-developed areas. Whereas the proportion of people of working age in work reached 75% in Denmark and south-east England and 70% in southern Germany in 1989, it was below 50% in all of Spain (except the extreme north-west), in Ireland and in much of southern Italy.

This pattern, however, is not universal. The proportion of working-age population in work in 1989, for example, was below 55% in much of the Netherlands and Belgium as well as in parts of central Germany, whereas the proportion was over 60% in northern Portugal and over 55% in Greece.

Official unemployment in the Community, as measured in the rates calculated by Eurostat for comparative purposes, ranged in 1989 from over 12% in southern Italy, much of Spain and Ireland (both north and south of the border) as well as in the Calais and Languedoc-Roussillon regions of France, and Hainaut in Belgium in 1990, to under 4% in southern Germany, northern Italy and central Portugal.

Since then, unemployment has been rising once again and, on average, the proportion of working-age population classified as unemployed in the less-developed regions was 8.5% in 1991 as opposed to just under 5% in the rest of the Community.

Estimating hidden labour supply

In Denmark in 1989, employment amounted to over 75% of the working-age population, and unemployment stood at 8%. This meant that only around 17% of people of working age were inactive and not counted as part of the labour force. While this proportion is considerably lower than in other parts of the Community, it is similar to that in other Scandinavian countries - all of which have given priority to making it easier for married women and other groups to participate in the labour force. It seems reasonable to suppose that over time - even a long time in a number of cases - regions outside Denmark could attain a similarly low inactivity rate.

To get an idea of the possible scale of this effect, an estimate of hidden labour supply can be made, based on the conservative assumption that a hard core of 20% (rather than the 17% in Denmark) of working-age population would remain inactive irrespective of the number of jobs on offer, and irrespective of the measures taken to facilitate participation. This is on a par with the inactivity rate in the USA.

Clearly, this can only be a rough assumption. It is possible that there are genuine, inherent, differences between regions as regards the proportion of the so-called inactive population who would like to work. This may be because of deep-seated social or cultural differences or because of differences in, for example, the proportion of women with young children who would prefer to stay at home, at least during their early years.

It is also possible that there are significant regional variations in the proportion of people over 65 who would like to work. Nevertheless it provides a useful indicator of the potential scale of under-employment or hidden labour supply across the Community as it progresses through the 1990s.

The estimates achieved in this way suggest that hidden labour supply was significant in almost all areas outside Denmark in 1989. Over much of Germany and France, it exceeded 10% of working-age population and, in the prosperous and developed regions of northern Italy, it exceeded 15%. In most of the poorer, less-developed regions, in Spain and southern Italy, the hidden labour supply rate exceeded 20%. This figure was also found, perhaps unexpectedly, in all regions of Belgium.

On average, hidden labour supply in the less-developed regions, expressed in relation to their population of working age, can be estimated at over 20%, in 1989, against a rate of under 13% in other parts of the Community. This difference is significantly greater than for unemployment. Taking hidden labour supply and unemployment together, just under 30% of people of working age were actual or potential job seekers in the less-developed regions in 1989, compared with under 20% in other areas.

The working-age population

Over the Community as a whole, the working-age population increased by around 1% between 1985 and 1989. There were, however, significant differences between regions. In general (but with exceptions) the increases tended to be higher in the south of the Community than in the north. Indeed in many of the most prosperous and most developed areas - in northern Italy, southern Germany, the Paris region and south-east England - there was little growth at all in the working-age population. In Greece, southern Italy and much of Spain and Portugal, the increase was more than 2%, in some cases significantly more.

On average, the increase in this group of people over the period was almost 3% in the less-developed (Objective 1) regions as against just over 1% in other areas. In broad terms, therefore, the differential rates of growth of working-age population added to the existing differences in rates of unemployment or under-employment between regions, thereby increasing the need for jobs in the southern regions of the Community and Ireland, as compared with the rest of the Community.

The change in working-age population recorded in each area depends not only on indigenous population growth, but also on inward and outward migration. Though migration flows have, in the past, tended partly to offset relatively high natural population growth in less-developed regions, the scale of movement over the past few years has been small.

Employment

Although there was a substantial increase in employment in the Community as a whole between 1985 and 1989, the experience in different regions varied significantly. In major areas - over much of France and Italy and parts of northern Germany - the numbers in employment actually declined. In the north of the Community, the numbers in employment rose considerably in many regions. This was the case over much of the UK, where unemployment was above the Community average at the beginning of the period, but also in areas of southern Germany where unemployment was below average.

In the south of the Community, employment increased at well above average in southern Spain, central Portugal, Sardinia and Brittany (at over 10% in the four years). By contrast, in the south of Italy, Greece and Ireland, employment either declined or rose at a relatively low rate.

Overall there was no general convergence between richer and poorer areas over this period. On average, employment in the less-developed regions of the Community increased by just over 6% between 1985 and 1989, marginally less than in the rest of the Community.

Unemployment and hidden labour supply

The effect on unemployment of differential rates of employment growth has not been uniform across the Community. Although the largest reductions in unemployment rates in the late 1980s were in parts of the UK and Spain (where employment growth was highest) and the largest increases were in southern Italy and Sicily (where employment fell), unemployment remained broadly unchanged over much of France despite a decline in employment. In most regions of the Netherlands, unemployment was only a little lower in 1989 than it had been in 1985, even though employment rose significantly over the period.

On average, the recorded rate of unemployment actually rose by around 0.5% of the labour force in the less-developed regions between 1985 and 1989, despite the growth in employment whereas, in the other parts of the Community, it fell by over 1%.

The estimate of hidden labour supply showed a similar pattern of change over this period. It declined quite significantly over much of Spain, Portugal and the UK, where official rates of unemployment also fell, and increased over much of France and Ireland where unemployment also rose or declined only marginally. There were, however, a number of exceptions to this trend. It fell substantially in the Netherlands as well as in parts of southern Italy - two areas where unemployment declined only slightly. Moreover, it increased in Brittany whereas unemployment showed an above-average decline.

In the less-developed regions overall, hidden labour supply (as a percentage of the working-age population) fell on average by slightly more than in other parts of the Community between 1985 and 1989. Nevertheless the average rate remained around a third higher in the former than in the latter, at over 20% as opposed to less than 13%. Taken together, unemployment and hidden labour supply declined over this period by only half as much in the less-developed regions (by 1.6% of working-age population) as in the rest of the Community.

Employment/population ratios

The deterioration in the position of the developing regions over this period is partly a consequence of fewer additional jobs being created and partly a reflection of their higher growth in working-age population (which was adding to a labour supply already in excess of the employment on offer, and which was only marginally reduced by outward migration).

The net effect of these differential rates of growth was that the rate of employment (i.e. the ratio of employment to working-age population) rose on average by 3 percentage points in the more developed parts of the Community between 1985 and 1989 and by only 1.5% in the less-developed regions.

For women, the difference in experience was even more marked. In the less-developed regions, the employment rate of women, which averaged 30% of the working-age population in 1985, increased to just under 33% in 1989. In other parts of the Community, the employment rate of women rose from 43% to over 49%.

Labour-force participation

In terms of labour-force participation, a major difference remains between the richer, more developed regions and the less-developed. Although labour-force participation (defined as employment plus unemployment as a percentage of working-age population) increased more in the peripheral regions of the Community between 1985 and 1989 than in other areas, this conceals the fact that much of the rise in participation in the former areas was associated with a rise in the numbers recorded as unemployed. Whereas in the more developed regions 42% of the growth in employment over this period can be attributed to increased participation, in the less-developed regions the figure was only around 30%.

Thus, a considerable proportion of people of working age who could have expected to find work had they lived elsewhere, remain effectively excluded from the labour market over much of the less-developed part of the Community. Most of these people are women, especially married women, since the participation rates of men are very similar from one part of the Community to another.

Employment opportunities for women

The importance of the employment of women varies significantly across the Community. Broadly, as reflected in the employment/population ratios, it is relatively high in the more developed northern regions and relatively low in the poorer, less-developed regions. There are, however, exceptions. In particular, it is lower than the Community average in parts of the Netherlands and Belgium (which are highly developed) and higher than average in Portugal and parts of Greece.

The importance of female employment has increased progressively over time over the Community as a whole. Of the additional jobs created in the Community between 1985 and 1989, significantly more went to women than to men. However, again, this was not the case in all regions. In southern and eastern Spain, where employment growth was relatively high, less than half the additional jobs went to women (even though the employment of women increased at a rate well above the Community average). This was also the case in Brittany and Northern Ireland, which also experienced comparatively large gains in employment.

In other peripheral regions, on the other hand - Ireland, central and northern parts of Spain, the south of France, and much of southern Italy and Greece - women did increase their share of total employment. Even where there was little or no increase in total employment - in Greece and much of southern Italy - the employment of women rose by more than the Community average.

Overall, the evidence of any convergence in the shares of female employment across the Community is patchy. Most areas where women's share of employment had been relatively low experienced a relatively large rise between 1985 and 1989. However, in the UK, Denmark and many parts of France and Germany, where women's employment was already high in 1985, its importance had increased further by 1989. Thus the relative disparities between areas changed comparatively little.

Part-time working

The scale of part-time working varies considerably across the Community. In general, it is comparatively low in the poorer, less-developed regions, such as in Greece, Portugal and Ireland, where it accounts for under 10% of total employment. In the more developed regions, however, although it is generally more important, there is little systematic tendency for the proportion working part-time to increase with the level of economic development in the region concerned (as reflected in incomes per head).

Whereas part-time working accounted for over 20% of total employment in 1989 in Denmark, the Netherlands and south-east England, its level is much lower over most of Germany, France and northern Italy. Clearly this is a reflection of many factors, economic, legislative and social.

There has been a tendency, however, for part-time working to increase particularly rapidly in the most economically successful and prosperous areas of Germany, France and northern Italy - for example, in Bavaria, in the Paris region and in Emilia-Romagna. In these areas, not only did the numbers employed on a part-time basis go up by more than 10% between 1985 and 1989, but they accounted for more than half the total rise in employment over the period.

At the same time, the number of part-time workers also rose significantly in some less-developed regions, such as northern Portugal, the most southerly part of Italy and Ireland. In many other similar areas, however - including Greece, central Portugal and most of southern Italy - it declined further over this period from levels which were already low.

Convergence in the sectoral distribution of employment

By and large, the peripheral regions of the Community have a higher proportion of people employed in agriculture and a lower proportion employed in industry than the more central parts of the Community. In 1989, in Ireland, Greece, and much of Spain, Portugal and southern Italy, over 15%, and in many cases over 20%, of employment was in agriculture and less than 30% in industry. By contrast, in the UK, (except for Northern Ireland), and most of the Netherlands, Belgium and Germany, agriculture accounted for less than 5% of employment. On average, developing regions had 19% of employment in agriculture as against under 5% in the rest of the Community and less than 28% in industry as against 34% in other areas.

Having a low proportion of the working population employed in agriculture does not necessarily imply a high proportion employed in industry, since much industrial employment in the Community is concentrated in the central triangle of southern and central Germany, northern Italy and eastern France. In these areas over 40% of jobs were in industry in 1989. Outside this area, only the west Midlands in the UK, Catalonia and the Basque region in Spain, and northern Portugal, have comparably high concentrations of employment.

Employment in services is not spread evenly across the Community. Service employment is, of course, particularly high in large cities like London, Paris, Brussels, Amsterdam and Rotterdam and, to a lesser extent, Madrid, where there is a large concentration of financial and business services. It is only slightly less high in the other, more prosperous, areas of the Community, such as south-east England, Denmark and the Netherlands. But it also tends to be high in tourist areas such as the south of France, Brittany and the Balearics. It is also high in much of southern Italy, where tourism is not developed but where there is a relatively high proportion of employment in public services.

By contrast, employment in services is relatively low not only over much of Spain, Portugal and Greece but also over much of Germany, particularly the industrial south where in a number of regions it accounts for less than 50% of those in work. On average, only just over half of employment in the less-developed regions was in the service sector in 1989 as compared with 61% in other parts of the Community and an average of 70% in the USA.

Convergence in employment structure

Between 1985 and 1989, employment in services in the Community as a whole went up at over four times the rate of increase in employment in industry, while jobs in agriculture continued to decline. By and large, changes in service employment moved in line with changes in total employment: those regions where the overall number of jobs rose at a relatively high rate also experienced a high rate of increase in service employment. There were, however, a few exceptions, notably the south-east corner of Germany and south-west England, where growth of employment overall was due more to rising employment in industry than in services.

In virtually all regions, the additional jobs created between 1985 and 1989 were predominantly in services rather than in industry and, in some regions, services accounted for practically all of the net increase in jobs over this period.

Overall, the increase in both service and industrial employment in the less-developed regions outstripped the rise in other areas between 1985 and 1989. For both sectors, the difference amounted to some 4 percentage points on average. Equally, the reduction in agricultural employment over the same period was greater in less-developed areas than elsewhere, though the difference averaged only 2 percentage points. There was, therefore, an unambiguous convergence in the sectoral pattern of employment in the peripheral regions towards that prevailing in the more developed areas.

However, the relatively high rates of job creation in services and industry in the less-developed regions did not prevent their overall employment growth lagging behind that in the rest of the Community. This outcome is a consequence of the very different initial distribution of employment between the broad sectors of activity in the two areas and, in particular, of the difference in the relative size of the agricultural sector. This means that, for every 1% reduction in agricultural employment, four times as many additional jobs in industry and/or services have to be created in the peripheral regions compared with elsewhere if the people released onto the labour market are to be absorbed.

In other words, in the less-developed regions, employment in industry and services has to grow at a higher rate than in other areas not just to cater for the significantly higher growth of working-age population and the larger numbers of unemployed (both revealed or concealed) but also in order to compensate for the steady contraction in the number of jobs in agriculture. This is likely to remain the case for many years given both the substantial numbers still employed in the agricultural sector in these regions and the long-term decline in employment in the sector.

Dependency ratios and working-age population projections

Peripheral regions not only have a lower proportion of their working-age populations in employment; they also tend to have comparatively large numbers of both young and old people relative to the number of people of working age. Accordingly, these regions tend to have greater numbers of people with little or no income compared with more prosperous areas. The so-called dependency ratio (the number of people aged under 15 and over 64 relative to the number of people in other age-groups) is less than 40% in parts of northern Italy, Germany and the Netherlands, but is over 50% in many regions of Spain, Portugal, Greece and Ireland, as well as south-west England, Wales and large areas of France.

Recent projections of future changes in the population of working age, which should be a good indicator of the growth or decline in the potential labour force, show that some growth is likely over the next 25 years in many of the peripheral regions of the Community - in Scotland, Ireland, Brittany, northern Portugal, southern Spain, the south of Italy and southern Greece. In many of the central, most developed and prosperous parts of the Community, however, a decline in working-age population is forecast. This is particularly so in Germany and northern and central Italy where in the majority of regions, falls of over 10% are projected in the period up to 2015.

Since these projections are determined, to a significant extent, by the population trends already in evidence (birth rates in particular) and since they make some allowance for possible migration on the basis of present movements, they indicate the challenge confronting the Community. Job creation will need to occur disproportionately in the peripheral regions simply to maintain the existing gap in employment and unemployment rates between these and the rest of the Community, let alone reduce it.

Fulfilling employment needs

If these projections of working-age population are combined with the estimates of hidden labour supply and the figures for the number of people currently unemployed, the need for future jobs in the less-developed parts of the Community is substantial.

As an indication it can be seen that, in order to close the gap between the less-developed regions and the rest of the Community in the ratio of employment to working-age population, employment would need to grow over the next 25 years by at least 1% a year more than elsewhere - a performance which is far in excess of what has been achieved over the recent past.

Of course, these projections cannot fully allow for the unknown but potentially-considerable migratory movements from central and eastern Europe and from the south of the Mediterranean, especially if unemployment becomes an even bigger problem in these places. To that extent, they may understate future employment needs in the Community, particularly in regions bordering or close to the countries from which immigrants are likely to come.

Labour mobility as a solution to imbalance

One approach to tackling the problems of labour-market imbalances and uneven economic development has been to encourage or assist people to move from areas with an excess supply of labour (in relation to jobs available) to areas where the reverse is the case. Indeed, difficulty in finding employment locally has always provided a strong incentive for people to move to find work elsewhere.

Usually, such movement has been from one region to another within the same country, but there have been a number of instances during the Community's existence of large-scale movements between European and neighbouring countries. In the 1960s, for example, there was a considerable migration of north Africans into France, of people from the new Commonwealth into the UK and of Turks and Yugoslavs into Germany. Within the Community, until comparatively recently, there were large movements north from Spain, Portugal, Greece and southern Italy into Germany and the Benelux countries, while migration from Ireland to other European countries still occurs on a significant scale.

Certain measures included in the Social Action Programme involve the removal of the remaining restrictions on the movement of labour from one member state to another. The underlying aim is to widen employment opportunities and ensure a more balanced labour market across the Community. However, labour movements have never been seen as a major means of correcting labour-market imbalance.

Moreover, the exodus of people from underdeveloped regions, by removing their income and skills, is likely to make it more rather than less difficult for such areas to generate self-sustaining development. Equally, a rapid influx of people into more prosperous areas can impose additional problems and costs in terms of increased congestion and in terms of pressure on local services, infrastructure and amenities.

It is, anyway, unlikely that any large-scale movements in labour will follow the removal of any remaining restrictions on labour movements. Language and cultural differences are likely to remain a significant obstacle to large-scale movements of labour. In addition, differences in business practices, especially as regards recruitment, promotion and the structure of pay, as well as in education and training systems, make it difficult for people to take up work in another country.

Migration between member states

The scale of inter-country migration which has occurred in the recent past has been limited. The result is that, in 1989, only 4% of the people living in the Community were not nationals of the country where they were resident. (The numbers of people living in one country who are nationals of another does not give a complete indication of past migration, since such figures leave out of account those people who have immigrated and have since taken up nationality).

Less than half of the non-nationals were from other Community countries. Only in France, Germany and Belgium was the proportion of non-nationals in the population significantly greater than the Community average. The highest immigrant population is found in Belgium, where it attains nearly 9%, over half of these originating from other Community countries. In Germany before unification (which has changed the average figure), the overall figure was 8%, with three-quarters of the people concerned being from non-Community countries, especially countries in the rest of Europe. In France, the total was just under 7%, with a higher percentage (about 40%) coming from other Community countries.

In relation to the size of their populations, the main Community countries to have supplied migrant labour to the rest of the Community are Ireland and Portugal. Irish emigrants living in other Community countries in 1989 totalled almost 18% of the current population of Ireland, while the figure for Portugal was almost 10%. For the other countries, only in the case of Luxembourg and Greece was the figure above 4%. For Germany, France, Denmark and the UK, emigrants to other parts of the Community amounted to less than 1% of their population in 1989.

The age structure of the immigrant population in Community countries tends to be different from that of the national population. For those coming from other Community countries, a relatively high proportion tend to be of working age. However, in the case of immigrants coming from outside the Community, a high proportion are children under 14 (over 25%).

The type of job taken by immigrants also tends to differ from those taken by nationals. A much higher proportion of the jobs they take up are in industry - over 40% for Community immigrants and around 50% for immigrants from other countries - with a lower proportion in both services and agriculture.

In the past, the people involved in migratory movements have tended to be mainly unskilled manual workers taking up jobs in construction, industry or menial services. With the exception of the continuing migration from Ireland, such movements have been on a relatively limited scale, and have been largely reversed over the past decade.

However, there is evidence that the rate of inter-country migration within the Community is now higher among professional and managerial workers than among manual workers, and this trend is likely to increase. The measures in the Single Market programme on the mutual recognition of professional qualifications and the comparability of vocational training qualifications serve to facilitate and encourage this trend. Over 50% of foreign nationals coming to work in the UK over the period 1985-88, for example, were managerial or professional staff. A large part of this migration, however, takes place within multinational companies, as managers and skilled personnel are moved from country to country to gain experience or to tackle a particular job. It is also usually for a limited period of time rather than permanently.

A resumption of the large-scale movements of unskilled manual workers which occurred in the past seems unlikely. Not only is the demand for such workers diminishing over time as skills become more important, but also an increasing proportion of manual jobs are no longer in manufacturing but in services, where the ability to relate easily to others and to communicate, often in more than one language, is becoming important.

Inter-regional migration

Labour movements within countries involve fewer obstacles than labour movements between countries. Nevertheless, in recent years the scale of outward migration from problem regions to other areas seems to have declined in southern parts of the Community. In Italy in particular, the large movements of mainly young people from the Mezzogiorno to the north in search of work was significantly less in the 1980s than in the 1970s. For Sicily, for example, net emigration averaged 0.1% of the population over the period 1980 to 1988 - half the rate for the period 1975–79 and substantially less than the rates of the 1950s and 1960s. The same pattern is evident for the Sud region and Sardinia.

In Spain, there seems to have been a slowdown in migration between the first and second half of the 1980s, with, for example, net outward migration from the Basque regions, Castilla-la-Mancha and Asturias falling between the two periods. For Germany and the UK, however, the pattern is somewhat different. In the former case, there is evidence of a general movement from the north (and east) to the south (and west) over the 1980s, except for Schleswig-Holstein, the most northerly region, which experienced a net influx of migrants. The scale of the movement, moreover, tended to be larger in the second half of the 1980s than the first half. In the UK, there also seems to have been some acceleration in the scale of inter-regional migration over the 1980s, with the south-west, East Anglia, Wales and the East Midlands all experiencing larger net influxes between 1984 and 1988 than over the previous five years and Scotland, in particular, experiencing a bigger outflow.

In general, however, the scale of inter-regional migration was relatively small over the 1980s and its effect in reducing local population, and therefore local labour supply, was relatively minor.

The impact of recession on cohesion

The broad evidence of the past two decades is that progress in achieving convergence in incomes and employment opportunities between richer and poorer regions of the Community is significantly affected by the overall rate of economic growth in the Community. In general, growth is good for convergence - a rising tide lifts weaker boats more effectively than stronger ones.

The significantly-lower rates of economic growth in the first two years of the 1990s compared with the second half of the 1980s, and the current forecasts of poor growth prospects over the next couple of years, therefore give cause for considerable concern - especially when compared with the greater employment needs of poorer regions.

It is to be hoped that the process of economic integration taking place under the stimulus of the completion of the internal market and progress towards economic and monetary union, supported by the Community's structural policies, will be sufficient to offset the forces acting against convergence. On the strength of past experience, however, it would be unwise to take success for granted.

NOTES

1. The views expressed in this chapter are those of the authors and should not be attributed to the Commission of the European Communities.

2. It should be emphasised that the employment figures used in this analysis are inevitably based on various statistical sources since the Labour-Force Survey statistics generally used for these kinds of comparisons only go back until 1983. For the recent period the LFS statistics show an increase of employment in Portugal of almost 3% a year, which is in line with GDP growth.

Part II

Aspects of the catching-up process

7 Catching up with the rest: the Irish experience

Kieran A. Kennedy

Introduction

"Catching up" in the EC context means the living standards of poorer countries approaching those of richer ones, i.e. real convergence, as distinct from nominal convergence in inflation, interest rates and budget balances. The most commonly-used measure of living standards in such comparisons is average GDP per capita. In some circumstances, however, this indicator may be seriously misleading.

Moreover, catching up, however measured, can take place in quite different ways. It matters a great deal to the poorer area, however, *how* real convergence takes place. For example, the GDP per capita of a poorer country or region may converge with that of richer ones either through relatively rapid GDP growth or through emigration and population decline. Convergence in average living standards also tells us nothing about the internal distribution of these standards. In particular, protracted high unemployment is a highly-visible indicator of exclusion from participation in society, which can pose a more severe threat to social cohesion than gaps in average income.

These and other points of relevance to the wider debate on economic and social cohesion in the European Community are illustrated in this chapter with reference to Irish experience. Table 1 gives some basic statistics on Ireland and the Irish economy and comparable EC-12 figures.

Table 1
Ireland - basic statistics (with comparable EC-12 figures)

	Ireland	EC-12
Population, 1992, millions	3.5	330
Population density, per sq. km.	51	145
Relative GDP per head of		
population, 1991	69	100
Relative GDP per worker, 1991	89	100
Unemployment rate, 1992%	17.8	9.5
% Employment by sector, 1990		
Agriculture	15	7
Industry	28	32
Services	57	61
% Gross value added by sector, 1990		
Agriculture	10	3
Industry	37	33
Services	53	64
Exports of goods as % GDP, 1991	56	22
Exports of goods Intra-EC	43	14
Exports of goods Extra-EC	13	8
Public debt/GDP ratio, 1991, %	103	62
Government borrowing as % of		
GDP, 1992	2.7	5.4
Inflation rate, 1992	3.0	4.3
Current balance of payments surplus		
as % GDP, 1992	5.5	0.5
% Population 14-24 in education, 1989	50	43

1. Long-term historical experience

Following the Act of Union of 1800, the whole island of Ireland formed part of an economic and monetary union with Great Britain which lasted from 1826, when the Irish pound was completely assimilated and all tariffs eliminated, until independence was achieved in the early 1920s. Independence involved the partition of the country, with Northern Ireland, which then accounted for nearly

30% of the total population of Ireland, remaining part of the United Kingdom. Even in the independent south, however, a fixed one-for-one link with sterling was maintained, and there were no transaction costs in exchanging the two currencies, so that monetary union with the UK effectively continued up to 1979, when the Republic joined the European Monetary System.

The nineteenth century

How did Ireland fare as regards real convergence in this situation? The data for the nineteenth century are not very reliable, but there is a good deal of evidence suggesting that Ireland experienced considerable convergence with Great Britain in terms of income per capita - at least following the Great Famine of 1846-7. It is estimated that in 1841, just prior to the Great Famine, income per capita in Ireland was about 40% of the British level, but that by 1913 it had risen close to 60% - a much greater increase than in Britain (Kennedy et al., 1988).

This convergence was achieved, however, in the context of a massive decline in population, mainly through emigration. During the Great Famine itself up to one million people died, but in the six years 1847-52, over 1.25m people emigrated from Ireland to North America as well as substantial numbers to Britain. In the course of the next 70 years, a further 3 million people emigrated, so that in 1921 the population was little more than half the pre-famine level. The singularity of this position can be illustrated by comparison with the rest of the UK. In 1841, the population of Ireland was over three times that of Scotland and more than half that of England and Wales. By 1921, it was 10% less than that of Scotland and only one-ninth that of England and Wales.

Ireland's average income *per capita* on the eve of the First World War, though well below the British level, compared favourably with much of the rest of Europe, but this position had not been achieved through vigorous economic growth. Though there was some rise in total product over the period 1841-1913, the rate was lower than in almost any other European country at that time. Rather, the improvement in living standards came about mainly through population decline and specialisation in favourably-priced livestock production, which itself helped to intensify the population decline. Needless to say, this form of convergence cannot be looked on as satisfactory, and serves as a reminder - admittedly an extreme one - that the way in which convergence takes place can be as important as the fact of convergence itself. Where convergence is achieved through massive migration, the income per head of the remaining population is an inadequate measure - because the level of population itself is a relevant variable in most countries' perceptions of national welfare.

Independence: the first 40 years

Although the catalogue of British misrule in Ireland is extensive, it must also be recognised that the newly-independent Irish state began life in 1922 with inherited advantages not possessed in the same degree by many of the European countries that have since outpaced it. The country could no longer be said to be overpopulated, having a relatively low population density; it had no national debt and possessed substantial external capital reserves; there was an extensive rail network; the banking system was widely spread; communications were satisfactory by contemporary standards; and education levels were not inferior to those generally prevailing. Yet in the next 40 years Ireland made no further progress in catching up with British income levels. This experience would be less disappointing if the UK had been a star performer, but in fact it has had the worst growth record in Europe this century - so that in merely keeping pace with Britain, Ireland's position deteriorated relative to continental West European countries. Furthermore, Irish emigration continued at a rate which meant a continuing decline in population, so that in 1961 the population, at 2.8 million, reached an all-time low, 10% below the level at independence.

Table 2
Composition of Irish merchandise exports (%)

	1929	1950	1990
Destination			
UK	92	88	34
Other EC	3	7	41
Rest of world	5	5	25
Total	100	100	100
Commodity			
Food and drink	86	80	22
Manufactures	} 14	7	69
Other		13	8
Total	100	100	100
Ratio exports: GNP			
(factor cost)	29	20	71

Source: *Statistical Abstract of Ireland.*

Why was Ireland's record of achievement so mediocre? Many explanatory factors - economic, social and cultural, including those inherited from the country's turbulent past - can be advanced. Here I simply draw attention to the significance of Ireland's trading pattern,[1] which is always a key factor for a small country and one that remains highly relevant in the EC context. Table 2 gives a summary breakdown of Irish exports by destination and by commodity composition since the 1920s.

At independence, over 90% of Irish exports were going to the UK, and in addition the financial, labour-market, institutional and other links were extremely close. This is not surprising given that Ireland was for so long a region of the UK. Nor would it necessarily have been a disadvantage if the UK had been a dynamic economy. But there are compelling reasons (to which I revert in Section 2) for the view that peripheral low-income areas find it difficult to catch up when the core is stagnant or growing slowly.

No other European country was as dependent on one market as Ireland was on the UK. No matter how hard Ireland tried, it was going to take time to reduce this dependence. The 1930s and 40s, moreover, were not auspicious times for diversifying the destination of trade, even if Irish policy had been directed more effectively towards that goal. Indeed, as late as 1950 the degree of trade dependence on the UK was virtually unaltered. The postwar period was much more favourable to diversifying both the destination and the commodity composition of Irish trade, and it is surely no accident that Ireland began to catch up with Britain as that process intensified.

The partition of Ireland, with Northern Ireland remaining in the UK, deprived the new state of the only region with substantial industrial development. Independent Ireland was heavily reliant on agriculture in relation both to trade (Table 2) and employment (Table 3), with only a minuscule manufacturing sector of which two-thirds was engaged in the processing of food and drink. In arguing that this was a constraint on the rate at which Ireland could develop, one must be careful to avoid special pleading, since the high share of agriculture in the 1920s was not dissimilar to what had prevailed in many European countries 50 years earlier (see Maddison 1982, Table C5). It might therefore be said simply to portray Ireland's latecomer status, rather than a constraint on future development. Nevertheless, it can reasonably be argued that the structure of activity which Ireland inherited at independence was not conducive to rapid development in the prevailing conditions. Real agricultural prices declined drastically from 1919 to the mid-1930s, and thereafter the long-term trend was downwards. The widespread resort to agricultural protectionism in the 1930s restricted market access almost exclusively to the UK, where the indigenous farmers were subsidised in a way that kept prices low. In this period, moreover, Ireland made matters worse for its own agriculture on the UK market by engaging in a trade war; but even without that, conditions were never long conducive to a strong agricultural performance until Ireland joined the European Community.

Table 3
Structure of Irish employment (%)

	1926	1951	1991
Agriculture	54	41	14
Industry	13	23	28
Manufacturing	(10)	(15)	(20)
Services	33	36	58
Absolute total (,000)	1,220	1,217	1,121

Source: Kennedy et al (1988) and ESRI, *Quarterly Economic Commentary*.

As regards the absence of a manufacturing tradition, Maddison's figures show that even fifty years earlier few of the sixteen developed countries in his sample had quite as small an industrial base as Ireland had in 1920, while the figures in Flora (1987) for about the 1920s suggest that, apart from Finland, Ireland was the least developed industrially among thirteen West European countries in terms of the share of the labour force in that sector. Inevitably, it would take time to build an industrial base, and in the prevailing conditions - the widespread protectionism of the 1930s and the absence then of a strong flow of mobile, export-oriented foreign manufacturing enterprise - it would have been very difficult to build an export-oriented industry even if Ireland had tried to do so.

Ireland in fact did not try to do so, but instead launched on a protectionist policy in the 1930s to develop domestic manufacturing. Initially, this brought about a considerable rise in manufacturing output and employment, but the protectionist phase soon ran out of steam because of the small size of the home market and the inability of the protected enterprises to penetrate export markets. The limitations of an introverted manufacturing sector became clear to the authorities during the 1950s and the thrust of policy thereafter was progressively outwards, though the measures only evolved on a piecemeal basis over a long period. The new strategy had three main elements: first, the use of grants and tax concessions to encourage export-orientated production; second, the attraction of foreign manufacturing enterprise; and third, the dismantling of protection in return for greater access to markets abroad, culminating in the establishment of a free-trade area with the UK in 1965 and accession to the EC in 1973.

2. The experience since 1960[2]

The general EC picture

A feature of the six member states which signed the Treaty of Rome in 1957 was their homogeneity in average income levels (except for Luxembourg which was 50% above the average). The poorest, Italy, was only 17% below the EC-6 average in 1960 in terms of GDP per capita, and the Italian situation arose from its own regional problem in the South rather than from general underdevelopment. The fact that at its establishment divergences *between* the member states of the EC were much less pronounced than the divergences *within* some of them partly explains why Community regional policy was so slow to develop and why, even today, it largely comprises national policies part-funded by the Community. Over the 30 years or so since the establishment of the EC the divergences between the original member states have become even narrower, with no country now more than about 5% below the overall average for the six.

Table 4
Relative GDP per capita in poorer EC countries
(Eur 12 = 100)

	1960	1973	1980	1985	1990
Ireland	61	59	64	65	69
Spain	60	79	74	73	78
Greece	39	57	58	57	53
Portugal	39	56	55	52	56
Mean	50	63	63	62	64
Ireland/UK ratio	47	54	63	63	66

	1960-73	1973-80	1980-85	1985-90
EC-12 real GDP growth rates (% p.a.)	4.7	2.4	1.5	3.1

Source: EC *Annual Economic Report 1991/92.*

The entry of three new countries in 1973 did not significantly disturb this homogeneity. The UK and Denmark already had income levels close to the overall EC average, and while Ireland's was only three-fifths of that average, its population was a tiny fraction of the total in the Community. Consequently it is only in the last decade, with the entry of Greece in 1981 and Spain and Portugal in 1986, that the Community has been faced with large divergences in living standards between member states with sizeable populations. Taken together, the four poorest member states - Ireland, Spain, Greece and Portugal - account for 35% of the area of the EC and 19% of its population, but only 13% of its GDP.

What has been the experience of Ireland and the other poorer member states in convergence towards the EC average over the last 30 years, bearing in mind that none of the four was a member for the entire period, though all had major trading links with the Community? As may be seen from Table 4, in the period 1960-73, when the whole western world experienced rapid growth, there was rapid convergence for all of these countries except Ireland. Even Ireland is not a clear-cut exception, since its living standards were converging towards those of the UK, the country with which it was then most closely linked. In 1960, three-quarters of Irish merchandise exports still went to the UK, and the growth in the volume of UK imports of goods and services from 1960-73 was only 5% per annum compared with 8.5% for OECD Europe. Therefore, although Ireland was now rapidly diversifying the destination and commodity composition of its exports, it still had a much lower export growth than the other three poorer countries because of its initial heavy UK dependence. After 1973, as EC growth slackened, convergence largely ceased, but with the pick-up in EC growth in the latter half of the 1980s there was a relative improvement for all except Greece. There is some evidence of a slowing-down in convergence again in 1991 and 1992 with the general reduction in economic growth (EC *Annual Economic Report, 1991/92*), though perhaps too much should not be made of short-term movements.

Although many other factors (including domestic policies) played a role, there are plausible theoretical reasons for attributing this pattern of experience primarily to a causal relationship between the rate of growth of Europe as a whole and convergence. When there is general economic buoyancy and the strong centres are pressing on the limits of capacity, forces enter into play which give the periphery a chance to outpace the centre. The law of comparative advantage presupposes full employment and, when such conditions apply to the centre, the less-developed areas are likely to enjoy greater scope to exploit their comparative advantage. The core regions begin to experience labour and skill shortages, congestion intensifies, house prices soar and environmental problems arise - thereby enhancing the attractions of the periphery as a location for mobile investment. Given the many reasons for expecting complementarity between capital accumulation and technological progress, the technology gap in the periphery is likely to be closed more rapidly in a period of high investment. There is a further point which is relevant to regional policy: not only does general buoyancy favour the catching-up process through market forces, but it also mobilises wider support for regional policy intervention, whereas in times of general slack even the most advanced areas tend to step up efforts to compete in attracting mobile international investment. If in fact there is a strong positive influence from overall EC economic growth to convergence, then the peripheral member states have a vital common interest in co-ordinated growth-oriented macroeconomic policies at Community level.

A closer look at the Irish experience

The data in Table 4, using the conventional measure of GDP per capita, suggest that Ireland has experienced a moderate degree of convergence towards the EC average since it first joined in 1973. Furthermore, the Irish population began to grow rapidly as the traditional pattern of migration was reversed and there was significant net immigration during the 1970s - though net emigration resumed again in the 1980s as the labour market deteriorated once more. I now want to take a closer look at this experience of apparent convergence using other measures given in Table 5 which throw light on it. The first of these is GDP per worker. Taking this measure at face value, Ireland has made striking progress since 1973 in reducing the productivity gap, and is now little more than 10% below the EC average. Indeed, on this measure Irish productivity is now higher than in Denmark and not much below that of the UK![3]

Table 5
Productivity and income in Ireland relative to EC-12,
various years 1960-90

	1960	1973	1980	1985	1990
			EC-12 = 100		
GDP per worker	73	69	75	83	89
GNP per worker	75	69	73	74	80
GNP per head of population	62	59	62	58	62
GNDI per head of population	64	61	65	61	66

Note: GNP comprises GDP and net factor payments abroad, while GNDI (gross national disposable income) comprises GNP and net foreign transfers.

Source: EC *Annual Economic Report 1991/92*; OECD *Labour-Force Statistics*, various issues; and OECD *National Accounts: Main Aggregates, 1960-1990*, Vol. 1.

Unfortunately this measure cannot be taken at face value, any more than the earlier measure of GDP per capita, because GDP movements give a distorted picture of economic progress in Ireland over the past 20 years or so - for a number of reasons. First, there is more than a suspicion that Irish GDP is artificially inflated to a significant but unknown degree by transfer pricing on the part of multinationals, and that the degree of overstatement has risen over time with the increasing volume of foreign enterprise. The outward-looking strategy proved far more successful in attracting foreign industry to Ireland than in developing indigenous industry - so that by 1988, foreign firms accounted for 44% of total manufacturing employment in Ireland, 55% of manufacturing gross output and 75% of exported gross output. Second, whether the published profit figures of multinationals are genuine or not, these profits are substantially repatriated and therefore do not augment Ireland's domestic income. Outflows of profits, dividends, and royalties have increased enormously in the past 20 years and in 1990 amounted to over IR£2 billion, or about one-third of the value of manufacturing GDP. Third, following the oil crisis in 1973 and for the rest of the 1970s and early 1980s, Irish governments embarked on an ill-advised policy of sustaining domestic activity through massive borrowing at home and abroad, resulting in a huge build-up of national debt which reached a peak of 130% of GNP in 1987. Corrective action, begun in the early 1980s but pursued effectively only since 1987, has now reduced the debt ratio to more manageable proportions, but it continues to be a severe constraint on the public finances, while the service of foreign debt involves a sizeable drain on national resources, amounting to over IR£1bn in 1990, or 4% of total GDP.

Accordingly, the growth of GDP in Ireland since 1973 has depended heavily on government borrowing and inward foreign investment, both of which gave rise to offsetting outflows which have substantially reduced the benefit of a higher GDP. For that reason GNP, which takes account of net external factor flows, is a truer measure of the income impact in Ireland.[4] As may be seen from Table 5, the degree of convergence in GNP per worker towards the EC level is more muted, but has still been taking place steadily.

Unfortunately, again, convergence in GNP per worker has not been matched by convergence in GNP per capita (i.e. per head of the whole population). As Table 5 shows, the gap in GNP per capita between Ireland and the EC average is much wider than in GNP per worker. It has converged only slightly since Ireland joined the EC, and is in fact no closer now than it was 30 years ago. The reason is the relatively small and declining proportion of the population at work in Ireland, which is now the lowest in the EC at 31%. The employment ratio is influenced by demographic factors, and to some degree Ireland's low ratio reflects social choices in favour of high fertility and spouses remaining at home. The major explanation of the low employment ratio, however, lies not in individual preferences but in the poor labour-market conditions, manifest particularly in the high unemployment rate (now the highest in the EC) which also adversely influences the participation rate and the age structure through emigration. The low employment ratio means, for example, that in Ireland every 10 workers have to support, on average, 22 dependents (defined as all those not in gainful employment), whereas in Denmark, at the other extreme, every 10 workers have to support only 9 dependents.

Finally, for completeness, Table 5 provides a measure - gross national disposable income (GNDI) per capita - which takes into account not only the foregoing considerations but also the beneficial impact of EC transfers. These transfers go only a small way towards closing the gap with the EC average, but since they have tended to increase over time, they have contributed to the marginal convergence that has taken place in GNDI per capita since Ireland joined the EC. The one really encouraging feature of Table 5 is that from 1985 to 1990, when Ireland adopted more sensible domestic economic policies, all four measures exhibited convergence, though not at the same rate. With the sharp deterioration in unemployment since early 1991 following the international decline in economic activity, however, this favourable position has not been maintained.

The household distribution of income

The dual divergence in Ireland between production and income and between income per worker and income per capita raises fundamental questions about the country's pattern of economic development. It also raises the issue of the internal distribution of income within countries, which has received far less attention in the EC than the distribution between states and regions. Yet the household distribution of income deserves more attention, both because it may directly affect economic and social cohesion and because it may act as a constraint on efforts to reduce inter-state and inter-regional inequality. In no member state of the EC, and only in a very small number of the 174 "level 2" regions, is average income more than 50% below the EC average, whereas it has been estimated that 15% of the households throughout the Community are below that level;[5] and while the poorer states have a higher incidence of poverty, only 37% of these households are located in the four poorer member states (ISSAS, 1991). In other words, every member state has its own poor, which does nothing to encourage the governments of the richer member states to give priority to eliminating divergences *between* member states.

Employment has a key role to play in ensuring a reasonable distribution of income. Where the economic system provides enough jobs for all who are willing and able to work, this will go a long way towards widely distributing the fruits of economic progress. On the other hand, high and protracted unemployment creates acute income-distribution problems. Studies at the Economic and Social Research Institute in Dublin have demonstrated the clear link between poverty and unemployment in Ireland. The poverty rate rose markedly during the 1980s with the large rise in unemployment, and three in every five households with an unemployed head fell below a poverty line set at

50% of average household income (Callan et al., 1989). Furthermore, the human misery for those directly involved goes far beyond the loss of income: one study, for instance, showed that the unemployed are five times more vulnerable to psychological distress than people in work (Whelan et al., 1991).

Many economic models either assume full employment or treat unemployment as transitory. In Ireland, however, labour surplus has been an endemic feature of the nation's history, stemming from the inability to create enough jobs to absorb the natural increase in the labour force: uniquely among European countries, the level of total employment in Ireland is lower now than in 1920. Historically, the pressure of surplus labour was relieved through massive emigration, but in recent years the most visible sign of the inadequate employment performance is high unemployment, though it has also resulted in low labour-force participation, in net emigration averaging 25,000 a year from 1982-90, and a rising proportion of the population in relative poverty. Ireland is in danger of intensifying an unhealthy dualism in its economy and society, in which an increasing minority is left further behind in terms of access to jobs, income and education, with the attendant risk that similar multiple deprivation will be transmitted intergenerationally to the children of this marginalised minority.

Such a situation also imposes a huge economic and social cost on the rest of the community. This cost must be met partly through high taxation for which there is no return in the form of goods and services. Furthermore, the sustained pressure on government and state agencies to be seen to be doing something about the problem puts a premium on short-term expedients and makes it difficult to be patient with policies where the fruits can only be expected to mature slowly (e.g. developing indigenous industry). It is highly unlikely, therefore, that Ireland will achieve EC income levels for its population as long as it carries such a high level of unemployment and associated dependency.

3. The outlook for the future

The Irish economy could be significantly affected by four major developments now in train in the EC: the completion of the Community's single market ("1992" for short), the Community Support Framework, economic and monetary union and the reform of the Common Agricultural Policy. The major Commission studies of these developments - such as the Cecchini Report (Commission of the European Communities, 1988) or "One Market, One Money" (Commission of the European Communities, 1990) - do not throw much light on their regional impact. There are, however, other studies which enable one to form a perspective on the likely impact on Ireland.

The single market and the Community Support Framework

The study by Buigues et al. (1990) of the impact of 1992 on European industry set out to evaluate the strengths and weaknesses in each EC country of what it called "sensitive industries", i.e. those likely to be significantly affected, for good or ill, as a result of the single market. The study concluded that of the four poorer member states, Ireland was possibly best placed to benefit, but this conclusion needs to be qualified in the light of the analysis by O'Malley (1990), who carried out the Irish part of the study. O'Malley confirmed that among the sensitive industries, which accounted for nearly half of all manufacturing employment in Ireland, those in a strong competitive position greatly outweighed those that might be vulnerable. The former, however, were dominated by foreign firms, whereas the vulnerable industries were largely made up of indigenous firms.

A subsequent study by O'Malley (1992) extended this work to take explicit account of economies of scale. Very little indigenous Irish industry was found to be engaged in activities with substantial economies of scale, so that it is not in a position to gain or lose much from growing economies of scale in the single market. On the other hand, the foreign companies in Ireland are heavily engaged in such activities and, given their past success, have considerable potential to benefit. The findings of both these studies suggest, therefore, that Ireland's potential to gain from 1992 is likely to depend, even more than in the past, on its ability to attract and retain foreign enterprise - at least until it has developed a more dynamic indigenous sector, which is likely to take time and, the studies suggest, may be even more difficult after 1992.

A recently-published paper by Bradley et al. (1992) represents the most comprehensive study of the future macroeconomic impact of EC developments on Ireland. Table 6 summarises the authors' findings on the overall impact of the single market and the Community Support Framework on Ireland. The figures relate to the estimated amount by which the specified variables will differ by the year 2000 from what they would have been had the single market and the CSF not taken place. The estimated impact of the single market on its own would be to raise GNP per capita in the year 2000 by 3% above the benchmark level. This is slightly less than the impact estimated for the EC as a whole in the Cecchini Report, implying that the single market would make for a slight divergence in Irish income per capita. When, however, the CSF is taken into account as well, the combined impact is estimated at close to 4% of GNP per capita, or virtually identical with the overall picture in Cecchini.[6] This implies that Ireland would share *pro rata* in the benefits, but that the process would do nothing to advance convergence in income per capita. It is important to add, however, that Ireland would be better off in terms of population (reduced emigration) and numbers employed as a result of the combined impact of the single market and the CSF, which would bring about an estimated fall of 2% in unemployment.

Table 6
Projected impact of 1992 and CSF on Ireland

	1992	CSF	Combined impact
GNP	5.1	2.7	7.8
GNP/Cap.	3.0	0.8	3.8
Employment 3.6	2.6	6.3	
Unemployment rate	-1.3	-0.9	-2.1

Source: Bradley et al. (1992).

Economic and Monetary Union

The analysis of the impact of EMU is necessarily more speculative, given that its precise nature and timing are uncertain. However, since Ireland has already incurred the costs of adjusting to the European Monetary System, since its exchange-rate policy is to keep the Irish pound firm and stable in the System, since the adjustment costs of the single market are already counted in the assessment of 1992, and since Ireland must in any case reduce its debt/GNP ratio, the extra step of EMU would not involve significant further adjustment costs. On the positive side, EMU holds out the prospect that the introduction of irrevocably-fixed exchange rates and a common currency will largely eliminate the interest-rate differential between Ireland and Germany and might bring about a fall in real interest rates. If so, this could have a dramatic impact on the debt/GNP ratio. Alternatively, the savings could be used to cut taxes or increase government spending in ways designed to encourage economic growth. The simulations by Bradley et al. suggest that a 1% fall in domestic real interest rates, with related cuts in direct taxation, could increase GNP by 1.25% after 5 years and by 2% in the long term, with a significant associated increase in employment.

The reform of the Common Agricultural Policy

The impact of CAP reform on Ireland has been the subject of a study by the National Economic and Social Council (NESC, 1992). The major impact of the CAP reform is, not unexpectedly, on the farming sector, with a probable decline of 16-17% in the value of gross agricultural output, of which 2-3% would be a volume fall and the rest a price fall. Because of compensation payments and savings on farm input costs, the decline in farm incomes would be much less. The impact is uneven among farmers, however, and those with the greatest decline in income are larger than average and make more efficient use of land:

they represent 16% of farmers, account for 28% of land, employ 40% of the workforce and produce 60% of agricultural output. The food-processing sector will have to adjust to reduced output, involving job losses.

For the country as a whole, the initial effect of the CAP reform is broadly neutral, with the loss in farm income being roughly offset by consumer gains. The long-run macroeconomic impact depends on what scenario is chosen, with estimates of the long-run reduction in GNP ranging from 0.3% to 1.2%. Broadly speaking, therefore, the CAP reform package does not threaten major losses to the Irish economy - and indeed the final agreed proposals were somewhat more favourable to Ireland than the earlier proposals assessed in the NESC study. What is perhaps more worrying, though impossible to quantify, is that there is little scope or incentive for Ireland to exploit its probable comparative advantage in certain agricultural products, an advantage not yet developed to the same extent as its European competitors for historical reasons.

The overall prospect

On balance, the overall impact of the EC developments now in train is favourable to Ireland but will do little in itself to advance convergence. Ireland will of course be affected by many other developments in the years ahead apart from those mentioned above. The economy has weathered the current recession in its major trading partners exceptionally well. Even the sharp rise in unemployment reflects not a fall in domestic employment but the curtailment of emigration as a result of poor labour-market prospects in the UK. The continued strong growth in industrial output and exports demonstrates the underlying competitiveness of the economy, and indicates that it is well placed to benefit from recovery in the world economy. The latest medium-term projections by ESRI suggest that the volume growth of GNP could average about 4% per annum for the rest of this decade. Even though this would be likely to bring about a 1% per annum growth in employment, unemployment will be slow to fall, and even by the year 2000 will probably have reached only the level prevailing early in 1991, before the current recession, i.e. about 15%.

Ireland will, however, experience a considerable alleviation of labour-market pressure on the supply side during the following decade. Because its birth rate remained high up to 1980 (at 22 per 1,000), the natural increase in the labour force will remain high throughout the 1990s - in the region of 22-25,000 per annum, or nearly 2% of the labour force. The sharp decline in the birth rate after 1980 means that the number of potential labour-force entrants will begin to fall in the late 1990s and will be down to 7,000 by the year 2006 (Sexton et al., 1991). If, therefore, Ireland could begin to make even modest progress in reducing unemployment in the 1990s, it would enter the next decade in a credible position to effect a much greater impact.

4. Policy issues

The preceding analysis does not provide any assurance that Ireland is yet well-established on a course towards convergence with its richer partners in the EC. Nor, for that matter, does it support alarmist views that Ireland will diverge further. What is certain is that if convergence is to take place, Ireland will have to improve considerably both on its past record and on its current prospective performance relative to most other EC member states. This raises the question of what policies could help to bring this about, and at what level these policies might operate.

The CSF, together with the proposed Cohesion Fund, can be regarded as the most visible sign of EC commitment to the poorer areas. Even the Commission itself, however, would not expect these funds alone to make a substantial contribution to convergence: rather, they are seen as compensation for the possible dislocation caused by the single market and EMU, and also as a stimulus to releasing the indigenous potential of the relevant areas. Can Community policy be expected to play a greater role in future?

The EC *Annual Economic Report 1991-92* expressed what I take to be a realistic view for the foreseeable future, namely that "responsibility for rapid economic and social convergence lies for the most part in the least-favoured countries themselves." Notwithstanding this view, the Maastricht Treaty set out in embryonic form the basis for developing a wider range of policies on economic and social cohesion at EC level. Obviously, the poorer member states have an important role to play in developing such policies and in ensuring that they are effective. Grandiose schemes that are badly designed or implemented could discredit the whole process. Since well-designed programmes inevitably take time to develop, the poorer states may be better served in the long run by steady progress than by a quick fix. In particular they must define more clearly and convincingly those areas of policy, in addition to the Structural Funds, which are essential to convergence and which can only be handled at Community level.

We might get some pointers to those areas by considering the alternative strategies by which Ireland itself might seek to improve its current prospects, and the extent to which it would be unable to implement these strategies without policy changes at EC level. The overall challenge facing Ireland is that while it has experienced good growth in the past 30 years - even making full allowance for the artificial inflation of output mentioned earlier - this growth has produced insufficient employment. In every five-year period since 1960, with the exception of the period 1980-85, the growth of real GNP has been in the region of 3.5 to 4.5% per annum; yet the current level of employment is only 10% higher than it was 30 years ago. How might this situation be changed? It seems to me that there are only four broad options.

A. The first, which I term the Korean style, would be to aim for a much higher growth of output in the reasonable expectation that this would also generate faster employment growth. In fact this is the only course by which Ireland could simultaneously achieve the objectives of convergence in income per capita and reduced unemployment and emigration. In this context one is contemplating a sustained growth rate of about 6% or more. In terms of domestic capability it is not inconceivable that such a growth rate could be sustained by Ireland, starting as it does with a strong competitive position, a large balance of payments surplus and a well-educated labour force (see Table 1). But it is most improbable that Ireland could maintain such a growth rate if the EC as a whole were growing at no more than about 2% per annum.

B. The second, which I call the American style, would be to aim, within the current prospective growth of output,[7] for a higher growth of employment in the market sector (i.e. a slower growth of productivity) through encouragement of more low-wage, labour-intensive activities. An inevitable corollary would be a slower growth in the pre-tax incomes of workers generally. There would also be a need for much greater flexibility in relative wages, and probably for a reduction in welfare benefits. The approach would not initially advance convergence in income per capita, but would probably leave Ireland better placed to do so once the enormous overhang of unemployment had been reduced. Apart from the problem of gaining domestic political support for such an approach, which would be formidable, this option could be constrained by demonstration effects arising from membership of the EC. Ireland has had long experience of the degree to which its labour-market conditions have been influenced by close institutional links and freedom of movement with a larger, richer neighbour, the UK. Income expectations are strongly influenced by the levels prevailing in the dominant partner and therefore tend to run ahead of domestic productivity. The subsequent pressure for productivity growth to validate the higher incomes puts pressure on employment unless output growth is accelerated. If deepening integration in the EC were to result in the higher wage levels in the richer member states being added to the reference group taken into account in formulating domestic wage claims, then it would effectively rule out this option.

C. The third option, which I call the Scandinavian style, would be to accept that the present prospective output growth will continue to be accompanied by high-productivity growth in the market sector, but to siphon off more of the gain to finance employment in useful public service and community activities and pro-active manpower policies for the long-term unemployed and unqualified first job-seekers. Domestically, this would call for higher taxation and reduced post-tax incomes and, furthermore, would make enormous demands on organisational and managerial skills to ensure that the activities involved were really worthwhile and did not just "make work". But the strategy would also be constrained by closer European integration. Economic union inevitably creates competitive pressures forcing a certain degree of harmonisation in taxation. In addition, freedom of movement and measures designed to encourage political cohesion (such as the concept of European citizenship or the Social Charter) give rise to pressures to harmonise state benefits and services. In such circumstances a poorer member state could encounter increasing difficulties in balancing its budget, as is amply demonstrated by the historical experience of Northern Ireland in relation to the United Kingdom. But even a rich country would find it hard to sustain a high tax/high public services economy in a Community where the other members were moving in the opposite direction: certainly fears about the future of the "Scandinavian system" in a closely-integrated Europe was a major issue in the referendum campaign in Denmark.

D. The fourth option would be to embrace the full logic of freedom of movement within the EC and upgrade the traditional Irish style, by not only tolerating emigration but actually welcoming and encouraging a much higher level of it than has been experienced in the past 30 years. This approach, however, would evoke so many negative echoes from the past that its adoption as an explicit policy choice would be seriously damaging to national morale. Moreover, it is very doubtful whether the approach would in fact enable Ireland to catch up. Modern regional economic theory suggests that labour outflows at a rate involving a reduction in population may merely reinforce the scale disadvantages of weaker areas while enhancing the advantages of the centre (Krugman, 1991). Also, while traditionally in Ireland the bulk of the emigrants have been among the least skilled, in recent times these have become relatively less mobile so that substantially-increased emigration could involve a major brain drain. Even if the approach did encourage convergence in income levels, it would not have a corresponding impact on economic welfare, because the bulk of emigration from Ireland is involuntary, in the sense that most of those who go would prefer to stay if they could get a job at home at or near the prevailing wage in Ireland for their level of skill.

While there are different variants within each of these four approaches, they do encompass the range of possible outcomes that need to be explored if Ireland is to significantly alter its current prospects. The approaches are not in all respects mutually-exclusive, though any given combination would of course require a coherent and compatible set of instruments that rule out other instruments. One could envisage, for instance, a coherent strategy that would put the main emphasis on A, while still encouraging a high degree of wage restraint and wage flexibility (B), coping with specially-deprived labour-market groups even at the cost of somewhat higher taxes (C), and recognising that for at least the next 15 years or so, some emigration is inevitable (D).

What then would be the policies that matter most to Ireland at EC level?

The Structural Funds, notwithstanding their inadequate level, have a very important role to play in supporting a higher level of investment in physical and human capital than could be financed domestically. The CAP will continue to be important to Ireland because of its relatively large agricultural sector and the significance of food processing in indigenous industry. But probably the single most important issue for Ireland is what EC macroeconomic policy will be in the years ahead. The reasons will be obvious from what has been said earlier. One of the concerns about EMU in this regard is that, while it provides convincing institutional arrangements for Community monetary policy, there is no fiscal authority of comparable weight, let alone an institutional counterpart responsible for the economic development of the Community. And even though monetary policy will be centralised there are fears that the balance will be weighted excessively towards price stability at the expense of employment and output. A continuation of the current high level of real interest rates at a time when EC unemployment is not far below 10% would be a major deterrent to reviving a buoyant European economy.

Given that its industrial base remains underdeveloped, Ireland will also be substantially affected by EC competition policy, and in particular by how the Commission addresses the issue of state aid. This is used extensively in all member states and, measured in relation to employment, is often much higher in the richer countries than in the poorer ones. In total in the Community it amounts to about 8-10 times the level of CSF support for the poorer countries. Some of these subsidies in the rich member states (for example, to indigenous mining industries) may not adversely affect the poorer members - indeed, they may reduce the competitiveness of the richer ones! - but others, such as support for mobile international firms, substantially negate the development efforts of the poorer member states. Moreover, they involve a huge windfall transfer to mobile international companies, since the competing subsidies probably have more influence on the location than on the volume of such investment. Only at Community level would it be possible to rationalise this situation.

The Community could also help by refraining from certain policies that would reduce the competitiveness of the poorer countries. For example, caution should be exercised in harmonising employment protection and welfare rights appropriate to richer countries but would be premature in the case of poor countries trying to catch up.

Finally, Ireland in my view would be best served by EC policies that will augment its own development efforts rather than by redistributive policies *per se*. In any event, elaborate inter-state redistribution of the kind envisaged in fiscal federalism is simply a non-starter now, though it may come to the fore at a future time as integration proceeds, especially if no convergence has been achieved. Fiscal federalism would not be an unmixed blessing for the poorer member states. Whether or not it would facilitate the realisation of their development potential would depend on the impact of the particular arrangements on their competitive position. Different policy programmes embody different incentive and disincentive effects: as a broad rule, federal support for ensuring comparable levels of public services in education and health would be preferable from a development viewpoint to income transfers or unemployment insurance schemes. If and when these issues become live ones in the future, the study of Irish experience, North and South, can provide some useful lessons.

NOTES

1. For a wider discussion, see Kennedy (1992b).

2. This and subsequent sections have benefited from earlier research reported in Kennedy (1992a).

3. The measure is inadequate, however, for comparing labour productivity, which should also take account of hours of work. Such data are not available for all the years in Table 5, but the most recent data from the EC Labour Force Survey, relating to 1989, indicate that hours of work in Ireland were 21% higher than in Denmark and 11% higher than in the UK - which would leave GDP per man-hour in Ireland still significantly below that of the other two countries. The higher average hours worked in Ireland are due to a variety of factors, among the more important of which are the much lower prevalence of part-time employment in Ireland, the somewhat smaller share of females even among full-time workers, and the higher share of the workforce in agriculture, where hours of work are well above average in all countries.

4. At the other extreme is Luxembourg, which has benefited from vastly-increased net factor income inflows from abroad - so that GDP as a measure significantly understates Luxembourg's living standards.

5. The household data are based on household expenditure, and therefore substantially understate the proportion of households below the average EC income level before taxes and transfers.

6. In making the calculations, the authors assumed that the CSF would continue unchanged in real terms beyond 1993. To the extent that the funds are increased further, as contemplated in the Delors-II package, the impact would be somewhat greater.

7. Purely to simplify the presentation of outcomes B and C, I am assuming that the growth rate of output would remain unchanged in the face of attempts to increase its employment content. In practice, of course, the resulting output growth rate could be higher or lower depending on the measures used.

References

Bradley, J., J. Fitz Gerald and I. Kearney (1992), *The Role of the Structural Funds: Analysis of Consequences for Ireland in the Context of 1992*, Policy Research Series No. 13, Dublin: ESRI.

Buiges, P., F. Ilzkovitz and J-F. Lebrun (1990), "The impact of the internal market by industrial sector: the challenge for the member states", *European Economy/Social Europe* Special Edition, 19-113.

Callan, T., B. Nolan and B. J. Whelan, D. F. Hannan with S. Creighton (1989), *Poverty, Income and Welfare in Ireland*, General Research Series No. 146, Dublin: ESRI.

Commission of the European Communities (1988), "The Economics of 1992" (Cecchini Report), *European Economy* 35, March.

- (1990), "One Market, One Money", *European Economy* 44, October.

Flora, P. (1987), *State, Economy and Society in Western Europe 1915-1975: A Data Handbook in Two Volumes. Vol. II. The Growth of Industrial Societies and Capitalist Economics*, Frankfurt: Campus Verlag.

Institute of Social Studies Advisory Service (ISSAS) (1991), *Poverty in Figures: Europe in the Early 1980s*, Luxembourg: Eurostat.

Kennedy, K. A., T. Giblin and D. McHugh (1988), *The Economic Development of Ireland in the Twentieth Century*, London: Routledge.

Kennedy, K. A. (1992a), "Real convergence, the European Community and Ireland", Presidential Address to the Statistical and Social Inquiry Society of Ireland, 14 May, *Journal of the Statistical and Social Inquiry Society of Ireland* XXVI (4), 1991/92.

- (1992b), "The context of economic development" in C. T. Whelan and J. H. Goldthorpe (eds.), *The Development of Industrial Society in Ireland*, Oxford University Press.

Krugman, P. (1991), "Increasing returns and economic geography", *Journal of Political Economy* 99 (3), June, 483-499.

Maddison, A. (1982), *Phases of Capitalist Development*, Oxford University Press.

National Economic and Social Council (1992), *The Impact of the Reform of the Common Agricultural Policy*, Report No. 92. Dublin: Stationery Office.

O'Malley, E. (1990), "Ireland" in "The impact of the internal market by industrial sector: the challenge for the member states", *European Economy/Social Europe* Special Edition, 247-261.

- (1992), "Industrial structure and economies of scale in the context of 1992", in *The Role of the Structural Funds: Analysis of Consequences for Ireland in the Context of 1992, op. cit.*

Sexton, J. J., B. M. Walsh, D. F. Hannan and D. McMahon (1991), *The Economic and Social Implications of Emigration*, Report No. 90, Dublin: National Economic and Social Council.

Whelan, C. T., and D. F. Hannan, S. Creighton (1991), *Unemployment, Poverty and Psychological Distress*, General Research Series Paper No. 150, Dublin: ESRI.

8 Spain in the EC: monetary stability versus economic growth?

José Folgado Blanco

1. The concepts of stability and growth

The question in the title of this chapter is of great importance, for two reasons. First, the Spanish economy experienced intense growth in the 1980s, but did so following a huge expansion in internal demand, which only heightened the conflict between stability and growth. This problem must now be resolved if Spaniards are to look forward to a more promising future. Second, the Spanish government recently presented its convergence programme for the next four years. This plan outlined a strategy with the dual objective of meeting the commitments of Maastricht, which aim primarily at stability, and maintaining the domestic economic expansion, which will make it possible to reduce the level-of-development gap of about 20% between Spain and the European Community average.

The difficulty of harmonising growth and development is well known. Economic theory holds that they are not only compatible but interdependent. Without stability, growth cannot be sufficient in scope and duration to promote full employment. The difficulty lies in attaining both objectives at the desired level and simultaneously coping with the distortions that occasionally stem from abroad or from domestic imbalances in the supply and demand of factors and products. It is not uncommon, moreover, for governments themselves to cause these distortions through the implementation of expansionary fiscal or monetary policies to speed up the rate of growth - often for obvious electoral reasons. The ensuing inflationary tendencies and imbalances in the foreign sector eventually require the implementation of stabilising measures, with negative effects on growth and employment. This is all too frequent an occurrence, and requires no further comment.

In this chapter I work on the basis of the criteria established at Maastricht for focusing the concept of monetary stability. Though in theory ideal stability would mean zero inflation, in practice it is extremely rare for a zero price increase not to entail excessively high costs in terms of growth and employment. I therefore believe that there will be monetary stability if the Spanish inflation rate closely approximates to that of the three most stable EC countries, i.e. a little under 3% according to present figures. Monetary stability also means that the peseta would have to enter the narrow band of the European Monetary System and not be subject to any serious fluctuations.

Clearly, when I suggest there is a possible conflict between stability and growth, I do not mean just any economic growth rate, however small. There will be tension between stability and growth if the price of stability is a growth rate in employment and activity that is equal or inferior to the growth rate in the most developed countries. In short, both aims are compatible only if we can speak of real and nominal convergence between Spain and the European Community.

2. Spanish macroeconomic evolution in the 1980s

Spaniards can look back with satisfaction on their country's initial experience as a member of the European Community. In the four years following our accession, national economic growth and stability evolved in an especially favourable manner. There were average annual increases of 4.7% in GDP, 3.2% in employment, and 13% in gross fixed investment. Aggregate demand rose sharply, especially in its investment component, which paved the way for a parallel expansion in aggregate supply, and there was restraint in price increases. The difference in Spain's level of development in comparison with the European Community average (measured in terms of GDP and purchasing power per capita) went from 71.8% in 1985, the year prior to Spanish accession, to 76.9% in 1989. Real convergence continued over the next two years (79.2% in 1991), but by then there was a serious conflict with the objective of stability, as we shall see later. Prices continued to evolve favourably, and the difference between Spain and the European Community was reduced; 1991 saw the maximum convergence with a differential of 1%.

This satisfactory balance in terms of growth and stability for the Spanish economy can be put down to factors of a domestic and foreign nature. The external reasons are sufficiently well known, so only a brief description is required here. First of all, the expansion of the US economy from 1982 onwards was a determining factor in increasing the growth of trade worldwide. Together with a marked fall in oil prices in the mid-1980s, which led to an improvement in terms of trade, this was the driving force in the performance of

European economies, whose sluggishness had led to the coining of the term "Eurosclerosis" in the early part of the decade. There was another important factor in the improvement of the business outlook and investment decisions throughout Europe: the passing of the Single European Act in 1987 and the concomitant "1992 effect".

We would have to include two further reasons to explain why the Community is now escaping Eurosclerosis for what could almost be termed Europhoria. First, the trade unions have learnt important lessons from the two energy crises, as shown in the low incidence of labour problems and restraint in wage demands. Second, new ideas have spread about the role of the public sector in the economy, and traditional welfare-state policies have been re-examined. The state's priorities are now to reduce spending and the public deficit, to effect fiscal reform through the lowering of direct taxation, and to deregulate the economic system, especially in the areas of labour, administration and finance. At the same time the entrepreneurial state has embarked on privatisation programmes, though to different extents in different countries. This new approach to the role of the public sector in the economy has not yet reached a close, but rather has been included as a criterion in the new European Union Treaty signed at Maastricht.

This international context, especially the European one, favoured the expansion of activity on firm and stable foundations, and contributed to the recovery of the Spanish economy. Nevertheless, the fact that, against all predictions, Spain performed better than average for new European Community members means we have to find domestic reasons. These can be divided into four groups. First of all (and here I am going against the standard analysis), I ascribe considerable importance to the process of reaching an open social consensus in Spain from 1979 to 1986. By social consensus I mean the process of dialogue, negotiation and agreement which took place at a centralised level between the organisations active on the labour market, with or without the direct presence of the government. This method of effecting wage policy through broad-based collective agreements has worked in different forms in different European countries; for the most part, it has succeeded in combining the aims of stability, competitiveness abroad, and growth in production and employment. However, it is also true to say that in some countries these agreements have imposed redistribution policies which have led to an upward drift in wages, and burdens on the state budget caused by tax concessions and higher social spending.

In Spain the first of these agreements was the *Acuerdo Básico Interconfederal*, signed in July 1979 by the Spanish employers' association (CEOE), and the main Spanish trade union, the Unión General de Trabajadores. The new constitution of the nascent Spanish democracy had been passed in December 1978. In the following year Spain experienced the highest incidence of labour unrest in living memory. But the *Acuerdo* gave formal legitimacy to the representatives of workers' and employers' interests, and later established the bases for new regulations on labour relations. This agreement and those that were to follow had the chief virtue of drastically reducing labour problems and social unrest. In 1980 the number of hours lost through strike action was 70% of the 1979 total, and in 1981 this figure fell a further 30%. This was of vital economic importance at a particularly delicate point in Spanish history: when the second oil crisis occurred, the country had not fully assimilated the effects of the first, because it was undergoing political transition and had a fragile industrial base. The reduction in labour problems was also politically important, because radical reform of Spain's institutional and regulatory framework was still needed to fit in with the new constitution. And it was important in social terms because a new model of labour relations was being shaped, based on free collective bargaining between both sides of industry, and on new regulations that were more in tune with the international situation and domestic political developments.

The process of social consensus in Spain had two other positive effects: it helped moderate wage increases, and eased the negotiation of more than 3,500 collective agreements in different sectors or businesses. Whereas wages had increased at an annual rate of 23.3% in the latter half of the 1970s - 8.7% above the European Community average - the rate of increase fell to 13.3% in the first half of the 80s, which was only 2.8% higher than the EC rate. Another great advance was that wage reviews ceased to be formulated using the previous year's rate of inflation; instead the inflation target for the year in question began to be used, and as this was set in the state budget, it would normally be lower each year.

The improved social and political atmosphere in Spain prevailed against a background of weak growth at the international level and particularly delicate economic conditions at home. It meant that business would be able to carry out a process of labour adjustment and financial renovation in the years prior to Spain's entry to the European Community. The ensuing recovery of profit margins is a key to undertanding the improvement in business expectations and the highly dynamic nature of investment in the country since the middle of 1985. Furthermore, the social consensus process allowed the government to introduce measures aimed at adjustment, renovation, and liberalisation of markets and factors - measures which were necessary but socially delicate.

These measures were the second element in Spain's positive performance in the European Community. Among them one stood out: the plan to modernise and adapt sectors and industries which had been especially affected by the economic crisis, such as shipbuilding, steel, fertilisers, and electrical consumer and other goods. The adjustment made unemployment rise to a record high for Spain and Europe: 22% in the first half of 1985.

Further, a series of liberalisation measures were implemented, directed at the labour market and introducing new, more flexible types of contract, though they did not in any way alter the strict legislation on permanent contracts. Rents and retail opening hours were also liberalised, and steps were taken to liberalise foreign commercial and capital trade.

Finally, I think it worth emphasising the fiscal measures aimed at stimulating investment in auxiliary capital and housebuilding. In general terms, a more balanced budgetary policy led to sustained, non-inflationary growth in the Spanish economy from the mid-1980s to 1988. It did so because it managed to reduce the deficit from 6.9% in 1985 to 3.1% in 1987, not only by means of automatic stabilisers but also by discretionary measures such as reform of the pension system and restraint in government consumption. Thus the structural deficit was cut from 5% in 1985 to 3.3% in 1987. However, since then things have only deteriorated, with concomitantly serious consequences for the economy as a whole, as we shall see later.

The positive results achieved in the initial phase of European Community membership are clearly due to a number of domestic and external factors acting in conjunction with each other, since they affect both aggregate supply and demand. However, after four years of growth and relative balance - all too short a period for our aspirations of real convergence - increasingly-serious problems have arisen, and these problems give the title question of this chapter its full meaning.

3. The present conflict between stability and growth

The drastic deceleration of variables underlying growth and the complete lack of improvement, or indeed the deterioration, in stability indicators are the most striking aspects of the Spanish economy in the run-up to the implementation of the single European market. In terms of annual variation rate, between 1989 and 1991 GDP fell from 4.8% to 2.4%, employment from 4.1% to 0.2% and investment from 13.8% to 1.6%. However, it is only fair to point out that in the context of economic cycles, nearly all countries in the industrial world have undergone this phase of economic cooling, so the process of real convergence in Spain has continued. Yet economic deceleration has been more marked in Spain, and at the same time underlying inflation has consistently failed to fall below 6.5%; this has meant a negative difference of approximately 4% compared to the best-placed countries in the European Community. The external current-account imbalance also remains high at 3% of GDP.

There are two sets of reasons behind the conflict between stability and growth which has recently surfaced, a conflict that risks making it impossible for Spain to attain the desired nominal and real convergence with the European Community over the next few years. These reasons are connected with budgetary policy and the rigidities that still exist in the Spanish economy, especially in the labour market.

The Spanish government soon lost the will to go on fighting for budgetary austerity. The control of public spending and public deficit are generally advisable in a period of great expansion of public-sector aggregate demand, yet such restraint was exercised for only three years, from 1986 to

1988. Since 1988 the aim of fiscal policy has been to follow a pro-cyclic course of additional incentive-creation for nominal spending growth. Public spending increased from 41% of GDP in 1988 to 45% in 1991. Although in this period the tax burden continued to increase, the deficit rose from 3.3% of GDP in 1988 to 4.4% in 1991. Furthermore, the structural deficit caused by discretionary spending in the civil service grew from 3.9% to 6% in the same two years. During this period, regional government spending was particularly vigorous, as was spending on social security and public investment.

The general strike successfully organised by the majority trade unions UGT and CCOO[1] in December 1988 may well have influenced government decisions and led to greater public spending. Indeed, the months following the strike saw the highest increases in public spending and the deficit. Yet the decision to include the peseta in the European Monetary System in June 1989 entailed banking on stability and giving greater importance to fiscal policy in inflation control, given that the chief concern of monetary policy became exchange rates. The general elections were brought forward to the autumn of 1989; after these it appeared that austerity measures were to be taken to control public spending, and thereby to make fiscal and monetary policy more coherent, i.e. to bring these policies more into line with the requirements for real and nominal convergence with the European Community. However, this was not to be the case, and consequently monetary policy has had to play the leading role in the fight against inflation. This was also due to the fact that wage performance was out of step with the price and cost moderation required for stability and competitiveness abroad. It is practically impossible for only one instrument (monetary policy) to influence two objectives (prices and exchange rates), so the authorities had to implement measures to make credits contingent and control capital inflow, with a view to decreasing the rate of growth of nominal spending.

The price of this lack of macroeconomic policy co-ordination was very high: investment in business stagnated, as we have seen, because financing through credit became extremely expensive. Yet virtually no benefits have ensued in terms of prices or in the foreign sector. In the latter this can be put down to the fact that interest rates were higher than in other countries, and thus sufficient foreign capital was attracted to keep an appreciated peseta in the upper band of the EMS. As for prices, their failure to fall, in spite of a deceleration in nominal spending and an improvement in exchange relations, is closely related to rigidities in some factor and service markets. There has been no coherence in macroeconomic policy, nor have measures been applied on the supply side.

If we are to believe the figures of our statistical institutes, we are indeed in for a surprise: at present we have the worst unemployment rate in Europe (15%), and yet our salary and unitary labour-cost increases have exceeded the average for European countries. The unemployment rate is probably somewhat lower, or even much lower, than this, though it is still sufficiently high to mean that an explanation for wage inflation has to be found elsewhere. This explanation is none other than the difficulty of making the Spanish workforce adapt to the needs of business in a sufficiently flexible manner. This difficulty is partly due to the rigidity of permanent contracts: where these exist, authorisation from labour organisations is required in the case of possible adjustments or geographical transfers. In this respect Spain and the Netherlands are the exceptions in Europe. The difficulty can also be ascribed to the lack of adequate training for the needs of industry, which is clearly demonstrated by the numerous unfilled posts.

4. Stability and growth in Spain in the context of EMU

On 9 June 1992, the convergence programme approved by the Cortes was put before the Council of EC Finance Ministers by the Spanish government. The summary of this programme clearly shows that the government is prepared to eliminate the present conflict between stability and growth. By means of a price-increase rate of 3% at the end of the period, and an average annual GDP growth target of 3.5%, the government aims to further nominal and real convergence. Moreover, in order to do so, it is confident that it can control public spending and the deficit to the extent of limiting increases to only 1% of GDP at the end of the period. This is well below the figure stipulated in the Maastricht Treaty. While experience shows that it is always good to be sceptical, it is encouraging to see the government taking a firm stand in the face of strong trade-union opposition to the programme, which aims to stiffen eligibility requirements and reduce unemployment benefit. These unpopular but nonetheless necessary and efficient measures led the trade unions to organise a half-day general strike on May 28.

In order to encourage real convergence the Spanish government has promised that public spending cuts will not affect investment, which will remain at 5% of GDP over the next five years. This objective is crucial, as in recent years growth has been limited and inflation increased by infrastructural inadequacies in transport, telecommunications, access to urban centres, and other areas.

It is quite clear that the fiscal policy of recent years has been the enemy of non-inflationary growth in Spain - and here I agree with the severe criticism voiced by academics and specialised national or international institutions. This criticism has focused on performance regarding the public deficit and public spending. Nevertheless, one must acknowledge that there are elements that inspire confidence and favour the growth and stability which Spain is aiming for within the European Community.

First, Spain has kept to the "golden rule" which holds that the sum of public deficit and public investment should be a positive figure. This rule was ignored in 1991 in Belgium, Germany, Greece, Ireland, Italy, the Netherlands and Portugal. Second, the accumulated Spanish public debt in 1991 stood at 46% of GDP, which is 16% below the European Community average: only Luxembourg and the United Kingdom enjoy lower totals. Not only does this easily meet what is stipulated in the Maastricht Treaty; it also means that the amount spent on interest payments is only 3.6% of GDP, which is well below the European Community average.

Obviously this does not guarantee that the Spanish government will display the necessary political will to reverse the recent trend towards huge spending increases, by constraining its own current spending and encouraging regional and local governments to follow suit. Such political will requires large doses of discipline under present circumstances, given the attitude of some of the governing party's own members and of the trade unions. This is not an easy problem, as there is not much room for tax increases. Indeed, direct taxes will have to be reduced if we want to see the flow of foreign investment continue, which is necessary for real convergence. There is, on the other hand, room for indirect tax increases, since the standard rate of VAT is 13%, but there is also too high a risk of aggravating inflationary tensions if at the same time we wish to achieve the objective of higher growth than the European Community average.

Furthermore, there are areas of rigidity which hinder non-inflationary growth in the Spanish economy, and which are currently having a negative effect. One such area is the marked inflation persisting in a large number of service sectors. If we break the Spanish Consumer Price Index down into its component parts, we can see that the annual rate of price increase for industrial goods has stayed under 5%, whilst for services it is twice as high. This is a difficult problem because this market is not subject to foreign competition, which means that measures have to be taken on an individual basis. In order to identify the costs of the regulatory mechanisms of a wide range of sectors, the Spanish Competition Tribunal[2] was commissioned to carry out a study of administrative prices, the situation of monopolies, and the conditions for professional activity during the 1992 parliamentary session as part of the national convergence programme.

Finally, Spanish hopes of progress and convergence within EMU will be conditioned largely by reforms needed in the labour market, which should aim to stimulate the job-search process and encourage the balancing of supply and demand. In relation to the former, the government has produced a White Paper on urgent measures on job creation and unemployment assistance; this courageous step is an attempt to reduce fraud in unemployment benefit claims and eliminate incentives for "staying unemployed". The second objective, a mechanism for a more flexible adjustment of supply and demand, is to be achieved in two ways: reducing rigidities that prevent labour-force mobility, and promoting professional training. This is the right way to approach to this goal, though its success depends on how well specific measures are implemented over the forthcoming months and years.

The less-developed countries of the European Community, including

Spain, will have to be careful in the design and implementation of their economic policies if they are to stay on the steep and narrow path of maintaining a faster growth rate than their more advanced partners (and thereby reducing the differences between them), without at the same time causing the inflationary tendencies which would soon eliminate the chance of real convergence.

A faster growth rate needs dynamism in investment, both public investment in infrastructure and private investment in equipment, industrial installations, and transport. Yet we will only see hundreds of thousands of businessmen investing if they feel confident that their investment will be profitable in the long and medium term. This kind of confidence existed in Spain during two important periods: from the 1960s to the end of the first half of the 1970s, and from 1985 until recently.

However, we must also pay attention to certain factors if there is to be the sort of profitability which retains enough domestic savings in Spain, and which attracts sufficient foreign funds to complement them (this would include investment from the Structural and Cohesion Funds). These factors are labour costs, ease of access to new markets and technology, social stability, flexibility in the adaptation of factors of production, the availability of an appropriately-qualified workforce and other factors affecting entrepreneurial expectations.

Since labour costs are important in the added value of companies, their evolution will play a determining role in investment profitability, and thus in the possibilities for real convergence. Traditionally low unitary labour costs have been the trump card which has favoured Spanish development. I am not entirely sure that this advantage is as great as it was, or that it will last. In its 1992-1996 macroeconomic projections, the government set its price and labour cost objectives. From our present position these may seem ambitious, but they are also necessary and in line with the aims of growth and development. The government correctly plans a gradual but steady deceleration in the rate of price increases, which will come down to 3% at the end of the period. So as to achieve this it has set a target for yearly wage increases of between 0.5% and 1% above the rate of price increases. However, this rise in purchasing power will not absorb the planned productivity increase of 1.7%. Thus unitary labour costs would allow business savings to keep in step with the aim of increasing investment in secondary capital by 7% per year; such a figure would make it possible to reach the aforementioned goal of job creation.

For less-developed countries and regions of the EC, a plan of this nature is attractive because their domestic aggregate demand for consumption and investment is highly dynamic: this will lead to more imports, and thus to a recovery of exports in other European Community countries, who in turn are rewarded for the solidarity they have expressed through the Structural and Cohesion Funds. Spain enjoyed a trade surplus with the European Community over a number of periods up until its accession. Since then the vigorous nature of investment and consumption has brought about a growing deficit, which means providing more work for industries in other European Community countries.

The key variable for Europe's future, and for Spain's future within Europe, is business expectations. If economic policy can gain coherence and credibility through the discipline of the Maastricht criteria, then there will be a commensurate improvement in business expectations, the foundations will have been laid for real growth conducive to convergence in levels of development, and the peril of a conflict between necessary stability and desired development will have been averted.

NOTES

1. Comisiones Obreras.

2. El Tribunal de Defensa de la Competencia.

Table 1
The convergence process in the European Community
(EC = 100)

	1960	1975	1985	1986	1987	1988	1989	1990	1991	60-75	75-85	85-91
Greece	38.6	57.3	56.7	55.9	54.1	54.3	54.1	52.6	52.5	19.7	-0.6	-4.2
Spain	60.3	81.9	72.5	72.8	74.7	75.7	76.9	77.8	79.0	21.6	-9.4	6.5
Ireland	60.8	62.7	65.2	63.4	64.5	64.7	67.0	69.0	68.9	1.9	2.5	3.7
Portugal	38.7	52.2	52.0	52.5	53.6	53.7	54.9	55.7	56.3	13.5	-0.2	4.3

Source: *European Economy* 50, December 1991.

Table 2a

Main Spanish economic indicators
% annual change

	GDP		Employment		Investment	
	Spain	EC	Spain	EC	Spain	EC
1980	1.2	1.3	-3.0	0.4	0.7	1.9
1981	-0.2	0.2	-3.0	-1.1	-3.3	-5.0
1982	1.2	0.9	-1.0	-0.8	0.5	-1.9
1983	1.8	1.6	-0.6	-0.7	-2.5	0.0
1984	1.8	2.3	-2.7	0.1	-5.8	1.2
1985	2.1	2.5	-1.0	0.5	4.1	2.4
1986	3.2	2.7	2.3	0.6	10.1	4.0
1987	5.6	2.9	4.5	1.1	14.0	5.5
1988	5.2	4.0	3.6	1.6	14.0	9.0
1989	4.8	3.3	4.1	1.5	13.8	6.7
1990	3.6	2.8	2.6	1.4	6.9	4.1
1991	2.4	1.3	0.2	0.4	1.6	-0.4

Source: INE and *European Economy* 50, December 1991.

Table 2b
Main Spanish economic indicators
annual rate of change

	Inflation (CPI)		Wages		Pub.deficit/GDP	
	Spain	EC	Spain	EC	Spain	EC
1980	15.6		13.8	17.3	15.0	-2.6
1981	14.5	12.1	15.3	13.0	-3.9	-5.3
1982	14.3	10.7	13.7	10.9	-5.6	-5.5
1983	12.2	8.6	13.8	9.7	-4.8	-5.3
1984	11.3	7.4	10.0	7.5	-5.3	-5.3
1985	8.8	6.1	9.4	7.0	-7.0	-5.2
1986	8.8	3.6	9.5	6.4	-6.0	-4.8
1987	5.2	3.2	6.7	5.6	-3.1	-4.2
1988	4.8	3.5	6.2	5.9	-3.3	-3.7
1989	6.8	5.2	6.1	6.1	-3.8	-2.9
1990	6.7	5.7	7.7	7.6	-4.0	-4.1
1991	5.9	4.9	7.8	7.0	-4.4	-4.3

Source: See table 2a.

Table 3
Fiscal policy indicators
in GDP %

	1985	1986	1987	1988	1989	1990	1991
Expenditure	42.7	42.1	41.0	41.0	42.4	43.3	45.0
Receipts	35.8	36.1	37.8	37.8	38.9	39.7	40.6
Public deficit	6.9	6.0	3.1	3.3	3.5	3.6	4.4
Structural deficit	5.0	4.4	3.3	3.9	5.6	5.8	6.0
Public debt	45.2	46.2	46.6	42.9	44.2	44.5	45.6

Source: Bank of Spain, European Commission and author.

Table 4
Macroeconomic forecasts 1992 - 1996
% annual change

	1991	1992	1993	1994	1995	1996
1. GDP and aggregate (% real growth)						
National private consumption	3.0	3.2	3.0	3.0	3.0	2.9
Public consumption	4.4	3.5	2.0	2.0	2.0	2.0
Gross fixed capital formation	1.6	3.2	5.1	6.2	5.8	5.4
Construction	4.3	2.7	4.0	5.0	5.0	4.5
Equipment	-2.5	4.0	7.0	8.0	7.0	6.7
National demand	2.9	3.3	3.4	3.6	3.6	3.4
Goods and services exports	8.4	7.9	7.9	8.0	8.1	8.1
Goods and services imports	9.4	8.0	7.1	7.0	6.8	6.6
Gross Domestic Product	2.4	3.0	3.3	3.6	3.6	3.5
GDP, current prices, '000m	54,775	59,751	64,591	69,483	74,378	79,405
% change	9.4	9.1	8.1	7.6	7.0	6.8
2. Prices and labour costs						
Private consumption deflator	6.3	5.8	4.6	3.7	3.2	3.0
GDP deflator	6.9	6.0	4.7	3.8	3.3	3.1
Compensation per employee	8.5	6.5	5.3	4.5	4.0	4.0
Productivity per employee	2.1	2.3	1.7	1.7	1.7	1.7
Unit labour cost	6.3	4.1	3.6	2.7	2.3	2.3
3. Employment and unemployment						
Active population	0.4	0.6	1.0	1.0	0.9	0.9
Employment : % change	0.2	0.6	1.6	1.9	1.9	1.8
change in 000's	30	76	203	245	250	241
Unemployment : % active population	16.3	16.3	15.8	15.1	14.3	13.5
in 000's of persons	2,464	2,478	2,427	2,335	2,225	2,125
4. Balance of payments						
Current acct balance, '000m pta	-1.598	-1.716	-1.830	-1.752	-1.785	-1.811
% GDP	-2.9	-2.9	-2.8	-2.5	-2.4	-2.3
5. Public administration						
Total receipts	10.4	11.4	8.8	9.6	8.1	7.8
Total expenditure	11.5	10.0	7.6	7.4	5.9	5.9
Capital requirements, '000m pta	-2,432	-2,372	-2,253	-1,845	-1,320	-793
% GDP	-4.4	-4.0	-3.5	-2.7	-1.8	-1.0
Public debt as % of GDP	45.6	45.8	45.8	45.3	44.1	42.3

9 Greece and European Monetary Union: a challenge or a helping hand?

Nicos M. Christodoulakis

1. Introduction

By almost all macroeconomic accounts, Greece is the odd man out in the process of satisfying the criteria set out by the Maastricht Treaty as the preparation for Economic and Monetary Union. The Greek public debt is approaching 100% of GDP, and shows no sign of coming down as long as the current fiscal policies are applied. Owing to high interest payments, the budget deficit stands at 14% of GDP even after the primary deficit has been brought down to 1%. Inflation persists at 15% despite the prolonged recession in the Greek economy. The exchange rate is depreciated by 10-12% annually against the Ecu currencies, but this is still not enough to correct the accumulated loss of competitiveness caused by inflation differentials with Greece's trading rivals. After the escudo joined the Exchange-Rate Mechanism in March 1992, the drachma was further isolated as the only currency left outside the band.

These negative macroeconomic indicators are accompanied by an adverse business climate in Greece, despite repeated government pleas to investors to exploit the opportunities available. The privatisation plan designed to drive the economy out of recession has been sluggishly implemented, reinforcing the private sector's fears that the public deficit will get out of control again in the near future.

Given this disappointing picture, is there any chance at all of Greece meeting the challenge of European integration? Despite the odds, the answer, in my view, can still be affirmative, for two reasons. First, because the task of stabilising the Greek economy is not an impossible one. Other countries in Europe and elsewhere have successfully implemented stabilisation programmes when faced with a similar deterioration of their public finances. Second, because there seems to be an unusually large consensus in Greek public opinion in favour of European integration in general and the Maastricht Treaty in particular. With efficient political and economic management this consensus can be transformed into support for national economic rehabilitation.

The process will not, however, be straightforward. Until now, the Greek authorities have been reluctant to comply with the fiscal and monetary convergence criteria, preferring to capitalise on the political dimensions of the agreement reached in Maastricht. It is only recently that policy-making bodies inside and outside government have tried to put economic policy on a path that will lead to macroeconomic convergence soon after 1997.

It is perhaps too early to judge how far the macroeconomic adjustment will have progressed by 1997. Most of the recent fiscal and monetary deterioration of the Greek economy is due to political factors. As new elections must be held by 1994, there might be a further rekindling of public spending that will prove disastrous for convergence. In the meantime there seems to be no institutional breakthrough that could enforce a different pattern of pre-election behaviour. The possibility of further public spending undermines the credibility of the stabilisation programme currently in force. If the programme is abandoned, the implementation of a new one will prove to be even more difficult. Yet neither the authorities nor the public seem fully convinced that monetary union *per se* is sufficiently beneficial for the country to justify the speed and extent of adjustment which is being called for.

It is therefore worth trying to evaluate the likely impact of Economic and Monetary Union on Greece. Economists are aware of the difficulty of doing a cost/benefit analysis for a country entering a currency union. The prevailing paradigm is a static model (see Mundell, 1961) that ignores important dynamic effects. As analysed elsewhere (CEC, 1990) the main benefits are expected to come from the reduction of transaction costs and the elimination of exchange-rate uncertainty. The most important costs stem from the loss of seigniorage brought about by the reduction of inflation and from the inability of the exchange rate to adjust any further to compensate for supply-side shocks. These costs will be felt not only under full EMU, but also during the period of participation in the Exchange-Rate Mechanism.

The second issue is the adulteration of stabilisation policies by electoral considerations. Since no change seems imminent in the functioning or the value-systems of the main political parties, there is a need to institutionalise the process of adjustment. As I shall explain later, the best option is for Greece to enter the ERM *even before the end of the stabilisation programme*, in order to gear fiscal and monetary policies to externally-imposed objectives and keep the adjustment process free from pre-electoral abuse.

The aim of this chapter is twofold. First, to analyse some stylised facts of the Greek economy, and discuss the effects on fiscal, monetary and exchange-rate policies that participation in the ERM and, subsequently, EMU is likely to have[1]. Second, to investigate the value of early participation from the point of view of providing institutional safeguards for the completion of the stabilisation programme.

2. Tax collection and revenue-maximising inflation

In Greece, as in many other countries, marginal tax rates are not indexed. With a high inflation rate, nominal income rises and, with the progressive tax structure unadjusted, bears higher taxation. Thus, fiscal drag leads to higher tax revenues without the administrative and political cost of explicitly raising tax rates.

There are, however, two opposing factors that tend to reduce and in some cases reverse the benefits of fiscal drag. One is the fact that fiscal drag multiplies the incentives for tax evasion and, as a result, the tax base is gradually diminished. The economy may end up on the falling side of the Laffer curve and, despite the higher tax rates on real income, real tax revenues may not increase. Although concrete evidence on this phenomenon is hard to produce, there are reasons to believe that the persistent inflation of the last 15 years in Greece is at least partly to blame for the spread of undeclared economic activity.

The second factor is the so-called Tanzi effect, which might be found in inflationary economies with considerable delays in tax collection. As analysed in Tanzi (1978), when tax obligations are not indexed and there is a lag between income realisation and actual collection of taxes, a higher inflation rate reduces the real value of state revenues. If the inflation rate is sufficiently high, the erosion of real revenues may be very significant, and even override the gains from the familiar inflation tax.

The impact of this factor is testable in actual economies. In what follows I investigate the effect of a change in inflation on tax payments for the Greek economy. I then derive the inflation rate that maximises the sum of seigniorage and tax revenues.

In Greece both direct and indirect taxes are collected with a delay which frequently exceeds a year. In the case of direct taxes this is due to the long gap between the end of the financial year and the time of tax evaluation and collection. Tax statements are submitted at the beginning of March for the previous calendar year and tax obligations are acknowledged at the end of May - at best. Payments are then scheduled through the rest of the year, but in many cases they are not collected in time. Disputes with the tax authorities, moreover, usually take a long time to settle, and it is not unusual for the authorities to settle at concessionary levels in order to avoid the complete repudiation of their claims. As an indication of the scale of the problem, in early 1990 there were unresolved cases involving as much as 500bn Drs, or about 5% of GDP.

The situation is similar regarding indirect taxes. VAT repayments are often deliberately delayed by firms, which, taking advantage of the rather lax monitoring system, use the cash as a substitute for short-term capital. In 1989 the Minister of Finance reported that more than 300bn Drs were overdue, or about 3% of GDP. Many firms were unable to repay their obligations simply because they had invested a large share of their VAT proceeds elsewhere. For indirect taxes, the official period for repayment is two months, so that delays are expected to be shorter than for direct tax collection.

The situation is aggravated at election time, when the parties in power tend to write off some of the disputed claims and deliberately delay the clearing of others. This has wider repercussions on revenues, as it provides incentives for further evasion and increases the administrative cost of future tax collection. During the last three election years (1981, 1985 and 1989) the average tax rate was substantially reduced.

Lags in tax collection may therefore have serious effects on an inflationary economy, reducing government revenues measured as a proportion of GDP. When the income elasticity of taxation is less than 1, the tax-reducing consequences of inflation become comparable with the gains that the government enjoys from seigniorage.

This point is demonstrated in the Appendix, which shows the effects of inflation and deflation on total tax revenues, that is the sum of tax payments and seigniorage. The inflation rate that maximises total revenues is found to be much lower than the rate that maximises only seigniorage. For a GDP growth rate of 2% per annum, seigniorage-maximising inflation is about 16%, a figure not far removed from the current inflation rate in Greece. However, the picture changes when one looks at total revenues (see Figure 1). In this case the seigniorage-maximising rate is already attained in the 0-6% per annum inflation range. At higher levels of inflation, the latter's revenue-generating capacity rapidly declines.

For the same GDP growth rate of 2% and assuming a real interest rate of 4%, revenue-maximising inflation is found to be less than 5% (as reported in Christodoulakis, 1992). This rate is considerably below the current level, and shows that the authorities need not worry that a fall in inflation will aggravate the accumulation of public debt. The reason is that the loss in seigniorage caused by the fall of inflation is outweighed by the reduction in the loss of real taxes due to delays in their collection.

Figure 1
Tax-plus-seigniorage revenues versus inflation rates

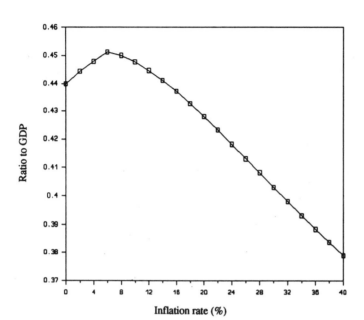

3. Monetary and exchange-rate policy

3.1 Monetary policy

A possible argument against monetary integration in the European Community is the fact that member states' central banks will surrender their independence to a supranational body, preventing national governments from using discretionary monetary policy to promote employment at home. By now, however, a sizeable body of literature in modern macroeconomics has effectively demonstrated that such discretion is mainly neutralised by the expectations of the private sector. When the latter "foresees" the authorities' expansionary motives, it raises prices, so that a rise in nominal demand does not, in the end, have real effects.

Political commitment is a necessary ingredient for an anti-inflationary policy to be credible. If governments lack that commitment, the private sector will ignore their pleas for reduced inflation, believing that the same governments will later find reasons to give in to expansionary policies.

The Greek authorities have at last begun to show signs of adopting this

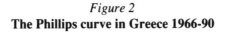

Figure 2
The Phillips curve in Greece 1966-90

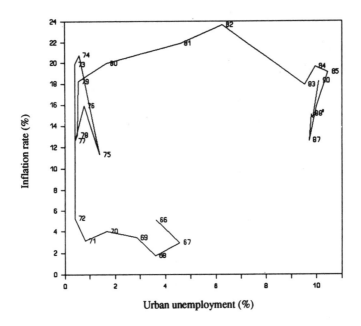

Urban unemployment (%)

dictum. This is logical, since in the past decade even short-run benefits from monetary expansion seem to have been lacking. This point has been demonstrated by Christodoulakis and Kollintzas (1991), in a study of the Phillips curve for Greece over the last 25 years. The curve is shown in Figure 2, divided into three periods. The first period ended in 1972, when the Bretton Woods system of fixed exchange rates was abandoned. It was a period of low inflation and moderate unemployment. During the 1970s, unemployment was kept at very low levels at the cost of a considerable rise in inflation. After 1980 the picture changed dramatically. Expansionary policies simply led to higher inflation without any improvement in economic activity. The Phillips curve became almost vertical. Unemployment remained around 9%, while inflation was reduced as a result of the monetary contraction of the 1985-87 stabilisation programme.

Corroborating evidence comes from comparing the movements of money supply and output in the postwar Greek economy. Dimelis et al. (1991) reported that all measures of monetary base were negatively correlated with output. Monetary policy in most of the period was found to vary counter-cyclically with output, but pro-cyclically with inflation. In a recent study, Gomme (1992) correlated inflation and output growth rates for a number of countries. Greece was found to have the second-largest negative correlation coefficient.

All these findings suggest that monetary policy in Greece has been - on average - unable to promote economic activity and has simply led to high inflation rates. It seems, therefore, reasonable to argue that the loss of discretionary monetary policy will not have serious output costs for Greece. On the other hand, participation in EMU will provide the economic authorities with an "institutional advantage" (Giavazzi and Pagano, 1988) that will enable them to make a credible commitment to an anti-inflationary policy.

3.2 Exchange-rate policy

This is apparently the most serious area of concern regarding EMU participation. Greek governments are accustomed to managing the exchange rate in such a way as to offset losses in competitiveness brought about by the higher inflation rate relative to the country's main competitors. There are, however, signs of change on this front as well: in 1990 and 1991 the drachma's depreciation fell short of the inflation differential with other European countries.

There are three main explanations for this change. First, the high-interest-rate policy followed by the Central Bank is attractive to foreign capital, so that pressure on the current account has considerably eased. Second, unit labour costs in Greece have deteriorated less rapidly than in the past. Measured over the total economy, they did not change significantly in 1989-90, and in 1991 actually declined to their 1989 level (see EEC Document II/194, 1991, Chart 5). As a result the real effective exchange rate improved in 1991, despite the fact that nominal depreciation was lower than inflation differentials. Finally, there has been a remarkable shift in the structure of corporate debt during the last five years. Several - mainly export-oriented - firms are now exploiting the new opportunities in foreign capital markets and making loans in foreign currency. As depreciation increases the debt burden in relation to their own capital, firms are no longer pressing for devaluation and are trying to improve their competitiveness by means of restructuring at the micro level.

The above remarks suggest that the ERM discipline will not be unsustainable for the drachma, assuming that the fiscal correction is successfully implemented. Nevertheless, the trade deficit continues to indicate a major imbalance in the Greek economy. This can be partly remedied by a corrective depreciation when Greece enters the ERM, and possibly by another one before EMU.

I now turn to the problems that Greece is likely to face under EMU conditions. The country will irrevocably lose the ability to adjust to productivity shocks via exchange-rate policies, as this instrument simply vanishes in a monetary union. Of course the country will still be able - at least formally - to use fiscal policies to face shocks, although the tight criteria set out in the Maastricht Treaty will make the room for manoeuvre very limited indeed.

It is, however, still an open question whether this loss will have serious consequences for Greece. First of all, if the disturbance is common to all members of the union the common currency can be adjusted vis-à-vis external currencies in response to the specific shock. Greece will suffer only to the extent of asymmetric shocks and of relative inefficiencies with respect to other member countries. At this point it is perhaps interesting to examine what has happened in the past. Historically, the major external shocks impinging upon the economy of Greece were not very different from those upon other European economies. Typical examples are the two oil shocks of 1973 and 1978, the widespread industrial action in Europe in the late 1970s, the impact of Chernobyl on agriculture, the dramatic fall in tourism from the USA during 1986, and more recently the uncertainty generated by the Gulf war. Although research measuring the shocks across EEC countries is not extensive, the findings so far suggest that asymmetric shocks in the EEC are considerably smaller than absolute shocks (see Pisani-Ferry and Italianer, 1992).

Though they may not be disproportionately large, shocks which are country-specific, or more severe for some members of the union than for others, remain a problem. If and when they occur, the countries most affected should be assisted by a Special Fund aimed at providing compensation for country-specific shocks and industry-specific disturbances.

4. EMU and geopolitical developments

Economic developments in Greece in the coming years depend crucially on the prevailing geopolitical climate in the Balkans and the Eastern Mediterranean. Before 1989, Greece had limited and controllable relations with its northern neighbours, and most of the geopolitical uncertainty was generated by the strained state of affairs with Turkey. With the collapse of the communist regimes, the regional roles of both Greece and Turkey are being redefined and the balance of power may change.

Greece is the most developed economy in the region, and its political institutions are by far the most advanced. It also shares a common religion with several peoples in the area, and this could form a basis for cultural affinity with the post-communist countries. There is also the possibility that Turkey may shift its foreign policy priorities towards becoming a major local power rather than pressing for imminent EC membership. The consequences of the above dynamics may be far-reaching as Greece would, in future, be the only country in the area with fully-fledged relations with Europe. Assuming that the Balkan countries keep their zest for eventual integration with Western European institutions, Greece will, both politically and economically, have a pivotal role to play in promoting economic co-operation and free trade with these countries, and in assisting institutional reforms.

The link between the prospect's of Greece resolving its economic problems and its chances of establishing a leading economic and political role in the Balkans is crucial. The reaffirmation of Greece as a major player in the Balkans would boost trade and increase its economic activity. The proximity of markets would minimise transportation costs which may compensate for the relative cost-disadvantage that Greek products now face in other world markets. The Balkan markets can thus provide a unique opportunity to raise demand for Greek production, improve the trade deficit and lead to higher economic growth.

Greece, if it successfully integrates into EMU, would be seen as a model country by its neighbours, and the most advantageous partner as they seek EC membership. Such a perception would further enhance economic and political ties between these countries, to the mutual benefit of both.

The picture would be starkly different, however, if Greece fails to prepare adequately for full participation in EMU within the next five to seven years. Such a failure, despite repeated stabilisation plans, would reveal a fundamental inability to adjust. Greece would be left with no coherent alternative in terms of economic development, nor with a viable strategy for international involvement outside Europe.

It is important to stress that failure to join EMU would undermine not enhance Greece's prospects of playing a major role in the area. This is because the other countries, as they seek closer ties with the European institutions, are unlikely to be attracted by a country that has itself failed to achieve this goal.

NOTE

1. The analysis of costs and benefits is here very selective, but papers considering various aspects of Greece's potential entry into the ERM or EMU are available (for a recent collection see EKEM, 1991).

References

Alogoskoufis G. and N. Christodoulakis (1991), "Fiscal deficits, seigniorage and external debt: the case of Greece", in G. Alogoskoufis, L. Papademos and R. Portes (eds.), *External Constraints on Macroeconomic Policy: The European Experience*, Cambridge University Press for Centre for Economic Policy Research.

Christodoulakis N. and T. Kollintzas (1991), "European Monetary Union: a chance for the economy of Greece to take off again", *Economicos* (Athens), September (in Greek).

Christodoulakis N. (1992), "Tax-collection lags and revenue-maximising inflation", Discussion Paper, Athens University of Economics and Business.

Commission of the European Communities (1990), "One market, one money", *European Economy* 44, October.

Dimelis S., N. Christodoulakis, T. Kollintzas and K. Prodromidis (1991), "Main stylised facts of the Greek business cycle: 1948-1989", Centre for Economic Research (KOE), Athens.

EEC (1991), "Indicators of price and cost competitiveness", DOC II/194/3/91.

EKEM (Hellenic Centre for European Studies) (1991), "Greece and EMU", Collection of papers, No. 9, October.

Giavazzi F. and M. Pagano (1988), "The advantage of tying one's hands: EMS discipline and central-bank credibility", *European Economic Review* 32, 1055-1075.

Gomme P. (1991), "Money and growth revisited", Discussion Paper, Institute for Empirical Macroeconomics.

Mundell R. (1961), "A theory of optimum currency areas", *American Economic Review*, 657-665.

Pisani-Ferry J. and A. Italianer (1992), "The regional-stabilisation properties of fiscal arrangements", this volume.

Tanzi V. (1978), "Inflation, real tax revenue and the case for inflationary finance: theory with an application to Argentina", *IMF Staff Papers* Vol. 25.

Van der Ploeg F. (1993, forthcoming), "Unanticipated inflation and government finance: the case for a common independent central bank", in F. Torres and F. Giavazzi (eds.), *A Single Currency for Europe*, Cambridge University Press for CEPR.

Appendix A

Tax-collection lags and revenue-maximising inflation

This Appendix has been taken from Christodoulakis (1992), where further details of the econometric estimation are given. Here we concentrate on investigating the effect of inflation and deflation on total government revenues. To find the inflation rate that maximises both tax and seigniorage revenues, I first estimate a tax-collection equation as a function of inflation, and combine it with a Laffer-type function of seigniorage. The general form of the adjustment equation for the collection of nominal taxes is found to be:

$$TAX_t = (1-\delta) \cdot TAX_{t-1} + \alpha \cdot Y_t + \beta \cdot Y_{t-1} + \gamma \cdot Y_{t-2} \qquad (1)$$

where TAX denotes taxes at current prices and Y is GDP at factor cost and current prices. Using cointegration techniques, parameters were estimated at $\alpha=0.124$, $\beta=0.377$, $\gamma=0.0167$, and $\delta=1.171$; all of them were found to be statistically significant at the 5% level. Parameter α denotes the rate of tax paid in the same period in which income is derived, while β and γ correspond to taxes due from previously-earned income.

Tax revenues as a ratio of output are then obtained by dividing (1) by current period output. Denoting nominal growth rate by $n=\pi+q$, where π is the inflation rate and q the real growth rate, a little manipulation yields:

$$\tau_t = [(1-\delta)/(1+n)]\tau_{t-1} + \alpha + \beta/(1+n) + \gamma/(1+n)^2 \qquad (2)$$

where τ is the ratio of tax revenue to output. The longrun value of τ is obtained as:

$$\tau = (\alpha n + \alpha + \beta)/(n+\delta) + \gamma/[(1+n)(n+\delta)] \qquad (3)$$

The second expression in the r.h.s. clearly decreases with inflation. Differentiating the first expression w.r.t. π we obtain that it too decreases with inflation as long as $\alpha+\beta-\alpha\delta>0$. In this case $\alpha+\beta-\alpha\delta = 0.355$, so that the tax to GDP ratio is strictly decreasing with inflation. The above finding suggests that for the economy of Greece a rise in inflation will be beneficial from the point of view of easing the accumulation of debt as a ratio to output.

To find the total revenue-maximising inflation rate one has to look at both taxes and seigniorage. Total revenue as a ratio of output, h, is given by the sum of taxes and seigniorage as

$$h(\pi) = \tau + (\pi+q)m \qquad (4)$$

where m denotes the demand for non-interest-bearing money as a ratio of output, estimated by Alogoskoufis and Christodoulakis (1991) to be given by

$$m = 0.60 \cdot \exp[-5.60(r+\pi)] \tag{5}$$

Seigniorage $(\pi+q)m$ as a function of the inflation rate exhibits the Laffer-curve property, and is maximised for an inflation rate of $\pi^* = 0.178-q$. For a growth rate of 2% per annum this gives an inflation rate of about 16%. However $h(\pi)$ is maximised at a much lower level. For the same growth rate and for a real interest rate of 4%, the optimal inflation rate is found to be slightly under 5%, a level well below the current rate of inflation in Greece.

Part III

The impact of Community policies

10 Fiscal federalism: a survey of the literature

P. Bernd Spahn

1. Theoretical aspects of multi-level government action

1.1 Allocation and federalism

There seems to be wide agreement among economists that macroeconomic stabilisation should be left to the central government - whether this be of a state or a supranational federation - while distribution and allocation functions may be exercised at lower levels. The strongest case for decentralisation is made for the allocation function. If there are various forms of public goods which can only be consumed jointly and provided uniformly, then these goods should be supplied at the level at which consumer preferences are relatively homogeneous. This is the essence of Oates' (1972) decentralisation theorem. Where regional preferences differ, the decentralised provision of public goods brings efficiency gains. Decentralisation would also make it possible to apply the benefit-pricing rule for public services, which is difficult to implement at the highest levels since regional tax discrimination is usually prohibited by federal constitutions. Although the efficient provision of regional public goods could eventually be effected at the central level, this would normally imply information requirements that are difficult to meet, and it would entail costs deriving from uncertainties (Tresch 1981).

The decentralised provision of government services also facilitates political decision-making, as it enhances the cost-effectiveness of supplying such services: political representation closer to voters and taxpayers can be expected to be both more responsive to demand and more accountable for policy actions (Cornes and Sandler 1986). This can also bring welfare improvements for regional polities, mobilising political resources through the greater involvement of taxpayers. Organisational diversity, institutional competition, and experimentation all contribute to stimulating innovation and creativity at the regional level.

The decentralisation theorem put on its head would recommend centralisation only for public goods the benefits of which are general and supraregional in nature. Defence would be the typical candidate. For the EC, it is not defence which has been the driving force behind regional integration, but the improvement of economic welfare through the creation of a single market and economic co-operation. Specific supraregional benefits can be expected in the fields of energy (common carriers), transport and telecommunications, environmental protection, research and technology policies (and to some extent higher education), as well as from foreign trade policy.

Apart from public goods, there are at least two further arguments in favour of a more centralised provision of public services: (i) increasing returns to scale in producing such services; and (ii) spill-over effects between lower-level jurisdictions of the federation. Although these arguments are often used in the literature, they are open to challenge. Increasing returns to scale were overstressed by communist rulers in Eastern Europe, with disastrous results. While such cost-reducing effects cannot be denied in principle, decentralisation has greater dynamic cost-reducing potential, through competition and process innovation. This may be true even with a degree of co-ordination at a higher level. After all, it is typical for modern industrial organisations to decentralise and to contract-out in order to reduce costs. Why should such principles not apply to government?

Moreover, neither increasing returns to scale - where they exist - nor regional spill-over effects preclude regional governments from co-operating with each other, and there is empirical evidence that this happens on a voluntary basis. Co-operation does, however, entail co-ordination costs, and these may be sufficiently high to open up the way for central government intervention.

These arguments do not, however, substantially support the concentration of expenditure functions within a federation. All they indicate is some scope for regulatory action and a catalytic role for central government. An optimal institutional design would seek to minimise organisational and co-ordination costs for such a framework.

Co-ordination costs in federal government have attracted little attention in the literature. Breton and Scott (1978) analysed the impact of organisational costs on the allocation of functions to different levels of government. While they were unable to derive firm conclusions on the problem of assigning expenditure functions, they emphasised the political elements embedded in such costs.

From an economic point of view, co-ordination costs - including political and organisational aspects - are the clue to the centralisation problem, and there is much scope for further research in that area. Whereas there is a general presumption in favour of a decentralised provision of public services, and not only for economic reasons,[1] managerial aspects may recommend some co-ordinated action, although not always centralisation. The principal-agent paradigm lends itself to the analysis of cost-minimising behaviour in multi-level government; also, regulatory federalism and questions relating to interjurisdictional competition seem to have found increasing attention in recent years (Oates 1991).

1.2 Distribution and federalism

Much of the work related to the analysis of distribution in a federation is tied to the Tiebout (1956) model, which investigates the optimality of the decentralised provision of public goods, hence its allocative aspects. Tiebout emphasises the role of the taxpayers in constraining local government by "voting with their feet", choosing that mix of local public goods and taxes that best suits their particular preferences.

This is not the place to discuss Tiebout's hypothesis in full - it has sparked off an extensive literature (see, for instance, attachment 1 in Walsh 1992). With regard to the distribution function, his main conclusion seems to be that in a world of free migration, movers create fiscal externalities for all members of the municipality they leave, as they inflict externalities onto residents of receiving jurisdictions. Such effects could be offset by a system of unconditional transfers between jurisdictions to the extent that they compensate for interregional externalities resulting from migration.

Migration would, however, effectively force regional governments to implement redistributional policies. The rich would leave municipalities with high redistributive taxation, as the poor would be attracted by such places. The locational neutrality of taxation, and for that matter of public assistance, would thus point towards centralising the distribution function.

Despite this argument, many federations employ distribution policies at lower levels of government. This may be explained either by altruistic motives or by the limited mobility of taxpayers. The former argument may have some bearing at the municipal level; at EC level, the latter is more decisive even if income differentials in the EC narrow, because cultural and language barriers are still likely to restrict migration to a large extent. Furthermore, primary incomes and wealth are not, as implied by the Tiebout model, independent of locational decisions. Migration can thus become rather costly for moving citizens.[2]

More recently, analysts seem to have agreed that the scope for regional redistribution policies is wider than the traditional view would suggest (see for instance King 1984). This is particularly relevant for the EC, where distribution policy is likely to remain at national levels, especially with regard to interpersonal redistribution. Yet in addition there may be scope for interregional redistribution which could eventually be effected via horizontal grants - as in Germany - or through the EC budget. Distribution policies may thus become a task shared between different levels of government, where some harmonisation of outcomes is achieved either by policy co-ordination or by compensatory interregional grants.

1.3 Macroeconomic management and federalism

As mentioned before, the traditional view would assign the stabilisation function to central government. There are a number of arguments supporting this view.

As with other traditional views on federalism, the general presumption in favour of central stabilisation policies has been challenged in recent years. Apart from a general scepticism about the usefulness of interventionist macroeconomic stabilisation policies, nurtured by monetarist and supply-side theoreticians alike, the literature on fiscal federalism has come to acknowledge the importance of automatic stabilisers embedded in the federal machinery. Built-in stabilisers may, however, work at all levels of government. Further, a federal system may establish co-ordinating machinery for budget policies, as for monetary and exchange rate policies. The EMS is an example of this. Hence, the transfer of exclusive powers for macroeconomic management to central government is by no means necessary to achieve stability in a federation. Yet the central government typically sets the pace for stabilising policy actions either by its own budgetary policies or through co-ordination. For the EC the latter seems to be the only feasible option, given its rather restricted budget. If the Community *in toto* is subject to an external shock, the fiscal and monetary responses must come from national policy actions, although these may have to be co-ordinated at some stage.

The case is more difficult for regionally-asymmetric shocks: where these occur and whenever they are permanent, markets should be allowed to react. Migration and/or capital flows may then alter relative prices in order to restore macroeconomic equilibrium. Where such shocks are temporary, some authors believe that a regional-policy response could achieve macroeconomic stabilisation more effectively than central government intervention (Gramlich 1987). Yet while sub-central governments may be better-placed to recognise the causes of economic disturbances, they may also have to be assisted in implementing stabilisation policies. This is a case for central government co-ordination. More recently, stabilisation schemes have been proposed that may work at the central level with little cost (Goodhart and Smith 1992; Pisani-Ferry 1992). They are designed to absorb only asymmetrical shocks, and they seem to avoid moral-hazard problems to a large extent. At least these models challenge the traditional view that a large central budget is needed to implement effective stabilisation policies.

2. The grant system and problems of assigning taxes

Any federation has to deal with the vertical as well as the horizontal assignment of financial resources to its different governments.[3] The vertical distribution of funds reflects to some extent the degree of centralisation of government outlays within a federation. Yet apart from expenditure, the question arises as to whether certain taxes are better suited for assignment to the central government than others.

A useful starting point for discussion of this issue is Musgrave's systematic treatment of it (1983). He would assign the following taxes to the central budget: (i) taxes with highly progressive rates - because of perverse incentives to migration; (ii) taxes on highly mobile tax bases (such as portfolio capital) - because of their distorting locational decisions; (iii) taxes whose base is unevenly distributed between jurisdictions (like natural resources) - because of geographical inequalities. On the other hand, sub-central authorities should exploit (iv) taxes on regionally-immobile tax bases, and (v) taxes relating to specific regional benefits.

These traditional criteria have also been challenged in recent years. It is, for instance, debatable whether progressive sub-national taxation does in fact lead to perverse migration effects. More recent studies (e.g. Goodspeed 1989) assert significant scope for regional redistribution policies with only moderate efficiency losses.

The essence of the allocative argument in taxation seems to lie in the benefit-pricing rule. The link between taxpayers' bills and the provision of public goods is the economist's main avenue towards establishing efficiency in the public sector. This offers, however, little guidance to answering the question of vertical tax assignment in a federation. While there may be distorting effects resulting from an inappropriate assignment of taxes, these may be blurred by fiscal illusion and intergovernmental grants.

Empirical evidence on existing federations reveals a wide variety of solutions to tax-assignment problems: income taxes are assigned to the centre in the USA, for instance, while they are more decentralised in Switzerland. Turnover taxes are decentralised in North America, while VAT is typically a central tax in Europe. Where this leads to vertical fiscal imbalances these can be corrected in many ways through unconditional grants and/or revenue sharing. Where the emphasis is on the income effect of taxation, such corrections through intergovernmental grants seem to entail few efficiency losses.

Yet central taxation is to be recommended where (i) taxes form *policy instruments* for achieving supranational policy goals; and (ii) where tax bases are difficult to define at the regional level - *the regional arbitrariness* argument. Agricultural levies, for instance, are policy instruments to be employed at the centre, while customs duties were handed over to the Community on grounds of regional arbitrariness.

In the longer run, a "carbon tax" may have to be added as a policy instrument to the arsenal of the EC's budgetary policy, whereas the regional-arbitrariness argument will increasingly apply to the taxing of portfolio capital with its high international mobility. While tax competition may become a severe policy constraint in this latter area, it is not necessary for capital taxation (or corporate taxation for that matter) to be centralised. All it requires, once again, is tax co-ordination, which could be effectively achieved at the horizontal level with "catalytic" functions for the Commission.

The tax-assignment problem has its complement in the grants system. As noted before, grants may be used to correct vertical fiscal imbalances in multi-layer government. Existing federations suggest solutions in this respect. At one extreme is Australia, with its emphasis on collecting taxes at the centre, while resources are redistributed downwards to the states; at the other lies the EC, which is largely dependent on grants from below, although these may be termed the Community's "own resources". Other federations, such as the US and Switzerland, have succeeded in assigning taxes so as to avoid sizeable vertical grants, yet often at the price of overlapping tax powers that some have called a "tax jungle".

A further strategy to correct vertical fiscal imbalances is revenue-sharing, whereby taxes are collected jointly and then apportioned vertically. This strategy is employed in Germany and - less explicitly - in the EC.

While the vertical effects of the grants system are important, the vital part is their horizontal redistributional effects. Grants are typically employed to reduce regional inequalities and to achieve social and economic cohesion through greater fairness in a federation. This is achieved by two types of grants: (i) horizontal compensation payments without central government interference - as in the German *Finanzausgleich*; and (ii) "asymmetrical" vertical grants, i.e. discriminating in favour of poorer regions. The latter practice is more widespread.

There is an extensive literature on the economic effects of grants and their corresponding policy objectives.[4] Where the aim is to stimulate specific regional activities because of existing regional spillovers, specific-purpose, open-ended, matching grants seem to be appropriate. They encourage regional activities by altering relative prices for the supply of such services - besides contributing resources for their financing. Where the aim is to equalise "fiscal capacities" in order to allow regional governments to provide similar levels of basic public goods, unconditional general-revenue grants are recommended. They are supposed to have a pure income effect, yet there is evidence that the fiscal impact of such grants is greater than expected.[5]

As to the further development of intergovernmental grants in the EC, a model like the German *Finanzausgleich* is likely to be unacceptable to member states. Political consensus on redistributive government finance is likely to lie far downstream. Grants will thus be of the asymmetrical vertical type, where conditional, matching variants are politically more acceptable since they can be tailored to compensating for regional spillover effects.

Intergovernmental grants seem to introduce high complexities into the workings of federal fiscal machinery, because of implicit strings attached to the political process. Often they imply joint decision-making and shared responsibility, as in the German "joint tasks", which entail political and administrative friction and hence organisational costs. On the other hand, such mechanisms tend to establish a broader political consensus and enable politicians to reach agreement in areas where there would otherwise be deadlock. Joint decision-making thus exhibits significant organisational benefits, despite its frictional costs. There is more specific literature on the impact of joint decision-making and grants on the efficiency of the public sector in Germany (Scharpf 1988), which emphasises costs while belittling the benefits of consensus-formation. The results are, however, far from being conclusive.

3. Conclusion

Federalism is here to stay. Given the need for greater economic and political co-operation in an increasingly-integrated world, and the sensitivities of nation states and their regions, federal structures are likely to become even more important than in the past.

Federal institutions exhibit costs and benefits which cannot be assessed in solely economic terms. Their political and organisational costs are also extremely important. Although an ideal fiscal machinery of a federal type cannot be designed in the abstract, well-balanced federal systems *can* evolve through free negotiations between equal partners who recognise and exploit the benefits of interjurisdictional co-operation. Federalism can thus contribute to enhanced economic welfare, to interregional fairness, and to stability through greater economic and political integration.

NOTES

1. Other writers approach the issue of decentralisation from public decision-making models (public choice): for instance, Downs (1957), Buchanan and Tullock (1962), and Olson (1963). A more radical approach is that of Brennan and Buchanan (1980), who argue that decentralisation is needed in order to prevent insatiable governments from behaving like revenue-maximising leviathans.

2. A case for decentralisation can also made on grounds of a better revelation of information, which is needed for optimal decisions in distribution policies (Wildasin 1990).

3. For a theoretical discussion of the division of functions between levels of government see, for instance, Oates 1972 (chapter 2), and on tax assignment within the "layer-cake" approach, Spahn 1988.

4. See, for instance, Oates 1972, ch.3; Gramlich 1977; and King 1984, chs. 3-5.

5. There is empirical evidence that grants have a greater impact on regional government spending than would result from the mere income effect. The fiscal stimulus of unconditional grants seems to be higher by about 40-50 cents in the dollar than predicted, a phenomenon known as the "fly-paper effect". See, for instance, Gramlich 1977.

References

Brennan, Geoffrey, and James Buchanan (1990), *The Power to Tax*, Cambridge, Mass.: Cambridge University Press.

Breton, A. and A. D. Scott (1978), *The Economic Constitution of Federal States*, Toronto: University of Toronto Press.

Buchanan, J. M. and G. Tullock (1962), *The Calculus of Consent*, Ann Arbor: University of Michigan Press.

Cornes, R. and T. Sandler (1986), *The Theory of Externalities, Public Goods and Club Goods*, Cambridge: Cambridge University Press.

Downs, Anthony (1957), *An Economic Theory of Democracy*, New York: Harper & Row.

Goodhart, C. and S. Smith (1992), "Stabilisation", in *The Economics of Community Public Finance*, *European Economy* special edition.

Goodspeed, T. (1989), "A re-examination of the use of ability to pay taxes by local governments", *Journal of Public Economics* 38, 319-42.

Gramlich, E. M. (1977), "Intergovernmental grants: a review of the empirical literature", in Wallace Oates (ed.), *The Political Economy of Fiscal Federalism*, Lexington, Mass.: Lexington Books.

Gramlich, E. M. (1987), "Federalism and federal deficit-reduction", *National Tax Journal* 40, 299-313.

Italianer, A. and J. Pisani-Ferry (1993), "The regional-stabilisation properties of fiscal arrangements" (this volume).

King, David (1984), *Fiscal Tiers: The Economics of Multi-Level Government*, London: Allen & Unwin.

Musgrave, R. A. (1983), "Who should tax, where, and what?", in Charles McLure (ed.), *Tax Assignment in Federal Countries*, Canberra: Australian National University Press.

Oates, Wallace (1991), "The theory of fiscal federalism: revenue and expenditure issues - a survey of recent theoretical and empirical research", in Rémy Prud'homme (ed.), *Public Finance with Several Levels of Government*, The Hague/Koenigstein: Journal of Public Finance Foundation.

Oates, Wallace (1972), *Fiscal Federalism*, New York: Harcourt Brace Jovanovich.

Olson, Mancur (1982), *The Rise and Decline of Nations: Economic Growth, Stagflation and Social Rigidities*, New Haven, Conn.: Yale University Press.

Scharpf, F. W. (1988), "The joint-decision trap: lessons from German federalism and European integration", *Public Administration* 66.

Spahn, P. B. (1988), "On the assignment of taxes in federal polities", in G. Brennan, B. Grewal and P. Groenewegen (eds.), *Taxation and Federalism: Essays in Honour of Russell Mathews*, Canberra: Pergamon Press/Australian National University Press.

Tiebout, Charles (1956), "A pure theory of local expenditure", *Journal of Political Economy* 64, 416-426.

Tresch, R. W. (1981), *Public Finance: A Normative Theory*, Plano, Texas: Business Publications.

Walsh, C. (1992), "Fiscal federalism: an overview of issues and a discussion of their relevance to the European Community", in *The Economics of Community Public Finance, op. cit.*

Wildasin, D. E. (1990), "Budgetary pressures in the EEC: a fiscal federalism perspective", *American Economic Review* (Papers and Proceedings) 80.

11 The regional-stabilisation properties of fiscal arrangements

Alexander Italianer and Jean Pisani-Ferry

1. Introduction[1]

The steps leading to the signature of the Treaty on European Union in Maastricht have refuelled the debate about whether a single European currency would need to be accompanied by a large budget at Community level, an equalisation scheme, a special "shock-absorbing" mechanism or a combination of these devices. One of the main arguments in favour of such a parallelism in the process of unification is that without a sizeable EC budget, monetary union would lack the automatic stabilisers needed to compensate states for the loss of the exchange rate as an adjustment instrument (a view taken by, for instance, Krugman, 1992 and Feldstein, 1992). As developed in Goodhart and Smith (1992), the case for regional stabilisation rests on the Keynesian assumption of market imperfections (especially price/wage rigidities) which prevent instantaneous market clearing. This is indeed a basic assumption in all the literature dealing with stabilisation properties of federal budgetary systems. It is therefore retained hereafter without further discussion.

The case for regional stabilisation is theoretically simple (see Wyplosz, 1991, and Frenkel and Goldstein, 1991). It basically holds that a federal budget provides a kind of insurance to states which enter a monetary union by guaranteeing that any of them which has to face alone an adverse economic shock (arising, for example, from a drop in the demand for its products) will automatically receive a net transfer of income from the rest of the union. This transfer will take place through higher transfers to individuals (unemployment benefit and means-tested transfers), possibly higher grants from the federal budget or the budgets from other regions, and lower tax payments, to at least partially offset the adverse effects of the shock. A federal budget would therefore make the monetary-union contract both less costly and more credible.

Presenting the issue in insurance terms is a way of saying that it is in principle disconnected from issues of static redistribution between the EC countries which might choose to participate in European Economic and Monetary Union (EMU). Even if all EMU members initially enjoyed the same standard of living, there would still be a debate over the regional-stabilisation function of the Community budget. What matters here is not average but marginal redistribution or stabilisation when any member state, even the most wealthy one, is hit by a shock. In other words, the issue is whether participating countries can take for granted, not only that the present value of expected welfare gains from EMU will be positive by the time they ratify the EMU treaty, but also that the present value of these gains will remain positive, whatever the future changes in their well-being in comparison to other EMU members.[2]

The logic of these arguments is indisputable. What remains a matter for debate is whether or not a *large* federal budget is necessary to ensure that participating countries will benefit from monetary union. As pointed out by several authors (Eichengreen, 1990, Sachs and Sala-i-Martin, 1991), a major difference between the proposed EMU and existing monetary unions is the very limited size of the Community budget. On the other hand, it is not enough to argue that a considerable federal budget is maintained in those monetary unions (especially the United States, but also Canada and Australia) from which the Community might draw inspiration. What has also to be assessed is to what extent those countries' budgets automatically offset regional shocks, and whether this is necessary for the stability of their monetary unions.[3] One can then begin to estimate the degree of shock-absorption necessary for EMU, and the mechanism through which this can be achieved.

2. Measuring regional stabilisation

2.1 Concepts

Before presenting different methods for evaluating the regional-stabilisation effect of a federal budget, it is necessary to define more precisely what has to be measured. In particular, a distinction must be made between the *stabilisation* and the *redistribution* properties of a federal budget. This distinction is based on the concept of the *primary* income of a region, i.e. before taxes are paid to, or funds are received from, the federal government; and *secondary* or *disposable* income, i.e. the primary income plus the transfers net of taxes received from the federal government. Redistribution occurs when, over the same period, the ratio between disposable and primary income is higher for a poor region (i.e. with low primary income) than for a rich one. Stabilisation occurs when for a given region, rich or poor, transitory changes in disposable income are smaller than those in primary income.

Obviously, redistribution and stabilisation can occur at the same time.

These notions are illustrated in Graph 1. The line Y shows the development over time of primary income (per capita) in a typical state in a federation, characterised by a cyclical movement around a trend increase. It is assumed that the average primary and secondary incomes in the federation remain unchanged. There are three possible lines for disposable income (YD) in the state concerned. If there were only a pure redistribution scheme through the federal budget (line YR), disposable income would develop so that the ratio between YD and Y would decline as Y increased. If there were only a pure stabilisation scheme through the federal budget (line YS), disposable income would follow the same trend as primary income but fluctuate to a lesser extent. Finally, redistribution and stabilisation schemes could operate at the same time (line YRS), so that with increasing primary income the ratio of disposable to primary income decreased but was less sensitive to cyclical movements.

Graph 1. Stabilization and redistribution

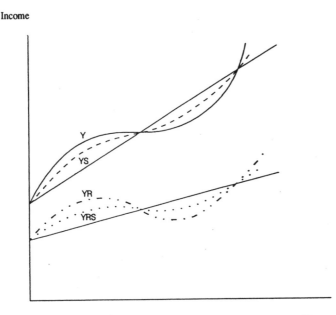

Income

Time

———— Y : primary income

· — · — · YR : only redistribution

– – – – – YS : only stabilisation

· · · · · · YRS : redistribution and stabilisation

In practice, one observes only the lines Y and YRS, so that it is difficult to disentangle redistribution from stabilisation schemes. Moreover, a pure redistribution scheme in general also contributes to stabilisation. In the example in the graph, this may be seen from the fact that at each point in time the slope of the line YR is smaller than that of the primary income line Y (dYR/dt < dY/dt). The converse does not follow, however: more stabilisation does not necessarily require more redistribution, since it can also be obtained from a pure stabilisation scheme.[4] In particular, it is not true that in order to obtain the same degree of stabilisation as in existing federations, the Community would need a sizeable federal budget: this could be done through a pure stabilisation scheme, as will be worked out below.

A second conclusion which follows from the preceding analysis is that, although the degree of stabilisation tends to increase with the degree of redistribution, there are no a priori grounds on which the one should be bigger than the other. In terms of Graph 1, this depends entirely on the relative difference in slopes between the two trend lines, and the difference in slopes between lines YRS and Y.

For the empirical measurement of the degree of stabilisation in existing federations, two methods have been employed. The most widely-used approach is that of regression analysis (time series and/or cross-section), using different types of estimators (3SLS, SURE, IV) to correct for simultaneity bias. An alternative approach is to calculate the properties on the basis of model simulations (introduced by Pisani-Ferry et al., 1992).

2.2 Regression analysis

For the regression analysis, two approaches can be distinguished, labelled "elasticities approach" and "income approach" by Bayoumi and Masson (1991). This may be explained as follows. Let us assume we are interested in the behaviour of a region's income within a federal or centralised economic union with a central government. An appropriate point of departure is equation (1), which gives an accounting definition of the disposable income (YD) of region i as regional GDP[5] (Y), less taxes and other contributions paid to the central government (TAX), plus transfers received from the central government (TR), plus the amount received by the region from central government expenditure on goods and services (G).[6] The inclusion of the latter term may be surprising at first sight, but public goods provided to the region by the central government have to be taken into account in the evaluation of the region's income.

(1) $YD_i = Y_i - TAX_i + TR_i + G_i$

Equation (1) may be rewritten in first difference form, thus:

(1') $dYD_i = dY_i - dTAX_i + dTR_i$

where it is assumed that government expenditure on goods and services is rigid in the short term ($dG_i = 0$)..

Since we are interested in the degree of stabilisation provided by the federal budget, an indicator of its stabilisation properties in the presence of region-specific shocks is:[7]

(2) $S_i = 1 - dYD_i/dY_i$

S_i would be zero in the absence of federal stabilisation, and reach 100% in the event that all shocks were absorbed without affecting regional income.

From (1') and (2), it immediately follows that

(3) $S_i = (dTAX_i/dY_i) - (dTR_i/dY_i)$

which can also be rewritten using elasticities as

(4) $S_i = h_{tax} \cdot (TAX_i/Y_i) - h_{tr} \cdot (TR_i/Y_i)$

where h_{tax} is the elasticity of tax receipts with respect to GDP and h_{tr} is the elasticity of transfer payments.

From equations (2) and (4) it follows that there are two ways of calculating the degree of stabilisation: the *income approach*, according to which variations in total disposable income are regressed on variations in primary income, and the *elasticities approach*, according to which individual tax and transfer categories are regressed on variations in income, multiplied by their share in primary income and then substituted in equation (4) to obtain the total degree of stabilisation. Most authors have used the elasticities approach until now, although Bayoumi and Masson (1991) argue that it may well overstate the role of taxes in stabilisation and understate the role of transfers.

Whichever approach one adopts, it is important that the specification of the equation be such that it measures stabilisation and not redistribution. In order to measure the latter, the equations should be estimated in levels or in log-levels. In the case of the income approach this yields (a similar equation can be used for a tax or transfer category in the elasticities approach):

(5) $YD_i = a_i + b \cdot Y_i$

with YD_i and Y_i measured as the level or logarithm of per capita variables relative to the federal average. The degree of redistribution according to this specification is measured as 1-b.

To measure stabilisation, the equation should be specified either in first differences over time (of levels or log-levels) or in levels with a time trend. In the case of the income approach this implies one of the following two specifications:

Table 1

Shock-absorption in regions through the central government: United States

Sample and income concept (y)	Dependent variable (x)	Estimation result	Share (x/y)	dx/dy "Redistribution"	dx/dy "Stabilisation"	Other features
ELASTICITIES APPROACH						
Sachs and Sala-i-Martin (1991)						
9 census regions, 1970-1988, per capita real income relative to US average	Real total personal taxes per capita relative to US average	$\ln(x)=.+1.275(*)\ln(y)$	25.8		32.8	Dummy variable and time trend for each region
	Real per capita federal transfers to individuals, state and local governments relative to US average	$\ln(x)=.-0.327(*)\ln(y)$	17.9		-5.9	Idem
von Hagen (1991)						
50 states, 1981-1986, real GSP per capita	Real per capita federal income tax payments	$\ln(x/x_{-1})=.+0.87\ln(y/y_{-1})$ (1981-2)	8.8		7.7	Intercept and oil dummy (6 oil states) for each year
		$\ln(x/x_{-1})=.+1.10\ln(y/y_{-1})$ (1983-6)	8.2		9.0	
		$x=.+0.38y$ (1980-6)	8.4	38		
	Real per capita federal direct payments to individuals	$\ln(x/x_{-1})=.-0.17\ln(y/y_{-1})$ (1982-6)	9.1		-1.5	Idem
		$x=.-0.088y$ (1980-6)	9.1	-8.8		
	Real per capita federal expenditure	$\ln(x/x_{-1})=.+0.036\ln(y/y_{-1})$ (1982-6)	19.9		0.7	Idem

Table 1 (continued)

Sample and income concept (y)	Dependent variable(x)	Estimation result	Share (x/y)	"Redistribution"	"Stabilisation"	Other features
Goodhart and Smith (1992)						
44 states (excl. 6 oil states and DC), 1981-1986, real GSP per capita (relative to US average for log-level models)	Real per capita federal payments relative to US average	$\ln(x)=..+1.528 \ln(y)$	8.4	12.8		Dummies for each year
		$(x-x_{-1})=..0.019(y-y_{-1})$ (1982)	8.5		1.9	Dummies for each year; current and lagged GSP change
		$(x-x_{-1})=..0.108(y-y_{-1})$ (1983-6)	8.2		10.8	
	Real per capita federal transfer payments to individuals (relative to US average for log models)	$\ln(x)=..-0.139 \ln(y)$	9.1	-1.3		Dummies for each year
		$(x-x_{-1})=..-0.011(y-y_{-1})$ (1982-6)	9.1		-1.1	Dummies for each year; current and lagged GSP change
	Real per capita total federal spending (relative to US average for log models)	$\ln(x)=..+0.477 \ln(y)$	19.9	9.5		Dummies for each year
		$(x-x_{-1})=..-0.040(y-y_{-1})$ (1982-6)	19.9		-4.0	Dummies for each year; current and lagged GSP change
INCOME APPROACH						
Bayoumi and Masson (1991)						
48 states, 1970-1986, nominal per capita personal income relative to US average	Nominal per capita personal income net of federal personal tax & social insurance payments and federal transfers & grants received, relative to US average	$x=..+0.803y$ (data averaged 1969-86) $(x-x_{-1}]=..+0.724(y-y_{-1})$ (1971-86)	- -	19.7	27.6	- State-specific constants
		$x=..+0.647y$ (1970-86)	-		35.3	Idem + time trend

(*) Weighted average of OLS estimates. Other estimates lead to similar results.

(6a) $dYD_i = a_i + b \cdot dY_i$

(6b) $YD_i = a_i + b \cdot Y_i + c_i \cdot \text{time}$

Since the findings of Bayoumi and Masson (1991) indicate that equation (6b) results in dynamic mis-specification, equation (6a) seems to be preferable. In either case, the degree of stabilisation S_i is measured by 1-b.

Table 1 provides some results for stabilisation and redistribution for the United States from the literature using the preceding classification. The seminal work in the area of stabilisation is Sachs and Sala-i-Martin (1989), updated in Sachs and Sala-i-Martin (1991), from which the results in the table are drawn. These authors, using the elasticities approach on the basis of equation (6b) with logarithms, found a degree of stabilisation equal to 39%. Their results are based on a grouping of states into 9 census regions.

Von Hagen (1991) also used the elasticities approach, but on the basis of equation (6a) with logarithmic growth rates. Moreover, he used individual state data and, unlike Sachs and Sala-i-Martin, did not take variables relative to the US average. On the basis of his tax and transfer categories (which represent smaller shares than those of Sachs and Sala-i-Martin), he found a degree of stabilisation of approximately 10%, i.e. considerably smaller than Sachs and Sala-i-Martin. It is clear, however, that this is not a realistic estimate. Suppose for instance that h_{tr} in equation (4) is zero. Even then, with the tax share equal to some 25%, stabilisation of 10% would imply a tax elasticity of 0.4, which is too low to be credible. Presumably, the fact that von Hagen excluded important tax and transfer categories is at least partly responsible for the low degree of stabilisation he found.[8]

This last conclusion seems to be confirmed by the results from Goodhart and Smith (1992). With the specification of their elasticities approach, which is in first differences of per capita levels, they found a comparable degree of stabilisation (12%) using the same tax and transfer categories as von Hagen. When extending transfers from federal transfer payments to individuals to total federal spending, the degree of stabilisation increases to 15%.

Bayoumi and Masson (1991), using the income approach, tested several specifications. Using equation (6a) they found 35% - virtually replicating the Sachs and Sala-i-Martin result of 39% of stabilisation - but also signs of considerable dynamic mis-specification. Using equation (6a), however, their preferred estimate resulted in a degree of stabilisation equal to 28%.

The conclusion on the degree of stabilisation in the United States on the basis of these results seems to be that it lies somewhere between 15% and 30%, given the problems associated with the Sachs and Sala-i-Martin approach on the higher side and the von Hagen approach on the lower.

Table 1 also provides results regarding the degree of redistribution. Using broadly the same approach as for the degree of stabilisation but applied to levels rather than first differences, the degree of redistribution found for the United States ranges from 20% (Bayoumi and Masson, 1991), to 22% (Goodhart and Smith, 1992) and 47% (von Hagen, 1991). The latter estimated his equations in levels without dividing by the United States average, while the other two results were estimated using log-levels on data relative to the United States average. Not dividing by the average values for the United States, which is necessary in order to obtain a correct measure of redistribution, may well explain part of the difference. The conclusion on redistribution in the United States is therefore that this is likely to be in the neighbourhood of 20%.

2.3 Model simulation

The regression analysis presented above was based on estimates using regional accounts. This has the advantage of relying on available regional data, but also two drawbacks: first, that only part of the budgetary data is available at the regional level, and second that this method is difficult to extend to other countries where similar data are missing.

Consequently, we propose a different method (Pisani-Ferry et al., 1992). Instead of using regional data, our method is based on simulations for the United States, France and Germany with a simplified neo-Keynesian model of a region within a federal monetary union. The model equations are representative of those of a fairly standard macroeconometric model, and its major behavioural parameters have been calibrated using simulations with existing country models, but special attention has been given to the representation of the operation of a two-level tax and transfer system: all major categories of federal and/or State and local taxes and expenditures are explicitly modelled, with tax and spending parameters calibrated in order to simulate the effects of current legislation.

This method has three advantages: first, as with the income approach for the regression method, the effect of the entire budgetary system is taken into account rather than that of one or two predetermined channels of redistribution; second, the use of both a common accounting framework and similar models leads to comparable country results; third, as macroeconomic variables are endogenous in the model, the assessment of stabilisation properties is made on an ex post rather than an ex ante basis. The main drawbacks are, first, that the simulation results may depend on somewhat arbitrary assumptions as regards the degree of economic integration within the country, and second that the calibration of the regional model's budgetary parameters rests on the quality of country-model estimates, which may not be as precise or specific as cross-section estimates.

Method and model

The method is simple. Suppose we have a macroeconomic model for a given country. Since stabilisation is the only concern, and assuming that asymmetric shocks can affect any region with equal probability, there is no point in specifying the economic characteristics of existing regions (or states or Länder). What should be measured is the extent of automatic stabilisation for the average (abstract) region, whatever the actual differences between (concrete) regions. It can therefore be assumed that economic structures as measured by, for example, the capital stock or the rate of unemployment, as well as the behaviour of private agents, are identical throughout the country. If there are n regions in the country, a "region" in the above sense can simply be defined as $1/n_{th}$ of the country's economy. A model of such a "region" can therefore be derived from the model of the country's economy as a whole. What needs to be defined in order to carry out this derivation is i) the operation of the budgetary system, and ii) the degree of economic integration (for labour, goods and capital markets) between the regions.

i) We have represented the major properties of the budgetary system in a detailed country macromodel, embedding information on, for instance, tax bases and elasticities and the economic characteristics of social insurance benefit in the model's equations. What is obviously missing in a model with a single government level is information on the assignment of taxes, contributions and expenditures to different government levels. This information could, however, be derived from national accounts and knowledge of the institutional characteristics of a country's budgetary system, and be combined with the model's aggregate information in order to build a region's model. The derivation of tax equations for regional and central governments is best understood in the two polar cases of generalised tax-sharing (in such a case, tax equations for different government levels only differ by a constant factor) and a clear assignment of different categories of taxes to different government levels (the only task is then to assign each tax equation to either one of the two government levels represented in the model); but it can also be dealt with in less clear-cut cases.

ii) In order to derive a region model from a country model, assumptions need also to be made regarding the degree of economic integration between regions. Since no strong basis exists for the modelling of interregional linkages within countries, a priori assumptions had to be relied upon. The choice was made to model interregional integration using standard international economic-integration assumptions. Stronger assumptions were introduced later to test the sensitivity of the results.

The *degree of labour-market mobility* resulting from integration within countries varies according to the country, and its contribution to stabilisation is a matter for controversy (see Commission of the EC, 1991, chapter 6, and Blanchard and Katz, 1991). The simulations presented here are based on two assumptions: that labour mobility between regions is not a significant channel of short-run stabilisation, and that regional wages respond neither to regional unemployment nor to regional inflation, but rather to economy-wide conditions. As a consequence, a region hit by a shock tends to exhibit higher-than-average unemployment for a protracted period, because neither migration nor a drop in regional real wages brings the labour market back into balance. Since this is clearly the case in which stabilisation has to operate through the federal budget, this kind of assumption can be considered appropriate for the simulations. However, these are quite extreme assumptions, and alternative simulations considering a higher degree of labour-market integration have been implemented (see Table 2 for the presentation of the different economic-integration assumptions, and Table 5 for the results of the corresponding alternative simulations).

Further, *goods-market integration* within a country can be measured in the framework of a macromodel by a) the share of trade with the rest of the country in regional GDP, b) the price-elasticities of exports and imports (to or from the rest of the country), and c) the relative impact of regional and national economic conditions on the behaviour of private agents, especially as regards investment and prices. Our simulations were carried out on the simplifying assumption that goods-market integration between regions is not significantly larger than between countries.[9] The variables and parameters from standard

Table 2
Alternative assumptions regarding economic integration

Degree of economic integration	*Low*	*High*
Labour markets		
Labour mobility between regions	0	50%[a]
Responsiveness of wages to regional economic conditions	0	50%[b]
Goods markets		
Export/GDP ratio	30%	75%
Share of demand from the rest of the country in the accelerator term of the investment equation	0	50%
Price elasticity of exports	0.7	1.4
Price elasticity of imports	0.5	1.0

[a] This 50% figure means that half of the new unemployed leave the region after the shock to work in another region. This compares to a figure of 65% found for the United States by Blanchard and Katz (1991).

[b] In this case, the evolution of wages follows both regional and national price and unemployment levels.

country equations were therefore retained in regional equations. Again, this assumption is quite extreme, but the alternative simulations did not change the results significantly. For instance, if one assumes a 75% share of trade instead of 30%, the impact of a regional shock is obviously reduced but the stabilising role of the central budget remains essentially unaffected (see also Tables 2 and 5).

Finally, *capital-market integration* can be assumed to be perfect within countries because regions share the same currency, and all financial assets, including stocks, can be considered to be perfect substitutes.

On the basis of the above assumptions, a small-scale standard model of a region's economy within a country was developed (for details, see Pisani-Ferry et al., 1992). The model is highly simplified as it attempts to capture in a compact fashion the standard short/medium-run characteristics of neo-Keynesian macromodels. The core behavioural equations consist of a wage-price block, investment and household demand equations, short-run equations for labour demand and unemployment, and "foreign" trade equations. For the sake of simplicity, no distinction is made between trade within the country and trade with the rest of the world, and the "region" is supposed to be small enough for it not to significantly affect rest-of-the-country variables ("small region" assumption). Since the focus is on differences in budgetary systems rather than on differences in agents' behaviour, no attempt has been made to differentiate between the United States, French and German models whose structure and essential non-budgetary parameters are identical.

The budgetary side of the model is more developed, although the equations remain unsophisticated. On the tax side, personal and corporate income taxes are represented as well as taxes on goods and services, VAT, and social security contributions. On the expenditure side, there is only one category for all expenditures on goods and services, but three categories of transfers to households are distinguished on the basis of their institutional characteristics: income-independent transfers (basically old-age and health benefits), which do not depend on a household's current income; income-dependent transfers (basically means-tested assistance programmes and, in Europe, family benefits); and unemployment benefit.

Intergovernmental grants are also taken into account, but basically considered to be exogenous, except in the case of Germany. For that country, two cases are distinguished: in the first (Germany I), which corresponds to a situation in which one of the wealthy Länder is hit by an adverse shock, the drop in regional income is supposed not to trigger intergovernmental transfers; in the second (Germany II), where a shock affects an already-poor region, transfers are supposed to compensate entirely for the loss in internal tax revenues. These two situations provide two extreme cases for assessing the properties of the German budgetary system.

The model was calibrated using parameters and multipliers from the *MIMOSA* multinational model (Equipe Mimosa, 1989). This model was chosen because it relies on a fairly detailed representation of major tax and expenditure categories. Its macroeconomic properties are comparable to those of other multinational models of a neo-Keynesian type, such as the European Commission's *QUEST* or the OECD *INTERLINK* models (see Whitley, 1991, for a comparison of their properties). The results should therefore not be model-dependent, but represent what could be obtained with a larger class of simulation models.

A three-year time horizon was chosen in order to eliminate the effects of lags in tax collection. This kind of horizon also corresponds to the approach of Sachs and Sala-i-Martin and others. The main tax and transfer parameters are given in Table 3.

An important issue is whether all categories of federal (or national) taxes and transfers have to be taken into account. Von Hagen (1991) limited his analysis of the US system to personal income taxes and transfers, leaving aside both corporate income tax and social security contributions. In part, this results from data limitations: the latter are levied in the state where companies are incorporated, which may not be the one where actual production takes place. The simulation method has the advantage of circumventing these limitations. It is implicitly assumed that establishments located in a region contribute to a firm's overall tax bill in proportion to their taxable profit (viz. wage bill).

However, there are also more conceptual problems with the treatment of corporate income taxes and employers' social security contributions. The cross-regional ownership of companies spreads the impact of a shock (and of the resulting tax-liability changes) across regions, thus providing a kind of insurance against regional shocks and reducing the stabilising impact of the tax system; in addition, the effects of a tax change may to some extent fall on the citizens of other regions through changes in the price of goods and factors.[10] It is therefore likely that a shock to regional enterprise income will only partially affect the region's disposable income. Consequently, the inclusion of corporate income taxes and employers' social security contributions is likely to lead to an overstatement of both the impact of a demand shock on the region's primary income and the stabilisation properties of the tax system.[11]

The inclusion of social security also raises intertemporal issues. In a fully-capitalised system, a reduction in the region's contributions would reduce the present value of future benefits by the same amount. It would therefore not imply more stabilisation than intertemporal income-smoothing through borrowing abroad. On the other hand, in a nationwide pay-as-you-go system, a decrease in social security contributions could have no impact whatsoever on the region's future pay-offs. All social security systems come between these two extremes. Here again, a decision to consider social security contributions as equivalent to federal taxes may lead to an overestimate of the stabilising character of the tax system.

Keeping these considerations in mind, the following choices were made for the treatment of individual tax and transfer categories. First, the characteristics of the personal income tax are captured by the aggregate elasticity of tax receipts with respect to households' taxable income. These parameters are taken from the *MIMOSA* model. Tax elasticity is higher in

France than in the other two countries owing to higher marginal rates.[12]

   Second, as the corporate income tax is modelled as the product of an apparent tax rate by taxable profits, apparent tax rates are well below legal marginal tax rates (see Table 3).

   Third, VAT is modelled in a simplified fashion as a consumption tax. The rates in Table 3 are obtained by dividing tax receipts by household consumption.

Table 3
Main tax and transfer parameters

	France	Germany	USA
Tax parameters			
Personal income-tax elasticity:			
federal taxes	1.40	1.30	1.20
regional taxes	-	1.30	1.00
Corporate income tax:			
apparent tax rate	0.14	0.17	0.09
regional governments' share	-	0.50	0.20
Social security contributions:			
employers' payroll apparent tax rate	0.20	0.16	0.20
employees' payroll apparent tax rate	0.20	0.19	0.08
regional governments' share	-	-	0.07
VAT:			
apparent tax rate	0.10	0.09	-
regional governments' share	-	0.35	-
Transfer parameters			
Income elasticity of income-dependent transfers:			
central transfers	-1.0	-1.0	-1.0
regional transfers	-1.0	-1.0	-1.0
Marginal replacement ratio for unemployment benefit:			
central insurance	0.6	0.75	-
regional insurance	-	-	0.13

Fourth, in the absence of reliable estimates for the elasticity of income-dependent transfers, a conservative evaluation was chosen; it is assumed that a 1% decrease in household income triggers a 1% rise in these transfers.[13]

Fifth, for unemployment benefit, the assumption was made that the marginal replacement ratio (of average unemployment compensation to average wage) was 50% higher than the average replacement ratio. The implied marginal replacement ratio is very low for the US, but since no federal unemployment insurance exists, this has little importance. For France and Germany, the marginal replacement ratios are rather high. Therefore, an alternative simulation was carried out assuming the marginal replacement ratio to be equal to the average ratio (see Table 5).

Table 4
Contributions of different channels to regional stabilisation
(baseline simulation)

	France	Germany I	Germany II	USA
Total stabilisation (%)	37.4	33.5	42.0	17.1
Transfers	*9.9*	*12.8*	*21.3*	*1.1*
Unemployment benefit	9.9	12.5	12.5	-
Income-independent transfers	-		-	-
Income-dependent transfers	0	0.3	0.3	.1
Horizontal transfers	-	-	8.5	-
Social security contributions	*14.5*	*12.5*	*12.5*	*8.7*
Employers' contributions	7.25	5.7	5.7	6.1
Employees' contributions	7.25	6.8	6.8	2.6
Taxes	*13.0*	*8.2*	*8.2*	*7.3*
VAT	1.6	0.6	0.6	-
Corporate income tax	6.5	4.1	4.1	3.4
Taxes on goods and services	3.3	2.2	2.2	0.7
Personal income tax	1.7	.4	1.4	3.2
Other	-0.05	-0.0	-0.0	-0.0

Germany I: without *Finanzausgleich.*
Germany II: with *Finanzausgleich.*

Results

In order to assess the stabilisation properties of the three budgetary systems, a demand shock consisting of a fall in the demand for exports by 1% of GDP was simulated with each of the country models. This is the most valuable simulation for the analysis of stabilisation. A supply shock in the form of a wage increase, for instance, will not give rise to much stabilisation from the budget side, since the tax increase induced by the nominal income increase will add to the direct negative impact on GDP. The model responses followed, as expected, the standard neo-Keynesian pattern, so there is no need to comment on the detailed simulation results. More interesting is the measurement of the stabilisation effect of the central budget.

Table 4 gives the contribution of different taxes and transfers to overall stabilisation in the three countries. Due to the non-linear character of the German system, two different simulations are reported for that country, with Germany I representing the system without interregional transfers and Germany II a case where they are assumed to have full effect. Table 4 is based on an analytical breakdown of the value of indicator S_i derived from equation (3) above.[14] A further refinement is that relative price effects have been taken into account, so that the expression for S_i is in fact (with p_i the deflator):

$$(7) \quad S_i = 1 - dYD_i/d(p_iY_i)$$

The US case may be analysed first because it is the one examined by previous studies. In terms of overall stabilisation effect, the 17% result lies between that of von Hagen (10%) and Goodhart and Smith (15%) on the one hand, and Bayoumi and Masson (28%) on the other. A breakdown of the effect will explain the difference between these findings.

First, a major contribution to stabilisation is provided by social security contributions and other employers' contributions to pension funds (almost 9%). The clear reason for this relatively strong effect is that these contributions are proportional to the wage bill; as the elasticity of employment with respect to output is assumed to be 0.7 and wages, which are set on a nationwide basis, remain approximately constant, a 1% fall in output leads approximately to a 0.7% drop in social contributions which is not matched by a reduction in transfers or the provision of health services. This single element explains a large part of the difference between our results and those of both von Hagen and Goodhart and Smith, who did not take social security into account. As we argued earlier, this difference could in reality be smaller due to the hybrid character of social security, as indicated by the fact that Bayoumi and Masson found that social security contributions added 2-3% to stabilisation.

Second, in spite of the assumption of an elasticity above unity, personal income taxes make a relatively minor contribution to overall stabilisation (3%), compared to a range of 8-11% obtained from the regression analyses. The reason for this rather surprising result is that personal income taxes are based on households' taxable income, which varies much less than regional output (because it is stabilised through the regional tax and transfer system). In the US case, the ex post elasticity of household income with respect to output is only 0.4. As the stabilisation effect of taxes is measured on an ex post basis, this significantly reduces the effect of personal income taxes.[15]

Third, corporate income taxes make for some 3.5% of regional stabilisation. The reason for this relatively strong effect is the high degree of variability in the tax base. However, the measurement may not be precise, because of the simplified way in which the tax base is modelled and the cross-regional effects of corporate income taxation.

Fourth, the contribution of transfers is minor, mostly because of the absence of a federal unemployment-benefit system in the United States. This is consistent with the results of von Hagen and Goodhart and Smith. It contrasts strongly, however, with those of Bayoumi and Masson, who found that transfers stabilised shocks to the tune of 10-13%. This is a striking contrast, since our approach is not open to Bayoumi and Masson's criticisms of the elasticities approach.[16] Further research is needed on this point.

For France and Germany, the stabilisation indicator is approximately twice as high as for the US. This is due to a number of factors: unemployment insurance, which contributes 10 percentage points (even more in Germany) to stabilisation; the social security system, which, with a larger share of GDP, contributes some 4 percentage points more to stabilisation; interregional grants in Germany, which contribute a maximum of 8.5 percentage points; and the operation of other taxes, which (mainly because of their share in GDP) explains some 5 percentage points of stabilisation in France.

To sum up, the results for France and Germany are similar in spite of France's more centralised budgetary system. If interregional cohesion is fully taken into account, the German budgetary system appears to achieve even more stabilisation than the French. However, there is evidence that the French system also involves important discretionary transfers to regions hit by a shock. These transfers are obviously not taken into account.

Table 5 summarises the results of simulations of the model under different, alternative assumptions (changes in economic integration, different replacement ratio). The baseline simulation results are affected to the extent that an alternative assumption has a direct impact on unemployment benefit (replacement ratio, labour-market integration), i.e. not very strongly. Furthermore, higher goods-market integration, while it may reduce the effects of a shock on a regional economy, does not affect the stabilisation results.

3. Asymmetric shocks

It is apparent from the preceding section that the degree of stabilisation provided by the system of fiscal federalism in the United States is rather low compared to

Table 5
Contributions of different channels to regional stabilisation
(alternative simulations)

Differences with baseline simulation in percentage points

Assumptions[a]	France	Germany I	Germany II	USA
1) Lower replacement ratio *for unemployment benefit* Total stabilisation (%)	-2.7	-3.6	-3.0	0.1
- of which: unemployment benefit[b]	-3.3	-4.2	-4.2	-
2) Higher labour-market integration[c] Total stabilisation	-4.1	-5.3	-5.3	0.1
- of which: unemployment benefit	-4.9	-6.25	-6.25	-
Higher goods-market integration[d] Total stabilisation	-	-	-	-

[a] See Table 2 for details.

[b] Replacement ratio = average ratio instead of 1.5*average ratio.

[c] Higher mobility between regions and higher responsiveness of wages to regional economic conditions. See second column of Table 2.

[d] Export/GDP ratio = 75%; share of demand from the rest of the country in the Accelerator term of the investment equation = 0.5; price elasticity of exports = 1.4; price elasticity of imports = 1.

other federations - of the order of 15-30%. Is a similar degree of stabilisation necessary for EMU? In all probability, the answer is no, because the automatic stabilisers in the Community member states themselves are presumably higher than those inside states of the American union.[17] On the other hand, the analysis has shown that even for a similar degree of stabilisation through federal flows in EMU, flows of the size observed in the United States or elsewhere would not necessarily be required, provided a suitable stabilisation mechanism were set up. Before discussing how such a system could work, it is worth briefly exploring to what extent it would be needed in EMU. The answer to this question depends on the size of the asymmetric shocks observed in EMU and on the availability of other adjustment instruments.

The main change in the third stage of EMU compared to the current situation is that the exchange rate will no longer be available as a means of adjustment, except when there are symmetric shocks. Until September 1992, the member states participating in the Exchange-Rate Mechanism of the EMS had largely renounced the use of this instrument. But even in the current situation of the EMS there is implicit agreement that such realignments will take place only in exceptional circumstances.[18] The loss of monetary instruments is therefore limited, especially when one takes into account the fact that the exchange-rate instrument has proved effective in the past only under certain circumstances.

Moreover, although the EMS countries will lose their monetary sovereignty after transition to the third stage of EMU, they will all (except for Germany) gain from the fact that the European Central Bank will take greater account of their economic situations than the Bundesbank currently does. The "anchor" role of the German economy at present focuses monetary policy almost exclusively on internal objectives, whereas monetary policy in EMU will have to take account of the average economic situation throughout the Community.

In principle there are two instruments other than national fiscal policy or federal fiscal flows which can compensate for the loss of monetary policy in EMU: temporary financing through capital movements or wage-price adjustments. The former will be facilitated in the truly integrated capital market which will be formed in the third stage of EMU. Indeed, the removal of all legal restrictions on capital movements as of July 1990 has not made exchange-rate uncertainty disappear, and this acts as a de facto impediment on capital movements other than speculative flows (Artis and Bayoumi, 1989, Atkeson and Bayoumi, 1991, Bhandari and Mayer, 1990).

All other things being equal, it is clear that a system of fixed exchange rates requires more flexible wage-price adjustments. Two important factors in this respect are labour-market flexibility and absolute wage differentials. Macroeconomically speaking, wage flexibility is mainly determined by price expectations and the impact of unemployment. In theory, wage flexibility in EMU could be enhanced by means of price expectations: excessive wage or price increases can never be compensated for by devaluation and can cause a permanent loss of competitiveness. For this reason, employers and trade unions can be expected to avoid inflationary wage-price spirals (Horn and Persson, 1988). This point is illustrated by Table 6, which shows that since the "hardening" of the EMS in 1983, all initial narrow-band EMS members (except Denmark) have improved their unit labour costs expressed in their *own* currency relative to Germany.

Table 6
Unit labour costs in manufacturing industry, 1991
(relative to Germany, 1983=100)

	B/L	DK	GR	E	F	IRL	I	NL	P	UK	EMS	Other
a. In own currency	88	111	294	120	95	72	111	80	202	106	89	167
b. In common currency	86	103	92	107	84	60	89	79	100	80	82	94
c. PM: exchange rate per DM	102	108	320	112	113	120	125	101	202	133	109	178

Source: calculated on the basis of Commission of the EC data. "EMS" is the arithmetical average of B/L, DK, F, IRL and NL. "Other" is the arithmetical average of the other five EC member states.

Absolute wage differentials between Community member states are currently substantial, owing to differences in productivity levels even between countries such as France and Germany (Centraal Planbureau, 1992, Chapter II.6). If the introduction of a single currency were, through wage-demonstration effects, to lead to a convergence of wage levels which did not correspond to differences in productivity, the process of adjustment to shocks would be severely hindered. Still, such effects are difficult to imagine on a scale like that observed for instance in Germany, mainly because of the more limited labour mobility between EC member states than between the two parts of Germany.

It follows from the preceding analysis that non-budgetary adjustment instruments could at least partly compensate for the loss of the exchange-rate instrument in EMU. However, in this context the question arises of the size of asymmetric shocks, which are after all the cause of the need for stabilisation. Bayoumi and Eichengreen (1991) compared supply and demand shocks for United States regions to those for Community member states. They found that supply shocks were larger and less correlated between countries in the Community than in the United States, and that supply and demand shocks were somewhat smaller in size than standard deviations of GDP growth rates. Bayoumi and Masson (1991) analysed absolute and asymmetric standard deviations of GDP growth rates for the United States and Canada, finding that asymmetric shocks represented one-sixth and one-third respectively of the absolute shocks. Table 7 summarises these findings, adding mean absolute values of relative GDP growth rates for the Community member states as a measure of asymmetric shocks (keeping in mind that actual supply and demand shocks will tend to be somewhat smaller). To the extent that the data are comparable, the data for the Community confirm the findings for the United States and Canada that asymmetric shocks to GDP growth are several times lower than absolute shocks. Nevertheless, asymmetric shocks in Europe seem to be higher than in Canada and especially than in the United States.

Still, the size of the asymmetric shocks in Europe seems to be manageable. This may be demonstrated by a simple calculation. If the (positive and negative) asymmetric shocks are on average equal to 1%, the negative shocks are on average 0.5% of GDP. With an efficient mechanism, stabilisation of these shocks by a given percentage, say 25%, would cost 0.125% of annual GDP. Even if the stabilisation mechanism is only 50% efficient,[19] the cost would be 0.25% of GDP.

4. A Community stabilisation mechanism

The discussion in section 2 demonstrates, in our view, that the federal experience is of limited value for EMU since the factors having the largest impact on stabilisation in such countries (personal taxes and contributions,

Table 7

Absolute and asymmetric shocks in the Community, the United States and Canada

% GSP/GDP

	B	DK	D	GR	E	F	IRL	I	NL	P	UK	EC	USA	USA[b]	CAN[b]
Absolute shocks[a]															
GDP	2.2	2.5	2.2	-	2.7	1.8	2.2	2.3	2.2	3.4	2.1	2.4	2.3	2.4	2.1
Supply	1.5	1.7	1.7	3.0	2.2	1.2	2.1	2.2	1.7	2.9	2.6	2.1	1.5	-	-
Demand	1.6	2.1	1.4	1.6	1.5	1.2	3.4	2.0	1.5	2.8	1.7	1.9	2.1	-	-
Asymmetric shocks[c]															
GDP	0.9	1.8	0.9	1.1	0.9	0.8	1.9	0.5	1.1	1.6	1.5	1.0	-	0.3	0.6

[a]*Source:* Bayoumi and Eichengreen (1991), except for the last two columns. Calculated as standard deviation of logarithmic growth rates. EC and USA are arithmetical averages of GDP for EC countries and Gross State product (GSP) for 8 US census regions. EC data for 1962-88, US data for 1965-86.

[b]*Source:* Bayoumi and Masson (1991). Standard deviation of first differences of logarithms of real per capita personal income (relative to average for last row). US data are for 1964-86, Canadian data for 1966-88.

[c]*Source, except for the last two columns:* calculated for 1981-90 using data from Commission of the EC as the mean absolute value of yearly differences of national GDP growth rates with the weighted growth rate of other EC member states. The value for the EC is the weighted average of that of the member states.

unemployment benefit) are not likely to be transferred to the Community level in the immediate future or the medium term. Stabilisation at the federal level, if required, would therefore have to be performed through a specific stabilisation mechanism.

The major choice to be made would be between an automatic stabilisation mechanism which would operate for asymmetric shocks of all sizes (here called *full stabilisation mechanism*), or one which would only be activated, either automatically or in a discretionary fashion, in the event of asymmetric shocks beyond a certain threshold of severity (here called *limited stabilisation mechanism*), and which would therefore serve as an insurance mechanism. Without going into this debate,[20] this section presents concrete proposals for the two types of mechanism, and some speculation on how they would have worked had they been available over the past decade.

A full stabilisation mechanism

The important role in many countries of unemployment benefit in the stabilisation process has led to a variety of European unemployment benefit schemes being proposed for EMU.[21] Nevertheless, the example of the United States, where the unemployment benefit system is mainly organised at state level, shows that existing federations can function with only a moderate stabilisation capacity at central level.[22] This could indicate that in EMU too there would be no specific need for a strong Community full stabilisation mechanism. Nevertheless, the example of a system of transfers based on unemployment rates will be used here to demonstrate how a system of moderate stabilisation capacity could work.

The proposed system, although based on unemployment rates, is not one of interpersonal transfers in the form of unemployment benefit. Instead, it is assumed to consist of payments to member states' governments, which then decide how to spend these funds. The way in which governments make use of these transfers is of paramount importance, but will not be further pursued here.[23] Let it suffice to say that the impact of these transfers on the degree of stabilisation obviously depends on the way the funds are used. A second question which will not be addressed is the way in which such a full stabilisation scheme would have to be financed. This could happen in several ways: in a countercyclical fashion through offsetting payments by member states experiencing higher-than-average economic activity, through the general Community budget (in which case adequate provision for the funds needed would have to be foreseen), or out of a separate stabilisation fund which would have to be constituted for this purpose.

The proposed system is quite simple and would work as follows. For each member state, national unemployment rates are measured at regular intervals on a harmonised basis. In the numerical example below, both monthly and yearly unemployment rates based on Eurostat surveys are used, but for the explanation of the system it is assumed that monthly data are available.[24] On the basis of the national unemployment rates of member state i in month t, $U_i(t)$, the weighted Community average excluding the member state itself, $U_{iEC}(t)$, is calculated for the same month. In a second step, the change in the unemployment rates with respect to 12 months earlier is calculated:

$$(8) \quad dU_i(t) \quad = \quad U_i(t) - U_i(t-12)$$
$$ dU_{iEC}(t) \quad = \quad U_{iEC}(t) - U_{iEC}(t-12)$$

In this way, seasonal variations are eliminated and a measure of a shock is obtained. The concept of stabilisation requires that for a member state to be a recipient, the shock which it suffers should be asymmetric and the unemployment change within it positive. Therefore, the member state would receive a transfer if the 12-month change in its unemployment rate was positive and greater than the average of its Community partners.[25]

$$(9) \quad dU_i(t) \quad > \quad 0$$
$$and \quad dU_i(t) \quad > \quad dU_{iEC}(t)$$

In order to control the size of the payments in terms of GDP, each percentage-point difference with respect to the change in the average of its Community partners implies a monthly payment $T_i(t)$ equal to a given percentage α of one-twelfth of last year's GDP of the member state concerned, say Y_i. In the example presented below, the value for α has been fixed at 1%. Furthermore, in order to put an upper ceiling on the system, relative unemployment changes above 2 percentage points are no longer compensated for. In the example, the maximum monthly payment to a member state is therefore equal to 2% of one-twelfth of its annual GDP. Altogether, this leads to the following rules for the monthly transfers:

$$(10) \quad T_i(t) = 0 \qquad \text{if } dU_i(t) - dU_{iEC}(t) \leq 0$$

$$\text{or } dU_i(t) \leq 0$$

$$\alpha \cdot [dU_i(t) - dU_{iEC}(t)] \cdot Y_i \text{ if } 0 < dU_i(t) - dU_{iEC}(t) \leq 2$$

$$\alpha \cdot 2 \cdot Y_i \qquad \text{if } dU_i(t) - dU_{iEC}(t) > 2$$

It should be stressed that the proposed system is only meant to serve as an example, and contains a number of arbitrary elements which would have to be the subject of political negotiations.

The first important choice concerns the use of the unemployment rate as the indicator of asymmetric shocks. In its survey form, the unemployment indicator has the advantage that it is available within a few months and is reasonably harmonised. An alleged disadvantage of using unemployment is, however, that it is a lagging indicator of economic shocks due to phenomena such as labour hoarding, so that the transfers could have a procyclical impact.[26] Since this disadvantage is a characteristic of many stabilisation schemes, and since discretionary fiscal fine-tuning in general is no longer considered by economists to be a feasible policy instrument, this counter-argument does not seem to be specific to this particular stabilisation instrument. This is not to say, of course, that instruments could not be devised which would a priori behave less procyclically.

A very crude idea of the link between changes in the unemployment rate and the occurrence of economic shocks may be obtained by regressing relative unemployment increases on relative GDP increases. A cross-section estimation for all twelve Community countries using annual time-series data for the period 1981-1990 gives the following result (with $y_{iEC}(t)$ the annual growth rate of GDP for the Community partners of member state i and standard errors in brackets):

$$(11) \quad dU_i(t)\text{-}dU_{iEC}(t) = \qquad -0.038 \quad - \quad 0.179 \ [y_i(t)\text{-}y_{iEC}(t)]$$
$$\qquad\qquad\qquad\qquad\qquad\quad (0.076) \qquad (0.050)$$

As can be expected due to the use of deviations from the Community average, the constant of this equation is not significantly far from zero. The coefficient which translates relative GDP shocks into relative unemployment shocks is, however, highly significant. According to this estimation, a relative decrease in the GDP growth rate of 1% will lead to a relative increase in the unemployment rate of 0.18%.

A second feature of the proposed system is that the payment is linked to the size of GDP. This has the advantages of simplicity and of putting a clear limit on the size of the system. On the other hand, there is a less direct link with the number of unemployed persons. But since the system is not an unemployment benefit scheme, this is not a serious drawback. Moreover, since the payment is equal to the product of the "excess" unemployment rate and GDP, this is equivalent to a payment per "excess" person unemployed equal to GDP per person of the labour force, which can be interpreted as a measure of productivity.[27]

A related question is whether it would be "profitable" for a government in this system to increase unemployment or for an individual to become unemployed, thereby creating a problem of moral hazard. First, the system is not an unemployment scheme and therefore does not create personal incentives. Second and more important, a one-time increase in unemployment which does not disappear will only lead to a transfer once, since the payment is based on changes in the unemployment rate. The long-term costs may therefore greatly outweigh the short-term "benefits". Thirdly, there is uncertainty since a costly national unemployment increase does not lead to a payment if there is a similar increase in the member state's Community partners.

As set out above, the size of the transfer has been set in the examples in such a way that the payment can reach a maximum of 2% of the GDP of the member state concerned. By way of comparison, it may be noted that the maximum observed transfer under the German *Finanzausgleich* over the period 1980-90 was approximately equal to 2% of Länder GDP in the case of Bremen, but hardly exceeded 1% of Länder GDP in all other cases. It should be noted, however, that the *Finanzausgleich* may only partly be considered a stabilisation mechanism.

A crude estimation of the degree of stabilisation implied by the proposed system can be made drawing on equation (11). Let us suppose that a member state's GDP grows one percentage point less than in the rest of the Community. According to equation (11), the unemployment rate in the member state will on average increase by 0.179 percentage points more than in the rest of the Community. Under the proposed system, the member state concerned would receive on an annual basis a payment equal to 17.9% of one percent of its GDP. In the example, where the annual payment is equal to 1% of GDP, about 18% of the shock to GDP will therefore be stabilised.

It is clear from this example and the results presented in section 2 that, depending on the size of the payment and the method used, a degree of stabilisation comparable to that in the United States could be obtained. Assuming a payment equal to 1% of GDP on an annual basis, the degree of stabilisation of the proposed system can therefore be assumed to be about 18%. It should however be noted that these calculations are only valid for relative unemployment shocks below 2 percentage points. Since the transfer payment does not increase beyond that upper ceiling (see Graph 2), the degree of stabilisation will in both cases slowly decrease with the size of the excess above the upper ceiling, as illustrated in Graph 3.

Tables 8 and 9 provide illustrations of how the proposed system would have performed in the past using a payment on an annual basis of 1% of GDP (i.e. $\alpha = 0.01$). For the monthly data, this covers the period from January 1984, the first month for which observations are available, until October 1991, the last observation. Unfortunately, monthly data for Greece are not available,[28] which is why the same exercise is also presented on the basis of yearly data, covering the longer time-span of 1981-1990.

Table 8 indicates for each member state excluding Greece the months for which transfers would have been paid out under the proposed system.[29] Since the system is symmetric (except for the fact that the Community unemployment rate is a weighted rather than an arithmetical average), it appears that transfers would have been paid in about a quarter of the cases (in 289 cases, i.e. 28% of the number of months multiplied by the number of member states). The annual payments show considerable variation, averaging around 11.2bn (1990) Ecu or 0.23% of 1990 Community GDP. This compares to an estimated annual transfer of 0.13% of (West) German GDP under the *Finanzausgleich* for stabilisation purposes over the same period. The distribution of the average annual transfers over the member states is uneven, reflecting divergent unemployment performances during the 1980s. There is no apparent link between relative prosperity and the size of the transfer payments, illustrating the fundamental difference between stabilisation and redistribution.

By way of illustration and in order to obtain an estimate for Greece, Table 9 presents the same exercise as in Table 8, but using annual average unemployment rates as a basis for the calculations. Although the period covered begins and ends earlier than that of the monthly data, the results in terms of annual average are hardly different from those in Table 8. It should of course be noted that the time-lag incurred for the transfer payments would strongly increase if the system operated on the basis of annual rather than monthly data. On the other hand, the German *Finanzausgleich* also works on an annual basis. From the results of Table 9, it appears that over the period concerned Greece would have obtained annual transfer payments equal to 0.284% of its GDP, which is in line with payments to some of the other member states. The maximum annual payment under both examples would have been about 17-21bn (1990) Ecu - considerably below the theoretical maximum, which lies around 1% of Community GDP or 48bn (1990) Ecu and would be reached if member states representing approximately 50% of Community GDP were each to receive the maximum payment.

A limited stabilisation mechanism

Given the high degree of national fiscal autonomy and the budgetary implications of a full stabilisation mechanism, an alternative would be to devise a limited stabilisation mechanism for the Community, functioning as an insurance policy in the sense that payments would be made only if the damage (i.e. an asymmetric shock) were to exceed a given minimum threshold. A simple proposal would be to add a threshold to the full stabilisation mechanism, in such a way that only relative unemployment shocks within a given interval would qualify for payment. Although this system will be presented here as working automatically, it could in practice be made operational in a discrete fashion. A shock above the threshold would be a necessary, but not a sufficient condition to qualify for payment. For instance, governments could be required to show that the origin of the shock was beyond the control of the member state.

A possible minimum threshold for such a limited stabilisation mechanism could be an unemployment change relative to the average of Community partners equal to 0.3%. Given the empirical distribution of unemployment shocks, this would eliminate a considerable number of cases eligible under the full stabilisation mechanism. In terms of equation (10), this would translate into the following rules for the transfer payments (assuming them to be automatic):

(12) $T_i(t) = 0$ if $dU_i(t) - dU_{iEC}(t) \leq 0.3$

                                    or $dU_i(t) \leq 0$

        $\alpha \cdot [dU_i(t) - dU_{iEC}(t) - 0.3] \cdot Y_i$ if $dU_i(t) - dU_{iEC}(t) > 0.3$

                        and $\alpha \cdot [dU_i(t) - dU_{iEC}(t) - 0.3] \leq 0.015$

$$0.015 \cdot Y_i \quad \text{if} \quad \alpha.[dU_i(t)-dU_{iEC}(t)-0.3] > 0.015$$

The system of equation (12) implies that the payment is initiated if the relative unemployment change is above 0.3 percentage points. As long as this change is such that the payment on an annual basis is below 1.5% of GDP, the monthly payment is proportional to the size of the excess shock, amounting to α percent of one-twelfth of the member state's annual GDP per percentage point relative change in excess of the threshold of 0.3 percentage points. For the simulations, the parameter α has been set at 2% instead of 1% for the full stabilisation mechanism. The maximum amount received by a member state in one month is therefore equal to 1.5% of one-twelfth of its annual GDP. The limited stabilisation mechanism is therefore twice as generous at the margin as the full system, in order to compensate for the fact that the initial average generosity per percentage point of relative unemployment increase is much smaller than under the full system. The maximum payment of 1.5% of GDP has been chosen so that the total cost would empirically be equal to that of the full system.

The degree of stabilisation implied by this limited stabilisation scheme depends on the distribution of the unemployment shocks. Again, a crude estimation can be made. The degree of stabilisation is less linear than for the full stabilisation scheme, however. For GDP shocks leading to relative unemployment changes below 0.3 percentage points, the degree of stabilisation is zero; for GDP shocks leading to relative unemployment changes between 0.3 and 1.05 percentage points, the degree of stabilisation increases from zero to reach a maximum when the relative unemployment change is equal to 1.05 percentage points (corresponding to a maximum payment of 1.5% of GDP); and for GDP shocks leading to relative unemployment changes above 1.05 percentage points, the degree of stabilisation decreases from its maximum.

The maximum degree of stabilisation thus reached may be calculated as follows. Let us suppose that a member state's GDP grows 1.05/0.179 = 5.87 percentage points below average Community GDP growth. Then the unemployment change relative to the Community average would be 1.05 percentage points. According to the limited stabilisation scheme of equation (12), the member state concerned would receive a transfer payment of 1.05% of its GDP. Therefore, the maximum degree of stabilisation of the limited scheme calculated in this way is equal to 1.5/5.87 = 25.6%.

The differences in the transfer payment and the degree of stabilisation (calculated assuming equation (11) to be valid in all member states) between the full and the limited stabilisation schemes are illustrated in Graphs 2 and 3.

The results of the automatic application of the limited stabilisation over the past decade are given in Table 10, using monthly data, and in Table 11 using annual data.

Table 10 indicates the months of each year in which a payment would have been made. The number of cases is reduced from 289 in Table 8 to 210 in Table 10, implying a historical application of the scheme in some 20% of all cases. On the basis of yearly data (Table 11), the limited scheme would have been applied in 31 out of 120 cases, i.e. some 25% of the cases. Depending on whether the monthly or the annual scheme had been used, the average annual costs would, by construction, have amounted to approximately those of the full scheme, i.e. 10.2-10.7bn (1990) Ecu per year on average or 0.210-0.221% of Community GDP, although the amounts have fluctuated, sometimes exceeding 18bn (1990) Ecu under both schemes. It is interesting to note that this is well below the maximum amount which theoretically could have been paid under the scheme, i.e. in the case where member states representing 50% of the labour force would each receive the maximum payment of 1.5% of their GDP, implying a total of approximately 0.75% of Community GDP or some 36bn (1990) Ecu.

5. Conclusion

The analysis presented in section 2 of this paper has provided a framework for distinguishing between *stabilisation* and *redistribution* in the context of tax and transfer payments between different levels of government, which is particularly important for federal states. If *regression* methods are used, redistribution should be measured through a specification in levels, whereas the measurement of stabilisation requires first differences. The seminal work of Sachs and Sala-i-Martin, intended to measure stabilisation, used a specification in levels but with a time trend, causing problems of dynamic mis-specification. Most later studies used either levels or first differences so that a clear distinction could be made between stabilisation and redistribution. Most of these studies (von Hagen, Goodhart and Smith) used the *elasticities approach*, estimating the contribution to stabilisation for individual tax and transfer categories. A more comprehensive approach is the *income approach* of Bayoumi and Masson, which is based instead on the total disposable income of a region after tax and transfer payments with the central government. An alternative to the use of regression methods is that of *model simulation*, which is the approach presented in this paper.

Our simulation analysis, despite its theoretical and empirical shortcomings, has proved to be a useful tool in shedding light on the debate concerning the degree of stabilisation provided by central governments in federal states, or for that matter in unitary ones. Focusing on the United States, it has been shown, in particular, that the elasticities approach gives an incomplete and therefore unnecessarily pessimistic picture of the degree of stabilisation. Our simulation approach suggests that the degree of stabilisation which we found for the United States (17%) is significantly higher than that of von Hagen or Goodhart and Smith, but more than half that found by Sachs and Sala-i-Martin. Since the latter's results are about halfway between stabilisation and redistribution, however, they have to be interpreted with care. On the other hand, our result for the United States is considerably lower than the 27-28% obtained by Bayoumi and Masson with their comprehensive income approach. Since both studies provide a breakdown of the total stabilisation effect obtained, the origin of the differences can be traced back. It seems to lie in the treatment of social security contributions, personal transfers and grants, and it requires further investigation.

In addition, our analysis has demonstrated that the main reason behind the relatively low degree of stabilisation in the United States compared to a federal state such as Germany or a unitary state such as France lies in the fact that there is hardly any federal unemployment insurance in the United States.

From our analysis, several conclusions can be drawn as regards stabilisation in the Community. First, the example of the United States shows that a monetary union can be viable with a degree of regional stabilisation through the central budget which is smaller than is sometimes believed to be necessary. Secondly, for an element of the central budget to play a significant stabilising role, it should primarily be income-elastic.[30] Thirdly, the major contribution to stabilisation in the countries which we examined comes from budget categories which are unlikely to be transferred to the Community level in the foreseeable future. Fourthly, the German *Finanzausgleich* shows that stabilisation need not arise from elements of the central budget and can be considerable on the basis of interregional transfers.

The need for stabilisation in EMU depends on the size of the asymmetric shocks and the availability of other adjustment instruments. Section 3 concluded that non-budgetary adjustment instruments could at least partly compensate for the loss of the exchange-rate instrument in EMU. As regards the size of the shocks, data for the Community confirm findings for the United States and Canada that asymmetric shocks to GDP growth are several times lower than absolute shocks. Nevertheless, asymmetric shocks to GDP growth in Europe seem to be higher than in Canada and especially the United States (keeping in mind that actual supply and demand shocks will tend to be somewhat smaller). Still, the size of the asymmetric shocks in Europe seems to be manageable. A simple calculation shows that a degree of stabilisation comparable to that in the United States could be obtained in the Community at a cost which would on average not exceed 0.25% of Community GDP.

The historical simulation exercise reported in section 4, with a concrete example of such a stabilisation mechanism for the Community, leads to some interesting conclusions. The first is that, based on an estimated annual cost equal to some 0.2% of Community GDP, a full stabilisation mechanism could be set up which would, on average, provide approximately the same degree of stabilisation as in the United States. The main reason why such a high degree of stabilisation can be achieved at relatively little cost is that, unlike in existing federations where stabilisation properties are usually a by-product of the tax and transfer system, the mechanism proposed here is explicitly designed for stabilisation purposes. Consequently, its efficiency in terms of the degree of stabilisation obtained in relation to the costs of the system is much higher.

A second conclusion, however, is that the full stabilisation scheme, although simple and operational, could not be free from the standard problems involved in stabilisation: identification of the shock, implementation lag and possibly a procyclical bias. Nevertheless, it was demonstrated on the basis of a cross-section/time series estimation for all Community member states that there is a clear link between the evolution of the unemployment indicator used for the system and relative shocks to GDP growth in the same year, without clear signs of a procyclical bias. Moreover, due to the fact that the scheme is based on changes in unemployment rates but consists of intergovernmental transfers, the problem of moral hazard with respect to individuals usually associated with Community unemployment benefit schemes is avoided.[31]

The third conclusion is that if, for any reason, the full stabilisation mechanism is not deemed to be desirable, a limited stabilisation scheme can be devised at equal or lower cost which, as a form of insurance, can provide a reasonable degree of stabilisation in the event of an individual shock above a certain threshold. The overall degree of stabilisation of both the full and the limited mechanisms largely depends on three parameters which would ultimately be politically determined: the minimum threshold for relative unemployment change which qualifies for payment, the size of the payment and the maximum annual payment per member state. Table 12 gives some examples of different scenarios, with their historical cost and estimated stabilisation properties.[32]

NOTES

1. This chapter draws on Pisani-Ferry, Italianer and Lescure (1992) and Italianer and Vanheukelen (1992). The opinions expressed are those of the authors and should not be attributed to the institutions to which they belong.

2. This is analogous to John Rawls' concept of the social contract underwritten by individuals in society.

3. Eichengreen (1990) estimates that a one-dollar decline in the income of a member state of the Community reduces its contribution to the Community budget by less than one cent (i.e. 1%). Gordon (1991) estimates that for a poor (a so-called "Objective 1") region, this would lead to a little over two cents (2%) in additional transfers. The maximum degree of stabilisation for a member state consisting solely of poor regions (such as Ireland, Portugal or Greece) is therefore about 3%. For the Community on average, this figure would be considerably lower.

4. The condition would be that $dYR/dY = dYS/dY$ at each point in time. This would hold, for example, with a redistribution scheme, so that $YD = Ya$, or a stabilisation scheme, so that $dYD/YD = a*dY/Y$.

5. In empirical work, either regional GDP or personal income is used.

6. For the sake of simplicity, no distinction is made between real and nominal terms in equation (1).

7. One could also measure the degree of stabilisation considering the relative variation of YD with respect to the relative variation of Y, i.e. $S'i = 1-(dYDi/YDi)/(dYi/Yi)$. Since YDi/Yi is generally smaller than one, this would imply $Si>S'i$.

8. Other possible explanations are the fact that he uses Gross State Product rather than personal income as regressor, that he uses individual state data rather than census regions and that the sample period is shorter.

9. There is little information available on the degree of goods integration inside federations. The intra-Canadian share in exports of goods from Canadian provinces amounted in 1984 on average to 18% of GDP, while the extra-Canadian share amounted to 22.5% (calculated from Ministère des Approvisionnements et Services du Canada, 1991). This compares to 13.5% and 11.3% for the intra- and extra-EC trade respectively of the member states of the Community in 1984 (see Commission of the EC, 1991).

10. We are indebted to J. von Hagen for discussions on this issue.

11. It is important to remember that this does not apply to employees' social security contributions.

12. More precise information could be derived from tax-simulation models.

13. It has been assumed, for the sake of simplicity, that the social transfers were "open-ended", i.e. that their amount had no limit. One has to admit, however, that such a limit may exist (e.g. in the UK, where they are subject to a ceiling.)

14. As is clear in the derivation of equation (3) from the accounting identity (1), any accounting identity giving regional disposable income can be used as a starting point.

15. As it is assumed that the elasticity of personal income tax with respect to household income is 1.2, the results imply a tax/output elasticity of 0.5. Von Hagen's estimates and those implied by Goodhart and Smith are twice as high, which probably implies a higher tax/income elasticity.

16. See above, section 2.2.

17. This assumes that member states have structural budget deficits sufficiently below the Maastricht criteria to allow them to let the automatic stabilisers work.

18. In the early years of the EMS, there were frequent parity realignments which compensated for the accumulated price differential with Germany to the tune of more than 100%. After 1983, this compensation decreased on average to 50%. See Emerson et al. (1992, Annexe E).

19. The efficiency of the stabilisation mechanism depends on several factors, such as the indicator on which stabilisation payments are based, the recognition lag, and the implementation lag. See also Goodhart and Smith (1992).

20. For an extensive discussion and a view in favour of automatic stabilisation, see Goodhart and Smith (1992). For a view in favour of a discretionary mechanism in the case of severe shocks, see Majocchi and Rey (1992).

21. See van der Ploeg (1991) and Wyplosz (1991).

22. See von Hagen (1991).

23. For an extensive discussion, see Goodhart and Smith (1992).

24. When the data were collected from Eurostat in early January 1992, unemployment data up to October 1991 were available (excluding Greece for which no monthly data are available), implying a recognition lag of 2-3 months.

25. We have chosen member states as the geographical units in this mechanism because of the fact that the stabilisation scheme in principle compensates for the absence of the exchange-rate instrument, which is national in nature.

26. Estimating Okun-type equations with current or lagged GDP growth rates did not produce significant differences, indicating that the procyclical bias may not be a problem.

27. This can be seen as follows. Let the "excess" unemployment rate be $ui(t)/Li(t) = dUi(t) - dUiEC(t)$, with $ui(t)$ the "excess" number of unemployed persons and $Li(t)$ the labour force. Then the payment is equal to a percentage of $ui(t)/Li(t)*Yi$. In other words, the payment per "excess" person unemployed is linked to $Yi/Li(t)$, i.e. GDP per person in the labour force, which is a measure of productivity.

28. For the purpose of the proposed system, such data would of course have to be collected.

29. Tables 8 - 12 are placed after the references at the end of this chapter.

30. This conclusion depends on the stabilisation measure which is used. In the example of footnote 7, the size of the budget category alone is sufficient to have an impact on the degree of stabilisation.

31. See also Goodhart and Smith (1992).

32. The degree of stabilisation of the full mechanism is calculated, as in the text, by taking the product of the size of the payment and the semi-elasticity from equation (11), the latter assumed to be equal to 0.18. For a given size of payment, the degree of stabilisation of the limited mechanism is calculated by multiplying the degree of stabilisation of the full mechanism by the cost of the limited scheme relative to the full scheme, taking the average of annual and monthly data. Thus, for a payment of 1% of GDP, the degree of stabilisation of the limited scheme is calculated as $0.18 \cdot [6.6+7.2]/[11.0+11.2]=11\%$.

References

Artis, M. and T. Bayoumi (1989),"Saving, investment, financial integration and the balance of payments", *IMF Working Paper* 89/102, Washington, 14 December.

Atkeson, A. and T. Bayoumi (1991), "Do private capital markets insure regional risk? Evidence from the United States and Europe", mimeo, October.

Bayoumi, T. and P. R. Masson (1991), "Fiscal flows in the United States and Canada: lessons for monetary union in Europe", mimeo, November.

Blanchard, O. and L. Katz (1991), "Regional evolutions", mimeo, November.

Centraal Planbureau (1992), *Centraal Economisch Plan 1992*, Sdu Uitgeverij, The Hague.

Commission of the EC (1991), *Annual Economic Report 1991-92, European Economy* 50, December.

Eichengreen, B. (1990), "One money for Europe? Lessons from the US currency union", *Economic Policy* 10, April, pp. 119-86.

Emerson, M., D. Gros, A. Italianer, J. Pisani-Ferry and H. Reichenbach (1992), *One Market, One Money: An Evaluation of the Potential Benefits and Costs of Forming an Economic and Monetary Union*, Oxford: Oxford University Press.

Equipe Mimosa (1989). "*Mimosa*: une modélisation de l'économie mondiale", *Observations et Diagnostics Economiques*.

Feldstein, M. (1992), "The case against EMU", *The Economist*, 13 June.

Frenkel, J. and M. Goldstein (1991), "Monetary policy in an emerging European Economic and Monetary Union", *IMF Staff Papers* 38 (2), pp. 356-373, June.

Goodhart, C.A.E. and S. Smith (1992), "Stabilisation" in *The Economics of Community Public Finance, European Economy* special edition.

Gordon, J. (1991), "Structural trends and the 1992 program in the European Community", *IMF Working Paper* 91/65, Washington, June.

Horn, H. and T. Persson (1988), "Exchange-rate policy, wage-formation and credibility", *European Economic Review* 32, pp. 1621-1636.

Italianer, A. and M. Vanheukelen (1992), "Proposals for Community stabilisation mechanisms: some historical applications" in *The Economics of Community Public Finance, op. cit.*

Krugman, P., "Integration, specialisation, and regional growth: notes on 1992, EMU, and stabilisation", paper presented at the Banco de Portugal/CEPR conference on "The transition to economic and monetary union in Europe", Estoril, 16-18 January 1992.

Majocchi, A. and M. Rey (1992), "A special financial support scheme in EMU: need and nature" in *The Economics of Community Public Finance, op. cit.*

Ministère des Approvisionnements et Services du Canada (1991), *Le Fédéralisme Canadien et l'Union Economique: Partenariat pour la Prospérité.*

Pisani-Ferry, J., A. Italianer and R. Lescure (1992), "Stabilisation properties of budgetary systems: a simulation analysis" in *The Economics of Community Public Finance, op. cit.*

Sachs, J. and X. Sala-i-Martin (1989), "Federal fiscal policy and optimum currency areas", unpublished manuscript, Cambridge, Mass.: Harvard University.

Sachs J. and J. Sala-i-Martin (1991), "Federal fiscal policy and optimum currency areas: evidence for Europe from the United States", *NBER Working Paper* 3855.

Van der Ploeg, F. (1991), "Macroeconomic policy co-ordination issues during the various stages of economic and monetary integration in Europe" in *The Economics of EMU, European Economy* special edition 1, pp. 136-164.

von Hagen, J. (1991), "Fiscal arrangements in a Monetary Union: evidence from the US" *Indiana University Discussion Paper* 58, March.

Whitley, J. D. (1991), "Comparative simulation analysis of the European multi-country models", paper presented to *SPES* Seminar, Paris, 27-28 June.

Wyplosz, C. (1991), "Monetary union and fiscal policy discipline" in *The Economics of EMU, op. cit.*, pp. 165-184.

Table 8

Full stabilisation scheme using monthly data
(months of activation and amount of payments)

	B	DK	D	GR	E	F	IRL	I	L	NL	P	UK	EC-11	Total payments (bn 1990 Ecu)	(% GDP)
1984	-	-	-	:	1-12	1-12	1-12	-	-	1-5	1-5	-	46	17.344	0.358
1985	6-12	-	-	:	1-10	1-11	1-12	7-12	-	-	4+11	2-12	51	11.851	0.245
1986	-	-	-	:	-	4-12	1-5	1-12	-	-	1+2	1-4+6-12	46	13.054	0.269
1987	1-3	4-12	11+12	:	-	1-9	-	1-3	4+6-12	-	-	-	34	7.576	0.156
1988	-	1-12	1+5	:	-	-	-	3-12	-	-	-	-	24	13.199	0.272
1989	-	1-12	-	:	-	-	11+12	1-7	1+2	-	-	-	19	8.043	0.166
1990	-	1-12	-	:	-	-	1-10	-	1	-	-	9-12	20	2.912	0.060
1991	1-6	1-10	-	:	-	1-10	-	1-2	1	-	-	1-10	49	14.041	0.290
Total months	16	55	4	:	22	51	41	40	11	5	8	36	289		
1.1984 - 10.1991															
Total: bn 1990 Ecu	0.349	4.988	3.282	:	11.625	19.836	1.135	29.431	0.033	0.369	0.115	16.859		88.020	1.817
% GDP	0.225	4.835	0.261	:	3.004	2.116	3.393	3.427	0.476	0.168	0.245	2.152			
Annual average	0.045	0.637	0.419	:	1.484	2.532	0.145	3.757	0.004	0.047	0.015	2.152		11.237	0.232
% GDP	0.029	0.617	0.033	:	0.383	0.270	0.433	0.438	0.061	0.021	0.031	0.275			

Table 9

Full stabilisation scheme using annual data

(bn 1990 Ecu and % of GDP)

	B	DK	D	GR	E	F	IRL	I	L	NL	P	UK	EC-11 (bn 1990 Ecu)	EC-11 (% GDP)
1981	0.490	-	-	-	4.784	-	0.389	-	-	-	-	15.653	21.316	0.440
1982	0.503	0.279	7.435	0.304	2.476	-	0.120	-	-	2.990	-	1.096	15.203	0.314
1983	0.209	-	4.783	0.581	1.964	-	0.614	-	-	3.565	-	-	11.715	0.242
1984	-	-	-	-	7.741	8.954	0.354	-	-	-	0.141	-	17.190	0.355
1985	-	-	-	-	4.054	3.098	0.389	1.071	-	-	-	1.630	10.241	0.211
1986	-	0.364	-	0.197	-	1.557	-	9.650	-	-	-	1.335	12.542	0.259
1987	-	1.412	-	0.427	-	5.601	-	-	0.024	-	-	-	6.186	0.128
1988	-	2.063	-	-	-	-	-	10.813	-	-	-	-	12.653	0.261
1989	-	0.948	-	-	-	-	-	-	-	-	-	-	2.063	0.043
1990	-	-	-	-	-	-	-	-	-	-	-	-	0.948	0.020
1981-90 (cumulative)	1.202	5.067	12.218	1.510	21.018	19.210	1.865	21.534	0.024	6.555	0.141	19.714	110.059	2.272
% GDP	0.775	4.912	0.971	2.843	5.431	2.049	5.577	2.508	0.355	2.983	0.300	2.516		
1981-90 (average)	0.120	0.507	1.222	0.151	2.102	1.921	0.187	2.153	0.002	0.656	0.014	1.971	11.006	0.227
% GDP	0.078	0.491	0.097	0.284	0.543	0.205	0.558	0.251	0.035	0.298	0.030	0.252		

Source: calculated using Eurostat survey data on average annual unemployment rates and DG-II data on 1990 GDP

Table 10

Limited stabilisation scheme using monthly data
(months of activation and amount of payments)

	B	DK	D	GR	E	F	IRL	I	L	NL	P	UK	EC-11	Total payments (bn 1990 Ecu)	(% GDP)
1984	-	-	-	:	1-12	1-12	1-12	-	-	1-3	1	-	40	18.576	0.384
1985	-	-	-	:	1-9	1-4	1-12	9-12	-	-	-	-	30	8.728	0.180
1986	11	-	-	:	-	10-12	1	1-12	-	-	-	5	18	12.030	0.248
1987	-	4-12	11-12	:	-	1-9	-	1-3	4+6-12	-	-	9	31	7.741	0.160
1988	-	1-12	1+5	:	-	-	-	3-12	-	-	-	-	24	13.990	0.289
1989	-	1-12	-	:	-	-	-	1-7	-	-	-	-	19	9.061	0.187
1990	-	1-12	-	:	-	-	11+12	-	1+2	-	-	9-12	20	3.466	0.072
1991	-	1-4	-	:	-	-	1-12	-	-	-	-	1-12	28	10.268	0.212
Total months	1	49	4	:	21	28	39	36	10	3	1	18	210		
1.1984-10.1991															
Total: bn 1990 Ecu	0.010	4.569	4.046	:	9.698	18.914	1.298	32.823	0.031	0.275	0.059	12.138		83.860	
% GDP	0.007	4.429	0.321	:	2.506	2.018	3.881	3.822	0.448	0.125	0.125	1.549			1.731
Annual average	0.001	0.583	0.517	:	1.238	2.415	0.166	4.190	0.004	0.035	0.008	1.549		10.706	
% GDP	0.001	0.565	0.041	:	0.320	0.258	0.495	0.488	0.057	0.016	0.016	0.198			0.221

Table 11

Limited stabilisation scheme using annual data

(bn 1990 Ecu and % of GDP)

	B	DK	D	GR	E	F	IRL	I	L	NL	P	UK	EC-12 (bn 1990 Ecu)	(% GDP)
1981	0.050	-	-	-	5.805	-	0.592	-	-	-	-	11.752	18.109	0.374
1982	0.076	-	7.318	0.290	2.631	-	0.039	-	-	3.296	-	-	13.649	0.282
1983	-	-	2.012	0.797	1.606	-	0.502	-	-	3.296	-	-	8.212	0.170
1984	-	-	-	-	5.805	12.284	0.502	-	-	-	-	-	18.591	0.384
1985	-	-	-	-	5.785	0.570	0.502	-	-	-	-	-	6.857	0.142
1986	-	-	-	-	-	-	-	12.881	-	-	-	-	12.881	0.266
1987	-	0.110	-	0.075	-	5.577	-	-	0.007	-	-	-	5.769	0.119
1988	-	1.547	-	0.536	-	-	-	12.881	-	-	-	-	14.964	0.309
1989	-	1.547	-	-	-	-	-	-	-	-	-	-	1.547	0.032
1990	-	1.277	-	-	-	-	-	-	-	-	-	-	1.277	0.026
1981-90 (cumulative)	0.126	4.482	9.330	1.698	21.632	18.431	2.045	25.762	0.007	6.592	-	11.752	101.858	2.103
% GDP	0.081	4.345	0.741	3.197	5.589	1.966	6.116	3.000	0.109	3.000	-	1.500		
1981-90 (average)	0.013	0.448	0.933	0.170	2.163	1.843	0.205	2.576	0.001	0.659	-	1.175	10.186	
% GDP	0.008	0.434	0.074	0.320	0.559	0.197	0.612	0.300	0.011	0.300	-	0.150		0.210

Source: calculated using Eurostat survey data on average annual unemployment rates and DG-II data on 1990 GDP.

Table 12

Different stabilisation scenarios, 1981-90

	Lower threshold for $dU_j(t)-dU_{iEC}(t)$*	Payment** (% GDP)	Maximum payment (% GDP)	Average annual cost				Number of cases out of total***		Average degree of stabilisation**** (%)
				bn 1990 Ecu		% GDP				
				Annual data	Monthly data	Annual data	Monthly data	Annual data	Monthly data	
Full stabilisation	0	0.5	1	5.5	5.6	0.114	0.116	39	289	9%
	0	1	2	11.0	11.2	0.227	0.232	39	289	18%
	0	2	4	22.0	22.5	0.454	0.464	39	289	36%
Limited stabilisation	0.3	0.5	1.5	3.5	3.7	0.072	0.077	31	210	6%
	0.3	1	1.5	6.6	7.2	0.137	0.149	31	210	11%
	0.3	2	1.5	10.2	10.7	0.210	0.221	31	210	17%

*   In addition, $dU_j(t)>0$ is required.

**   Payment per percentage point relative unemployment increase above threshold, in % GDP.

***   For the annual data, 120 observations are available; for the monthly data, 1034.

****   Assuming a semi-elasticity of 0.18. Average of annual and monthly data.

12 The implications of cohesion policy for the Community's budget

Horst Reichenbach

1. Introduction

In 1980 I wrote an internal working paper for the Commission with the title "The pre-federal integration phase in the MacDougall report: a possible scenario for 1985?" In it I focused on the budgetary expenditure necessary to promote economic efficiency and equity in the process of deepened European integration. I left aside external aid and agricultural expenditure and will do the same in this chapter.

I assumed then that the scale of "market intervention", i.e. expenditure for agricultural guarantee support and for fisheries, would stay constant at 0.55% of Community GDP. Reality turned out quite different. In fact, the further rises in agricultural expenditure were a major ingredient of the budgetary crises of the 1980s. This item alone now represents 0.67% of Community GDP, and even in the financial perspectives of the "Delors-II" package there is still 0.64% of GDP provided for the Common Agricultural Policy. The significance of this increase in CAP spending, compared to its 1980 level of about 0.1% of Community GDP, can be appreciated by relating it to present expenditure for internal policies other than structural operations - a mere 0.06% of GDP in 1992.

In my 1980 paper I developed two projections: one in which structural and other internal expenditure in 1985 would represent 0.5% of GDP, and one in which it would represent 1.0%. 1985 was intended to be seen as a hypothetical rather than a calendar year, reflecting a certain degree of deepened integration. This would include the gradual build-up of the Community's political structures, the completion of the common market, and further steps, falling short of monetary union, towards economic and monetary policy integration.

This scenario is in fact rather similar to stage two of economic and monetary union as set out by the Maastricht Treaty. Today, I am confident that the 0.5-1.0% projections cater broadly not only for the second stage of economic and monetary union but also for the third - in other words, that a single currency is sustainable with quite modest Community expenditure on the promotion of economic efficiency and equity.

2. Guidance from fiscal federalism

I would now like to draw some policy-relevant conclusions from the literature on the subject over the twenty years since Wallace Oates' seminal work.[1] I will do so in the form of five theses.

i) *Theoretical and empirical evidence cautions against a mechanistic view of federal structures and their transposition to the Community*

Theory provides no prefabricated models for the structure of unions in general or of the Community in particular. Moreover, empirical evidence shows that federations function with widely-varying degrees of expenditure- and revenue-centralisation. Much depends on the political process embracing the constitutional foundations of the union, the rules of co-operation between levels of government, the characteristics of the democratic system and the sharing of power between executive and legislative branches of government.

ii) *More emphasis should be placed on the dangers of centralisation than was suggested in the MacDougall Report*

There are two main facets to this. First, the case for public involvement must be carefully scrutinised. Market failures do not by themselves justify state involvement; their costs have to be set against the cost of such involvement in terms of administration and public-sector inefficiency.

Second, a question arises as to which level of government is best suited to performing a given function. In this respect, there are clear advantages to decentralisation. Public goods and services can be better tailored to people's preferences; democratic control is more effective, reducing the risk of excessive bureaucracy; and innovation and efficiency are encouraged through competition between jurisdictions. For any task to be undertaken at Community level, therefore, the burden of proof is on those proposing to centralise, and their proposals should be substantiated by careful analyses of the benefits of centralisation compared to its costs.

iii) *The efficiency grounds for assigning expenditure responsibilities to the Community level rest largely on conventional arguments of economies of scale and spill-over effects*

The allocative and distributional aspects of public policy cannot be entirely separated since it is costly to correct the negative distributional consequences of efficient policies. Nevertheless a distinction must be drawn between "efficiency" and "equity" grounds for assigning expenditure responsibilities to the Community.[2]

iv)   *Interpersonal redistribution policies at Community level will impose excessive uniformity costs for some time to come, as will unconditional general-purpose equalisation grants*

As far as expenditure assignment on equity grounds is concerned, a distinction needs to be made between interpersonal redistribution on the one hand and interregional transfers on the other. The conventional conclusion from fiscal federalism that interpersonal redistribution should be carried out at the highest level of government is based on the assumption of near-perfect labour mobility. As this assumption does not apply to the Community, neither the MacDougall Report nor any subsequent work on the subject has seriously advocated that interpersonal redistribution should primarily be a Community responsibility; on the contrary, recent literature has challenged the traditional view, pointing to the importance of geographical proximity for such redistribution.

However, there have been two interesting suggestions for more limited Community involvement. First, the idea of a Community unemployment fund has been put forward. This originated from the Marjolin Report, was revived in the MacDougall Report and resurfaced in the context of stabilisation policy under economic and monetary union. Politically, this idea has never been taken seriously, and I think rightly so, because the case for centralisation has not been convincingly made. Italianer and Pisani-Ferry, in their chapter in this volume, show that stabilisation can be achieved by other means more in line with the principle of subsidiarity.

The second idea was put forward by Helm and Smith, following the "positive freedom" approach of Sen and Dasgupta: "Each citizen", they argue, "is entitled to a common minimum standard of living, met by a mixture of minimal monetary payments and the provision of a bundle of basic social primary goods such as health, education and housing."[3] Helm and Smith rightly point out that such an approach largely depends on the degree of altruism prevailing among member countries. Only the political process can provide an answer to the question of when (or whether) sufficient altruism will prevail for the Community to acquire responsibilities in this respect.

Regional transfers fall into two broad categories: general-purpose equalising grants and specific-purpose grants. For the former, the same basic rules apply as for minimum standards. Whether the Community will take some responsibility for fiscal equalisation largely depends on the feelings of solidarity between member states and their mutual confidence that funds are being wisely spent. The time is certainly not right now and the early stages of economic and monetary union will add very little. In my view, it is only under full political union that this matter could become the subject of serious negotiation between the member states.

v)   *For the next decade at least, specific-purpose grants will continue to be the main explicit EC instrument for interregional transfers; as such they should flow from richer to poorer regions and serve specific allocative purposes*

Specific-purpose grants serve two purposes at once. On the one hand they give rise to interregional transfers. In existing federations, they represent on average about 2.5% of national GDP and reduce regional income differentials by about 6%. On the other hand, they serve allocative purposes influencing the provision of public services at lower levels of government in a wide spectrum of fields covering welfare, health, education, transport, vocational training, research and regional policy. They are thus complex policy instruments on which an extensive theoretical and empirical literature exists.

My colleague Declan Costello, in a recent unpublished paper, has pointed to the substantial discordance between the theoretical predictions of the intergovernmental grants literature and the results of empirical tests of the effects of grants on recipient outlays, the so-called "fly-paper" effect. Actual changes in expenditure patterns by the recipient authorities are considerably larger than theoretically predicted. In the Community jargon this means that there has been more "additionality" than predicted.

The Community Structural Funds and the Cohesion Fund agreed on at Maastricht fall into this category of specific-purpose grants. Not surprisingly, therefore, their design and the evaluation of their effect has been a central and continuous activity over the last fifteen years. They were a key aspect of the "Delors-I" package and even more crucially a part of the "Delors-II" package presented in 1992. For the Community, they are also a key determinant of budgetary fairness. One of the main findings of the MacDougall Report was that in economic unions, public finance has a considerable regional redistributive effect, meaning that through federal or central budgets resources are transferred from the rich regions of the economy to the poorer ones.

I believe that the "resource-flow principle", whereby resources flow from richer to poorer regions and serve specific allocative purposes, should also be reflected in EC public finance. With the chapter on economic and social cohesion, a clear Treaty foundation was created for implementing the principle. The Maastricht Treaty has further highlighted the importance of the cohesion objective.

The resource-flow principle should also be used more widely for assessing budgetary fairness. As a natural corollary, regressive elements in the present "own resources" system should be corrected, at least for the less prosperous member states, as foreseen in the protocol on economic and social cohesion in the Maastricht Treaty.

3. Expenditure assignment on efficiency grounds[4]

An expenditure of about 0.1%-0.2% of Community GDP would suffice to strengthen the economic efficiency of the completed internal market, and there is no convincing evidence that more would be needed in the third stage of economic and monetary union. This conclusion is arrived at mainly by applying the conventional arguments of scale economies and spill-over effects, but also in the knowledge that, in practice, the choice of policy is based on incomplete information and policy is not implemented without cost. The design of public intervention is therefore complex, especially given the wide divergences in social and cultural factors in the Community.

Leaving aside market intervention, I can see an economic rationale for Community spending on environmental protection, Europe-wide infrastructure, research and development and, to a lesser extent, higher education. In accordance with the principle of subsidiarity, such expenditure should largely replace less efficient national spending and complement the completed internal market with an element of positive integration.

There are three main reasons for EC involvement in environmental policy: the spill-over effects of pollution; the need to protect the integrity of the internal market; and the benefits of enhanced negotiating power in international fora. Clearly, expenditure on environmental protection is only part of the Community's involvement and there are good reasons for dividing regulatory and expenditure functions between different levels of government. Therefore, even if the Community is active in, for example, defining common norms of pollution or the concerted introduction of "ecological taxes", this does not necessarily imply significant expenditure at Community level.[5] In accordance with the "polluter pays" principle, direct EC expenditure on environmental protection should remain limited to no more than a small percentage of member states' direct environmental spending. On member states' expenditure no reliable comparable data exist, but the information available suggests that there are wide differences, with amounts varying between 0.1 and 1% of GDP.

In the field of infrastructure, the predominance of national perspectives in the Community has led to insufficient cross-border links, inefficient network design, unnecessary duplication of infrastructure in border regions and technical incompatibilities. Community involvement to rectify these deficiencies is largely a matter of the EC playing a co-ordinating and planning role. As for environmental protection, the Community provides significant support for infrastructure through the Structural Funds and the European dimension will be strengthened through the financing of the Cohesion Fund decided on at Maastricht. In addition, limited finance should be made available on a case-by-case basis to ensure that adequate trans-European networks are developed to cope with the increased cross-border traffic resulting from the single market. The bulk of finance, however, will still have to come either from private or from national public sources and may to some extent be recovered through user charges.

In the field of research and development, the principal rationale for EC involvement stems from economies of scale and the spill-over benefits of research results across frontiers, which will grow as economic integration deepens. The Community's increasing involvement should reduce the fragmentation of national efforts, improve the coherence of long-term strategic objectives and exploit economies of scale. The precise question, however, of how Community spending on R & D ought to evolve cannot be fully answered until a detailed scrutiny has been carried out of Europe's needs in specific research areas and the role of government in this respect. At present, Community expenditure on R & D represents 4.5% of member states' spending in general and about 11% of their spending on industrial technology. Further increases could prove beneficial; indeed, the greatest potential for future expenditure increases on internal policies other than the Structural Funds probably lies in this field.

In the field of higher education the main task is to contribute to the lowering of professional and cultural barriers to the movement of persons by promoting the cross-border mobility of students and teaching staff, co-operation between universities and the learning of foreign languages.

Community expenditure on Europe-wide infrastructure, R & D and higher education carried out mainly on efficiency grounds is likely also to have a significant positive impact on interregional equity. Since all less-prosperous EC regions are also peripheral ones, improved Europe-wide infrastructure will bring them nearer to the centre by reducing communication costs. Regional disparities in R & D input and output are considerably greater than income disparities; Community R & D efforts will help close this gap and make industrial innovations more easily accessible for backward regions. Similarly, access to European centres of excellence in higher education will be particularly valuable to the youth of the less-advanced parts of the Community and benefit their home regions - provided, of course, that they return there with their new vintage of knowledge and skills.

4. Expenditure assignment on equity grounds

As outlined above, specific-purpose grants will, for some time to come, be the most appropriate instrument for effecting interregional transfers at Community level in pursuit of economic and social cohesion. As such they have both a redistributive and an allocative role. As always, however, when one instrument has to contribute to two different objectives, it cannot be expected to be optimal with respect to both objectives taken separately. Part of the criticism of the Community's Structural Funds is due to this unavoidable conflict. The same will apply to the new Cohesion Fund. This implies that regardless of whether further improvements in the design and implementation of the Structural Funds are desirable, there will always be scope for criticism.

4.1 Redistributive aspects of structural operations

The redistributive role of structural operations is determined by their scale and their distribution between member states and regions. For structural operations to exhibit a positive redistributive effect, the resource-flow principle must be respected, i.e. resources must flow, in net terms, from richer regions of the Community to poorer ones. The extent of regional transfers undertaken in applying the principle is a matter of political choice, but this choice is not made in a vacuum or arbitrarily. It will be guided by a number of qualitative and quantitative factors, such as objective indicators of regional disparities; an appreciation of the distribution of the overall costs and benefits of integration; the potential scale and effects of integration; the degree of homogeneity in terms of citizenship, culture and language; and the economic effectiveness of the transfers.

Scale
In the context of the 1988 reform of the Structural Funds, Directorate-General XXII (Co-ordination of Structural Funds) sought some yardstick for a politically-attractive yet fairly objective justification for the future scale of the Funds. The doubling of the Funds which was decided upon reflected both the political will in favour of a substantial increase and the fear of regional costs in the process of completing the internal market. Similarly, in the run-up to the "Delors-II" package DG-XVI (Regional Policy) made an attempt to quantify "catch-up" needs, in particular the additional investment requirements in Objective 1 regions with respect to different categories of infrastructure. This was certainly a useful exercise for a rough quantification of these regions' absorption capacities. Beyond this, however, the definition of needs itself is such a controversial subject that it could not facilitate the political negotiations on the scale of the structural operations. On the basis of its own political

evaluations, therefore, and the Maastricht Treaty, the Commission proposed another "doubling", this time restricted to Objective 1 regions covered by the Cohesion Fund, with smaller increases for other Objective 1 regions and other Objectives (67% and 50% respectively). This proposal would lead to structural operations amounting in 1997 to 0.47% of Community GDP.[6]

The Marshall Plan for the reconstruction of post-war Europe is often mentioned as an example of a timely and generous programme of aid. During 1948-51 the USA granted about 1% of its GNP to Europe every year; this represented on average about 2% of the recipient countries' annual GNP (with considerable differences between countries; see Eichengreen and Uzan). Compared to this, the proposed Community effort of 0.47% in 1997 looks modest, but it should be seen as a much longer-term commitment. The cumulative amount of about 4% of US GNP during the years 1948-51 is still higher than the cumulative amount of Community structural spending of 3.6% over the twelve-year period 1986-97, which takes in the third enlargement of the Community and the "Delors-II" proposals.

Seen from the angle of recipient member states, the situation is very different for the three smaller ones (Ireland, Portugal and Greece) on the one hand and Spain on the other. While the smaller states can be expected to receive very substantial amounts over 1986-1997 (at an annual average of 3.3% of their GDP and 36.6% cumulatively), the sums for Spain are more modest (0.9% annually and 9.5% cumulatively), but still higher than the cumulative 8% disbursed to Western Europe by the Marshall Fund.

Another possible comparison is the flow of funds through explicit interregional transfer mechanisms in existing federations, such as Germany in 1990 before unification. In terms of flow of funds, the Community compares favourably, since the four most generously-treated German Länder received between 0.8 and 2.9% of their regional GDP in 1990 through explicit interregional transfers, whereas the figures for the Community range from 0.9% for Spain to 3.6% for Greece on average between 1986 and 1997, but rising much higher in 1997, from 1.4% for Spain to 5.5% for Greece, on the basis of an overall volume of 0.47% of GDP as proposed in the "Delors-II" package.

In assessing these figures, however, it should be borne in mind that regional disparities in the Community are much wider than in Germany, so that the redistributive effect of equivalent transfers as a ratio of GDP is much lower. In the MacDougall Report a redistributive effect of about 10% was postulated for the pre-federal phase - a quarter of what had been observed in existing economic and monetary unions on average. The structural operations of the "Delors-II" package would provide for a redistributive effect in 1997 of about 5% for Ireland, Greece and Portugal and about 1.5% for Spain, amounting to an average of 4.2% - well below the level postulated in the MacDougall Report.

Distribution of funds
The distribution of funds between member states is another sensitive political issue. It has important implications for the redistributive effectiveness of the

structural operations as well as for their allocative role. With respect to interregional redistribution, a net fund - that is, one which would be exclusively concentrated on the less-prosperous member states - would of course be the most effective, and during the successive reforms of the Structural Funds this idea has often been discussed. The new Cohesion Fund agreed on at Maastricht is a pure example of this idea. It demonstrates how much redistributive considerations have been at the forefront of its creation.[7]

The 1988 distribution of the Structural Funds between member states and regions has been analysed in a recent IMF discussion paper (Gordon, 1991), which found that "transfers were carefully targeted" but objected that "otherwise-identical regions were treated differently depending on the country to which they belong". In my view, however, there are no grounds for criticism here, as the result reflects the mixed Community responsibility vis-à-vis member states on the one hand and the regions on the other.[8] This means that member states with the same level of average GDP should be treated differently if their internal regional disparities are significant. The clearest demonstration of this is Germany before and after unification. Even if the change in the average level of German GDP compared to the Community average has been rather limited since 1990 and Germany as a whole continues to be one of the more prosperous member states, Community support in favour of Germany through the Structural Funds is set to increase dramatically because Eastern Germany will become an Objective 1 region.

Similarly, the degree of Community involvement in a specific region must depend on the financial capacity of the country in which the region is situated, since under the principle of subsidiarity the primary responsibility for regional assistance lies with member states as far as they are able to cope with their regional problems. Consequently, a French region with the same GDP per capita as a Spanish one should receive less Community and more national support than the latter.

4.2 Allocative aspects of structural operations

Eligibility and flexibility

The reduction of regional disparities can only be attained if Community assistance improves growth performance in the recipient economies. A necessary condition for this is that structural operations should cover those activities which are the most promising for raising the growth potential of the poorer regions. This can only be achieved by measures affecting the supply side, i.e. through improvements in the factor endowment of the economy, or by making existing endowments more productive, or both. The bulk of Community structural operations correspond faithfully to this requirement: the main areas of intervention are infrastructure (related to capital and land as direct or indirect production factors) and vocational training (related to labour). There is thus no need to change the basic orientation of these structural operations with respect to eligibility,[9] but the growing awareness of the importance of education and health for labour productivity makes an extension of present eligibility to cover these fields desirable.

Within broadly-defined areas of intervention, flexibility is necessary to identify the specific measures which are likely to be the most effective for regional development. This is the core task of programming and partnership at the beginning of the contract between national authorities and the Commission, but changing circumstances make it imperative to have flexibility in the implementation of the contract as well. Indeed, one of the inherent dangers of grants is that inertia will prevent funds from being allocated according to changing needs. It is therefore very important to limit fixed a priori allocations to the minimum necessary for planning and to allocate the rest according to reassessed needs and priorities which will depend on actual performance.

Evaluation and monitoring
For this inbuilt flexibility to operate, there is a need for a sophisticated system of ex-ante evaluation and permanent monitoring. The evaluation has to ensure that programmes and projects are sound in a cost/benefit sense. It should also provide a set of indicators against which performance in the implementation phase can be effectively monitored.

Additionality
Community grants can have a positive allocative impact only if they are not offset by reductions in national spending; they must be *additional* to national expenditure, not replace it. This might seem straightforward enough, but analytically and empirically the issue is complex, as the grant literature and practical Community experience testify.

At present, the Structural Funds' regulations require that the increase in the appropriations for the Funds has "a genuine additional economic impact" and "results in at least an equivalent increase in the total volume of official or similar (Community or national) structural aid in the member state concerned". This condition is monitored on a regular basis, and with few exceptions compliance has been observed.

In future the interplay between Community structural operations and national budgetary expenditure, whether at central, regional or local level, will become even more important since national budgetary policies are crucial to the convergence process designed to lead to the final stage of EMU. In a number of member states considerable efforts will have to be undertaken, in particular with regard to budgetary discipline as part of their convergence programmes. Compatibility between this discipline and development efforts will henceforth have to be achieved in a new and more demanding context.

Economic conditionality
Conditionality can be used in a negative sense (as a stick) or a positive one (as a carrot). In the negative sense, the disbursement of funds allocated to a

particular member state can be blocked if pre-defined conditions are violated. In the positive sense, additional transfers could be triggered by the fulfilment of certain conditions.

The final word on the conditionality of the Cohesion Fund has perhaps not been said. Nevertheless, this case can serve as an illustration. According to the protocol on economic and social cohesion in the Maastricht Treaty, the Cohesion Fund is to provide Community financial contributions for member states "which have a programme leading to the fulfilment of the conditions of economic convergence as set out in Article 104c". I interpret this as positive conditionality: additional transfers from the Cohesion Fund will be made available if member states follow a path of budget discipline. If, on the other hand, a member state has an excessive deficit according to an Article 104c(6) Council decision, and that member state does not respect the budgetary targets set in its convergence programme, the protocol conditions will not be fulfilled, and no Cohesion Fund financial contribution will be triggered in its favour. I would advocate going one step further, in fact, in the direction of positive conditionality, and favour disbursing a supplementary tranche of Cohesion Fund assistance if the member state's fiscal convergence performance is significantly better than foreseen in its convergence programme.

For the Structural Funds neither the Treaty nor present regulations stipulate any economic conditionality beyond the additionality requirement mentioned above. In future, Marshall Fund experience might be instructive. Eichengreen and Uzan, analysing the role of conditionality in their study of the Marshall Fund's economic effects, conclude: "If the overall record of conditionality regarding fiscal and monetary policy was mixed, informal pressure for market liberalisation and economic integration was more successful".

Following this insight, I would support the provision of incentives for structural adjustment rather than the imposition of conventional IMF-type macroeconomic conditions. More operationally I would suggest the incorporation in Community Support Frameworks of commitments to concrete policy measures aimed at improving supply-side performance. Depending on national circumstances, these could include the reduction of state aid and steps to ensure a better allocation of capital and greater labour-market flexibility. If the commitments were honoured, supplementary Structural Fund assistance would be made available as part of the overall increase in the scale of the Funds.

5. Conclusion

To sum up, public intervention to promote economic efficiency will have limited implications for the EC budget. Even in the perspective of economic and monetary union, the Community is unlikely to need to spend more than 0.1-0.2% of GDP for internal policies other than agriculture and structural operations. Such spending should be concentrated on R & D, Europe-wide infrastructure, environmental protection and higher education. In addition to improving economic efficiency in conformity with the principle of subsidiarity, Community expenditure in these fields can be expected to have a positive impact on interregional equity.

Specific intervention to promote interregional equity is a recurrent bone of contention in most if not all economic unions since its scale and distribution are largely matters of political choice. The Community will not escape this at times painful decision-making process. Nevertheless, properly-designed instruments for interregional transfers can make an important difference. To improve the effectiveness of Community structural operations, four design elements require particular attention: eligibility and flexibility, evaluation and monitoring, additionality and economic conditionality.

NOTES

1. Spahn (1993) and Walsh (1992) also provide a survey and discuss the relevance of the literature for the European Community.

2. Helm and Smith (1989) provide a synopsis of both sets of grounds. With regard to the former, they have enriched the traditional arguments of economies of scale and spill-over effects with an original contribution based on game theory, which is nevertheless more relevant to regulatory questions (i.e. tax competition) than to the assignment of expenditure functions.

3. Ibid; p. 4.

4. This question has been more fully analysed by my colleague Declan Costello in an unpublished paper which is available on request (EC Commission, Directorate-General for Economic and Financial Affairs).

5. In fact, Community spending for environmental projects is quite significant, but it is mainly undertaken through the Structural Funds and specific research programmes. Direct Community expenditure for environmental purposes has hitherto been very small.

6. Cf. my 1980 paper in which I gave a range of 0.4-0.8% of GDP as the scale of structural operations flowing from the pre-federal integration scenario of the MacDougall Report.

7. In my view the Cohesion Fund is the result of an implicit Spanish renegotiation in line with that which led to the British budget rebate, the Greek renegotiation which gave rise to the Integrated Mediterranean Programmes, and the more marginal Portuguese one by which the PEDIP programme was agreed upon. All of these are country-specific or highly concentrated, being intended to overcome a specific equity problem.

8. Also relevant in this context is the practice in all mature economic unions whereby small regions are treated more favourably than large ones. The Community is no

exception in this respect.

9. An area of intervention about which doubts have sometimes been raised is the Community's assistance to private investment. Since this takes place mainly through the co-financing of state aid, this is primarily an issue of competition policy rather than of eligibility for Structural Fund intervention.

References

Commission of the European Communities (1975), *Report of the Study Group "Economic and Monetary Union 1980"* (Marjolin Report), Brussels.

Commission of the European Communities (1977), *Report of the Study Group on the Role of Public Finance in European Integration* (MacDougall Report), Brussels.

Costello, D., "Inter-governmental grants: what role for the European Community?", unpublished internal Commission paper (DG-II), available upon request.

Costello, D., "Public intervention to promote economic efficiency: implications for the Community budget", unpublished internal Commission paper (DG-II), available upon request.

Costello, D., "The redistributive effects of interregional transfers: a comparison of the EC and Germany", unpublished internal Commission paper (DG-II), available upon request.

Eichengreen, B. and M. Uzan (1992), "The Marshall Plan: economic effects and implications for Eastern Europe and the former USSR", *CEPR Discussion Paper* 638.

Gordon, J. (1991), "Structural funds and the 1992 program in the European Community", *IMF Working Paper* 65/91.

Helm, D. and S. Smith (1989), "The assessment: economic integration and the role of the European Community", *Oxford Review of Economic Policy* 5 (2).

Italianer, A. and J. Pisani-Ferry (1993), "The regional-stabilisation properties of fiscal arrangements", this volume.

Oates, W. E. (1972), *Fiscal Federalism*, New York: Harcourt Brace Jovanovich.

Reichenbach, H. (1980), "The pre-federal integration phase in the MacDougall Report: a possible scenario for 1985?", TFC/5/80 of 26.3.80, unpublished, available upon request.

Reichenbach, H. (1983), "EC budgetary imbalances: a conceptual framework", *Finanzarchiv* 41 (3).

Spahn, B. (1993), "Fiscal federalism: a survey of the literature", this volume.

Walsh, C. (1992), "Fiscal federalism: an overview of issues and a discussion of their relevance to the European Community", *Federalism Research Centre Discussion Papers*, Canberra.

13 The regional impact of Community policies

Bernhard Seidel

1. Introduction[1]

Social cohesion, that is the harmonisation of working and living conditions, has been a firmly-rooted aim of the European Community since the passing of the Single European Act. Clearly this represents an ambitious target if one bears in mind the stark differences in economic performance of the member states and their various regions. In the poorest regions economic output per head of population amounts to only one-ninth of that in the richest. Economic weaknesses and unfavourable local conditions often go hand in hand, so that geographical remoteness, a poor communications network, inadequate infrastructure and shortages of skills significantly hinder the catching-up process, even if the difference in labour costs offers incentives to move production away from the central regions of the EC.

The worry in this situation is that efforts to boost growth within the Community, as envisaged in the single market programme and monetary union project, will have positive effects only in regions which are already economically-advanced. Apart from some of the southernmost areas of the Community, to which long-term autonomous development opportunities will be given, it is the central areas which have emerged at the forefront of the single market's activities. The political opening-up of eastern Europe will only slightly alter this picture. The focus of economic success may shift eastwards, stretching towards the Prague-Vienna-Budapest axis, following enlargement of the EC to take in the EFTA countries.

The process of German unification has now shown that unequal achievement does not necessarily mean a difference in income. Large transfer payments can facilitate a regional redistribution of disposable income - a process which is clearly different from income-formation. But the German experience also shows the financial strains which are linked with such a strategy. It has entailed a complex financial balancing-act between East and West, to which, moreover, there was little alternative, given the unique political situation of East Germany in Europe. The experience is therefore unlikely to be repeated elsewhere in the EC; it would far exceed the financial capacities and political will of the member states. It is therefore necessary to continue with the previous approach to improve start-up conditions in the less-developed regions of the Community, and to compensate for certain geographical handicaps through incentive schemes which will counteract its centripetal forces.

2. Measuring the regional effects of EC policies

In order to determine the effects of economic policy intervention, simulations are often carried out on the basis of econometric models. The effects are defined as the difference between a projection of the current situation and the estimated cost of the policies in question.

For regional analyses with a European dimension, however, such an approach is unsatisfactory. Even if the necessary data were available, the model would become too complex in the face of the exponentially-increasing number of variables which would have to be considered. On the other hand, case studies analysing the costs and benefits of individual development programmes in selected regions are not extensive enough. In this chapter, therefore, I offer a measurement of the financial flows from the Community level to the regions.

In what follows, the following assumptions are made. First, per capita income is the yardstick for measuring regional disparities. Second, Community expenditure has a direct or indirect effect on incomes. If lagging regions are helped by grants from public funds - whether for developing infrastructure, stimulating private investment or raising household income - the overall effect is to counteract the regional income gap. But if it is the better-off central areas of the Community that benefit, regional disparities will only be reinforced. The third assumption is that the revenue side of the Community financing system does not exacerbate disparities. The method described is obviously subject to the restriction that it applies only to policy areas affecting the budget. Moreover, direct effects must also be distinguished from indirect ones where support to backward regions through the promotion of infrastructure and industrial investment is concerned. A strengthening of investment no doubt also benefits regions' supply of the necessary goods and services. Spin-offs like this, however, are extremely difficult to pin down.

On no account should the direct effect of Community funds measured here be equated with their actual income effects. The latter will vary according to supportive instruments and measures and will depend not least on the degree of efficiency in the planning, implementation and monitoring of structural policy. The strength of the immediate knock-on effect is determined by this and by the rates of financial incentive themselves. The lower the rate of incentive, the greater the economic effect - as long as the incentive remains attractive. The lower the financial involvement of the Community itself, the more the member states pay in terms of support. Considering Community expenditure on its own exaggerates the balancing-out tendency of regional support. Therefore the immediate multiplier effect of Community production is substantially less in the lagging regions (higher level of overall support, greater Community participation) than in the more advanced ones (lower level of support, less Community involvement). But of course there are also indirect benefits deriving from the removal of infrastructural bottlenecks.

The tendency for the regional divide within the Community to be evened out depends on the extent to which the stimuli provided by payments in individual policy areas are concentrated on the backward regions. This may be illustrated in compressed form by a concentration curve derived from the Lorenz curve.

For this purpose the Community regions (*NUTS* Level 2) are ranked by per capita income (as a measure of their level of development). The aggregate payments are then compared with the aggregate populations of the regions thus ranked. The resulting graphs show how far payments are concentrated on the population of backward regions; whether they tend, paradoxically, to work *against* the elimination of regional disparities; or whether, being evenly distributed, they are neutral from a regional-policy viewpoint. A curve following a line emerging at 45° from the centre of the co-ordinate system would imply equal per capita distribution. A concave curve signifies disadvantageous treatment of the poorer regions, while a convex curve indicates preferential treatment.

3. The main areas of EC policy and their regional impact

3.1 Structural intervention

The Regional Fund
European Regional Development Fund investment grants - about 10% of the EC budget in 1990 - are the main factor in evening out the regional disparities in the Community. The compensatory effects have even increased over the years, a result that is undoubtedly linked with the reform of the Structural Funds. In 1989 and 1990 an average of some 80% of investment support grants went to the 20% of the Community's population living in the poorest regions (see figure 1). However, following their accession Spain and Portugal required an initial period of adjustment before making full use of the Regional Fund, with the result that they were not able to extract as much benefit from the first few years

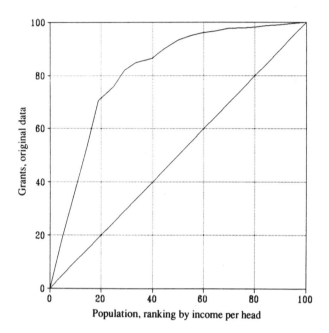

Figure 1
Concentration of ERDF investment grants
(total 1989-90, EC-12)

of their membership as other backward regions had been.

This applies to basics such as infrastructure measures. When it comes to investment support for industry the differences are even more pronounced (figures 2 and 3). In the backward regions of Spain and Portugal, which economically are among the weakest in the Community, the main thrust of regional assistance, even more than in other regions, has been directed at infrastructure measures. Poor infrastructure has always been a major obstacle to private investment in these areas. Empirical studies show that the existence of infrastructure serving companies (and households) is a crucial factor in attracting private investors to such regions.[2] In this situation not even the attractive financial incentives of Community investment support, with investment grants rising to 70% of total costs, have sufficient bite. In 1986 and 1987, for example, the poorer regions of the Community, containing 10% of the Community's population, received less than 5% of investment subsidies to trade and industry, with the lowest fifth receiving no more than 40% of this money.

Overall the calculations show, as expected, that the financial impact of European regional policy is largely in line with the desired compensatory function. In this process the promotion of infrastructure plays something of a pioneering role, with investment in trade and industry lagging somewhat

Figure 2
Concentration of ERDF investment grants
(infrastructure 1986-87, EC-12)

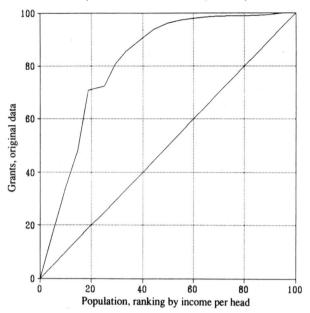

Figure 3
Concentration of ERDF investment grants
(industry 1986-87, EC-12)

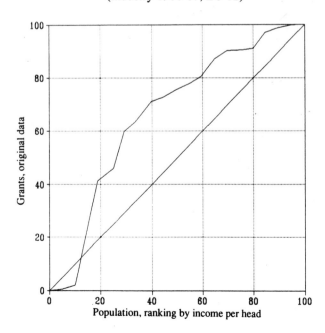

behind, with the result that the take-up rate has not been uniform throughout the regions. However, as far as it is possible to draw conclusions from the short period under study, there is a noticeable trend towards greater regional equalisation in the latter area too.

The Social Fund

Like the Regional Fund, the European Social Fund - the most important Structural Fund, with 7% of the EC budget in 1990 - is a strong force in evening out regional imbalances in the Community. However, the regional concentration of aid is not quite so pronounced (figure 4). Nonetheless, in 1989 approximately half of the strictly regional resources were tied to measures in the poorest regions, with a fifth of the Community's population. Over the years this regional concentration has become somewhat more pronounced. This is undoubtedly due to some of the funds being committed to the underdeveloped regions and to better co-ordination of the various Community operations that come under the support programmes. Finally, it is evident from the Social Fund's gentler curve compared to that of the Regional Fund that despite long and continous growth in the 1980s, long-term and youth unemployment in the Community is not only the problem of a small number of underdeveloped regions but is relatively widespread.

Figure 4
Obligations of the European Social Fund
(1986-89, EC-12)

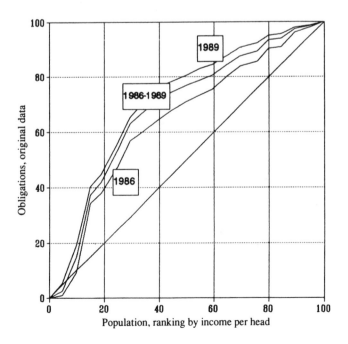

With a clearer sense of purpose than was the case with the Regional Fund, the Community channelled Social Fund resources to Spain and Portugal from the earliest days of their membership. Comparison over time indicates that the better treatment for backward regions occurred in the late 1980s, i.e. mainly in the Community of Twelve, thus obviously benefiting the Spanish and Portuguese regions.

EAGGF-Guidance Section
With about 2bn Ecu, the Guidance Section of the European Agricultural Guidance and Guarantee Fund accounts for over 4% of the EC budget. It promotes the improvement of agricultural structures, in particular by granting investment subsidies. These resources thus chiefly benefit rural areas which, compared with regions dominated by manufacturing and service industries, are more in need of help. The reform of the Structural Funds caused the objectives of regional policy to become even more closely identified with those of the agricultural structures policy.[3] This regional-equalisation function can also be detected in the concentration of EAGGF investment subsidies to the Community's poorer regions (figure 5). In 1986 and 1987, for example, about half the subsidies on average went to the poorest regions of the EC, where a fifth of the Community's population lives. On the other hand, the top 40% of the rich regions received only 20% of the Guidance Fund's investment grants.

Figure 5
EAGGF-Guidance Fund investment grants
(1986-87, EC-12)

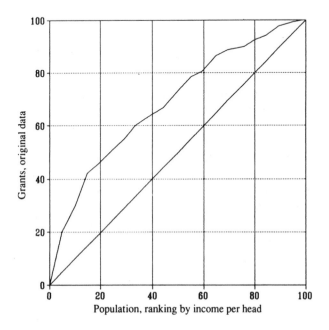

Grants, original data

Population, ranking by income per head

Figure 6
Concentration of ECSC loans
(total 1986-87, EC-12)

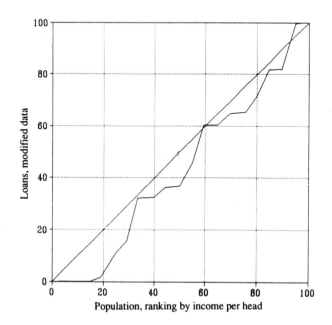

ECSC credits

At roughly 1bn Ecu (1986 and 1987), ECSC credits are among the more modest financial flows. For a number of regions, including some of the poorest, there is simply no material basis for such payments. This is all the more true for the Community of Twelve. The 15% of the population in the poorest regions derives virtually no benefit from them (figure 6). This is particularly true of Portugal and Greece. Overall, ECSC loans exacerbate regional inequality. Under the Community of Ten and over the period 1985-87, the distributive effects of ECSC loans were largely neutral. No broad trend is in evidence. Between 1986 and 1987, under the Community of Twelve, inequities of distribution in the true poverty area widened, though the overall regional distribution of ECSC loans actually became more even than before.

Figure 7
Concentration of ECSC subsidies
(1986-89, EC-12)

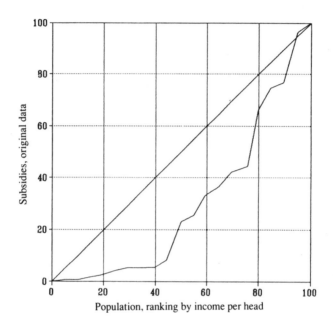

ECSC aid
The same applies to ECSC readaptation aid as to credits. It favours companies and workers in structurally-weak regions dominated by the coal and steel industries. In relation to the Community average, these regions are not necessarily those with the lowest incomes, even though their economic outlook may be poor and structural help badly needed. On the other hand, most of the Community's poorer regions derive no benefits from this specific form of sectoral aid (figure 7). In any event, the aid is of no great size: in 1989 it still amounted to little more than 60m Ecu.

ECSC aid is even more unevenly distributed than the corresponding readaptation credits, and if anything tends to boost overall regional income inequalities. The adverse regional effects of this trend fell off somewhat between 1986 and 1989, although in 1989 the Community's poorest regions, accounting for 40% of the population, received less than 5% of ECSC aid while the more prosperous regions with more than a fifth of the Community's population received something over a fifth of this aid.

European Investment Bank loans

Unlike ECSC aid, loans granted by the European Investment Bank amounting to the rather substantial sum of 7bn Ecu (1986 and 1987) have an altogether equalising effect on regional income-distribution. It is plain from this that the rectification of regional imbalances is one of the EIB's objectives. However, the curves in the poverty area drop below the 45° line (figure 8).

Spending on infrastructure is by far the greater part of the EIB credits. There are significant differences between the distribution of spending on industry and spending on infrastructure. Industrial credits overall are more unevenly distributed - thus helping to counteract regional income disparities, within the limits set by their size - than infrastructure credits. As far as poverty is concerned, their effects are not regressive. Yet the curves for infrastructure spending stick relatively closely to the 45° line and in both the years under observation are strongly regressive in the poverty area after the end of each period.

Figure 8
Concentration of EIB loans
(total 1986-87, EC-12)

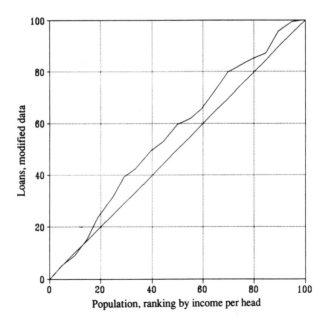

3.2 Other forms of structural intervention

Research and development expenditure
With little more than 1.5bn Ecu from 1983 to 1990, the amounts granted by the European Community to businesses and research institutions for R&D projects as part of contractual research (excluding research into fusion) comprise no more than a tiny fraction of the EC budget. Subsidies benefit developed regions more than regions whose development is lagging behind. Over the same period, at least two-fifths of these resources were spent in the economically-strongest regions of the EC-12, with roughly one-fifth of the Community's population. The lowest fifth of the population, from the weakest economic regions, received less than a tenth of the Community's R&D expenditure (figure 9). R&D support thus tended, if anything, to counteract the levelling-out of regional disparities.

Figure 9
Regional concentration of R&D contracts
(CEC contributions 1983-90, EC-12)

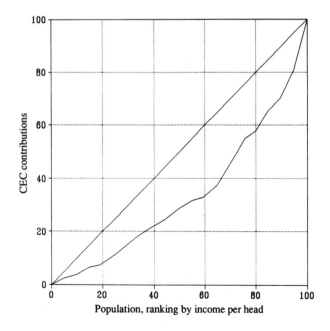

This is not surprising. For one thing, highly-skilled staff are required to carry out research and development, and as a rule they are less numerous in underdeveloped areas. For another, businesses have a tendency to locate their own research operations within a reasonably comfortable distance of company headquarters or to employ local institutes in order to ensure smoother communications between company management and their researchers. Finally, the fact that universities and research institutes have been established in less-developed areas on regional-policy grounds has not yet resulted in any practical reversal of this trend. As long as the Community's economic structure remains regionally imbalanced, the centripetal effect of R&D operations, despite substantial financial incentives for regional diversification, will continue to be a fact of life.

Agricultural guarantee payments

Much more difficult than measuring the impact of Community structural assistance is the evaluation of the net advantage to a region of agricultural guarantee payments. They are chiefly designed to maintain farmers' incomes at an adequate level. They do this not by raising them directly but by supporting the prices paid to farm producers. The income advantage for the farmer, all

Figure 10
Concentration of CAP guarantee payments
(total 1986-89, EC-12)

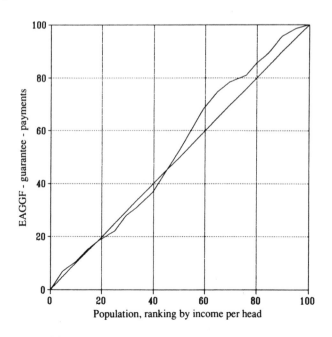

Figure 11
Concentration of CAP guarantee payments
(sugar 1986-89, EC-12)

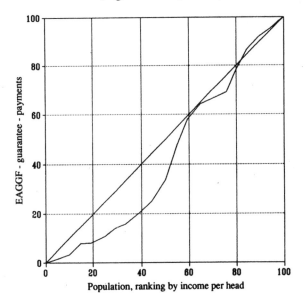

Population, ranking by income per head

Figure 12
Concentration of CAP guarantee payments
(cattle [meat] 1986-89, EC-12)

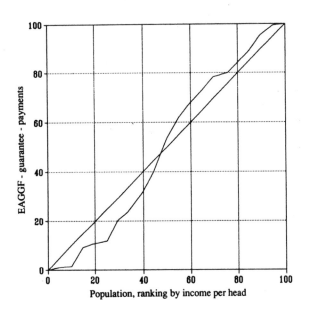

Population, ranking by income per head

Figure 13
Concentration of CAP guarantee payments
(sheep- and goat-meat 1986-89, EC-12)

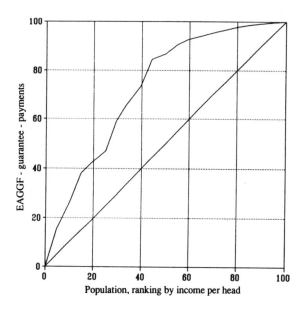

Figure 14
Concentration of CAP guarantee payments
(fruit and vegetables 1986-89, EC-12)

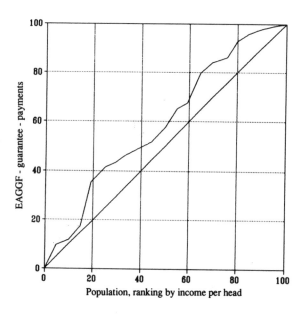

other things being equal, is equivalent to the difference between the Community price and the world market price, multiplied by the total volume sold at home or abroad. The sum total of these amounts for all Community farmers is not simply identical with the sum spent by the EAGGF on intervention.

In terms of safeguarding incomes under the market-regulation system, the regional origin of the Community products on which guarantee funds are spent is immaterial. I have therefore sought here to trace regional effects on the basis of production. This called for a different approach. Each group of intervention products was divided up separately. With regard to aid to producers, it is safest to assume that such aid benefits producers directly rather than indirectly via market stabilisation.[4] This is why the EAGGF financial reports list payments made separately by member state, and also by regional production for each individual country separately. In respect of the other costs of the system, the incidence of which, being relatively independent of the place or country of intervention, is more widespread owing to the interdependence of national farming markets, support spending was also broken down in accordance with regional production structure, but across the EC. Spain and Portugal were generally dealt with separately since under their treaties of accession these countries are still subject to transitional provisions, with the result that they do not benefit from the CAP to the same extent as the other member states. For this reason, country-specific spending was regionalised.

The calculation covers the period 1986-1989 and includes all the major products subject to market organisation, accounting for more than nine-tenths of all price-support payments, or 56% of the Community budget. It shows that for the Community as a whole no effect on regional income equalisation is discernible. Only some of the poorer regions benefit from guarantee payments

The regional distribution effects vary in respect of the individual products (figures 11-14). In the case of sugar it is the richer regions of the Community (EC-12) that benefit; in the case of cereals, milk, oilseeds and beef the poorer regions are also put at a disadvantage, with the regional-equalisation effects being confined to the economically-stronger northern regions. Thus 70% of guaranteed expenditure, or fully 40% of the entire Community budget, is in effect working against the Community's regional policy objectives. Only in tobacco, olive oil, sheep- and goat-meat and, to a lesser extent, wine, fruit and vegetables are the poorer regions of the Community of Twelve favoured to any extent. These products attract less than 20% of guaranteed payments.

3.3 Overall effects

Because of the difficulty of summing up the different effects of various EC measures one can draw only broad conclusions (figures 15 and 16). An examination of the regional concentration of aid from the Structural Funds (Regional Fund, Social Fund and EAGGF-Guidance Section) - amounting to more than one-fifth of the Community's budget for 1990 - shows a clear trend towards the elimination of regional disparities. In 1986 and 1987 half this money on average went to the regions with the poorest 20% of the Community's population, whereas the 40% living in the economically-powerful areas received little more than 10%.

If, in addition to the Structural Funds, one takes into account the Community's other structural policy operations of financial significance - EIB credits and ECSC credits and aid, amounting to 25-30% of the Community budget - a substantial dilution of the equalising effect is apparent. This is partly because ECSC money has no impact whatsoever on regional equalisation and partly because EIB credits are significantly more dispersed throughout the Community region by region. While the bottom fifth of the regions' received over half the resources provided by the Structural Funds, they received little more than 40% of the actual structural assistance provided. As a form of aid, credits play a minor part and their levelling effects have undoubtedly been overstated.

Owing to the relatively small amounts involved - little more than half a million Ecu for the period 1985-87 - the curve remains virtually unchanged even if financial contributions to R&D contracts are included in this spending, despite their adverse impact on regional equalisation.

But taking into consideration guarantee payments under the Common Agricultural Policy - roughly three-fifths of the Community budget - we find a

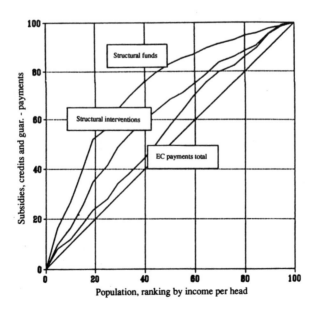

Figure 15
Regional concentration of EC payments
(1986-87, EC-12)

Figure 16
Regional concentration of Income
(1988, EC-12)

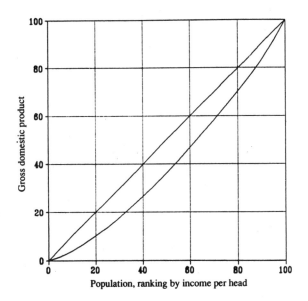

marked levelling-off in the financial incentives for regional equalisation, and farm policy as a whole doing little to support regional-policy objectives and hence working against the Structural Funds' equalising effect. The concentration curve clearly approaches the diagonal, that is to say assistance in the form of financial-policy incentives was not on the whole geared to regional poverty measured on a per capita income basis.

4. Outlook

If the Community is to achieve its aims of regional and social cohesion, a stronger concentration of funds on backward regions appears necessary. Moreover, guarantee-price levels in agriculture should be cut back and greater stress placed on regional differentiation in agricultural policy. The European Commission's efforts are already turning in this direction, as shown by the CAP reform and by suggestions for increasing structural expenditure in the "Delors-II" package. It should not, however, be forgotten that their success depends not only on the availability of Community finance but also on its efficient use.

In this context it is important that Community funds should not simply serve as a substitute for those of the member states, and that the recipient regions be capable of absorbing the large amounts of available funds; for even now signs are beginning to appear that the preconditions are not always being met, especially in the least-developed regions such as Greece and the Italian Mezzogiorno. If this trend continues, the increase in the volume and diversity of structural support within the Community could lose much of its hoped-for effects.

NOTES

1. This contribution represents the main results of a study carried out on behalf of the European Parliament: Fritz Franzmeyer, Peter Hrubesch, Bernhard Seidel, and Christian Weise, "The regional impact of Community policies", European Parliament, Directorate-General for Research, Research and Documentation Papers, Regional Policy and Transport Series 17 (Luxembourg: Office for Official Publications of the European Communities, 1991).

2. Cf. Biehl and Dieter, "The contribution of infrastructure to regional development" (Commission of the European Communities, 1986), especially p. 114 ff., 347 ff.; and C. W. Nam, G. Nerb and H. Russ, "An empirical assessment of factors shaping regional competitiveness in problem regions" (Commission of the European Communities, 1990), especially p. 29 ff.

3. See Commission of the European Communities, *Guide to the Reform of the Community's Structural Funds* (Luxembourg: Office for Official Publications of the European Communities, 1989).

4. This is also true for refunds, guidance premiums and co-responsibility levies.

5. Measured by GDP per capita.

14 The efficiency of the Structural Funds

Philippe Goybet and Moreno Bertoldi

1. Introduction[1]

The aim of this chapter is to discover whether it is possible to reach an objective assessment of the efficiency of the Structural Funds, as administered by the Commission since 1989.

This is a complex and difficult task. Firstly, though in some cases (Ireland, Portugal and Greece) the scale of the Funds' involvement may exceed 10% of total investment, in others (such as rural areas and regions in industrial decline) it does not amount to a major macroeconomic contribution, no matter how great the effect on productive potential. Thus, it is not possible to apply the same analytical methods and models to all structural policies.

Secondly, the Structural Funds do not consist of a set of independent projects to each of which one can apply a cost/benefit analysis. Rather, they are intended to be a comprehensive and integrated approach, creating synergies and positive spin-offs through a series of co-ordinated measures to improve human capital, set up infrastructures and promote productive activity. Moreover, when the volume of aid involved takes on significant economic proportions, an assessment of the efficiency of entire economic systems is called for. This is the case both for short periods, focusing on demand, multiplier and accelerator effects, and long periods, where supply effects predominate, contributing to growth in productivity and competitiveness, the reduction of transport costs and the breaking-down of geographical isolation.

2. The reform of the Structural Funds

The Single European Act opened the way for a radical reshaping of the Community's structural-intervention policy. In replacing the project approach by a co-ordinated policy based on a multi-year programme, the reform sought coherence and efficiency. Its main features were as follows:

i) Focusing structural intervention on clearly-defined objectives.

ii) Increasing the sums available. Thus, the Funds would double in real terms (from 7 to 14bn Ecu) between 1987 and 1993, with 60bn Ecu committed for 1989-93.

iii) Introduction of new structural-policy methods based on partnership, programming, synergy between structural allocations and complementarity between Community and member-state expenditure.

iv) The additionality principle, whereby Community finance would "top up" national expenditure, increasing the Funds' impact and obviating withdrawals by member states on grounds of budgetary constraints.

v) Simplification and harmonisation of administrative procedures to make for greater efficiency and transparency.

vi) Dovetailing of structural policy with other Community policies, notably in the areas of competition, public procurement and the environment.

The Community's structural intervention is concentrated on five objectives concerning specific regions or whole member states.

Objective 1 is economic growth and recovery in regions which are underdeveloped by comparison with the Community average. This covers a total of seven countries or regions and 21.5% of the EC population and represents an expenditure of 39bn Ecu over the period 1989-93.

Objective 2 is to rehabilitate regions seriously affected by industrial decline. It covers 60 regions and 16% of the EC population, with an expenditure of 7.2bn Ecu.

Objectives 3 and 4 are to assist the long-term unemployed and first-time workers respectively (7.45bn Ecu).

Objective 5a is the adaptation of agricultural structures along the lines of the CAP reform (3.4bn Ecu).

Objective 5b is the development of rural areas. It concerns 56 regions and 5% of the EC population (2.86bn Ecu).

Clearly, these objectives are ambitious and the sums allocated are significant. What matters is to discover whether the means suit the ends and whether the choices made in the different regions really meet the criteria of efficiency.

3. The lessons of economic theory

3.1 Neo-classical theory

The Community's structural-intervention policy seems generally in agreement with neo-classical theory, which holds that the factors of production are remunerated according to their marginal productivity and that growth is a function of increases in capital, labour and technical progress, the latter factor being exogenous and calculated as a residual. In fact, in lagging regions or those in industrial decline, capital ownership per head is lower than in the Community's more advanced regions, so that marginal capital productivity there is higher and Community aid enables a better allocation of resources. It is also fair to suppose that Structural-Fund assistance contributes to the acceleration of technical progress through the training of workers and the reduction of transport costs.

However, it is clear that in the light of neo-classical theory, structural intervention is a second-best course of action. In fact, if return on capital is higher in less-developed regions, capital should migrate naturally towards them, thus making for an optimal allocation of resources. Yet this does not take place, and neo-classical theory is unable to explain why; and it is therefore also incapable of explaining the main reasons for economic growth or giving useful policy directions.

Recent developments in growth theory have opened up new avenues of research, overturning the neo-classical hypotheses of constant returns to scale and exogenous technical progress and positing externalities arising out of an increase in the input of the factors of production. The latter may be human capital, R&D expenditure or public investment. The new theoretical developments, by making at least part of technical progress endogenous, attempt to resolve some of the inadequacies of traditional neo-classical models and to offer an explanation of different rates of growth.

3.2 Growth through the accumulation of human capital

According to this approach, it is the stock and evolution of human capital which determine differences between countries in growth rate and income level. This theory also suggests that the economic capacity to exploit the opportunities offered by human capital strongly depends on the kind of production in which a country specialises. By seeking to modify that country's initial human capital and, to a lesser extent, its unfavourable economic specialisation, the EC's Structural Funds can help it to move to a higher growth path.

For these reasons the Funds, through their emphasis on training, investment support and the modernisation of production technology, seem to fit in, at least from a theoretical standpoint, with the view that human capital is the key to faster growth, though one might criticise the lack of explicit accompanying measures in favour of higher-value-added and technology-intensive production.

3.3 Growth through the accumulation of knowledge

In this second category of theoretical models of endogenous growth, technical progress is the fruit of research and development. The latter is itself dependent on the share of human capital directly devoted to research, achieving increasing returns through the accumulation of a stock of public knowledge.

In the light of this approach, the Structural Funds do not seem to be wholly targeted on the requirements for strong and swift growth in the regions concerned. In fact, the Funds are only indirectly concerned with the promotion of R&D-intensive activities; above all, the kind of human capital formation resulting from the Funds' activities is only marginally related to research. In this respect, the Funds' effectiveness seems limited.

However, if one extends the model to take account of international trade, the picture is somewhat different. In fact, significant externalities can derive from a country's import-export activity and its capacity to create a favourable environment for foreign direct investment in technologically-advanced production. By opening up countries' markets, by training more highly-qualified personnel, and by creating favourable investment conditions, the Structural Funds contribute to the internationalisation of their economies. Moreover, the Funds are themselves part of the wider and more complex movement towards the single European market. This movement should help to increase the stock of knowledge in the Community as a whole and in its less-developed regions in particular, where the stock of knowledge is markedly smaller. As such the Structural Funds have a positive impact on growth rates.

3.4 Growth through the accumulation of public capital

Finally, some economists consider that public capital is a source of increasing returns and externalities for private capital. It gives rise to externalities since, through a process of accumulation, it helps to increase the overall efficiency of the economic system by breaking down geographical isolation, reducing transport costs, creating infrastructural support and supplying services which increase firms' productive efficiency and cut their management and information costs.

The Structural Funds seem well-suited to this approach. Less-developed countries and regions are inherently under-equipped - a problem which the state, with its limited resources, finds it difficult to cure. Structural assistance comes in most useful here, supplying a set of goods which complement the private factors of production and increase the system's overall efficiency. In this way the Funds make possible greater productivity and returns in the public sector than would have been obtained in the private sector by, for example, subsidising the factors of production.

The returns-on-public-capital approach, therefore, leads to rather different policy conclusions from the previous two, particularly concerning the effectiveness of structural intervention. The stress on infrastructure considerably helps to increase productive potential and to create a virtuous cycle of growth in production and productivity. By comparison, assistance in the development of human capital is a less-widely accepted approach, and assistance to firms themselves definitely seems a sub-optimal choice. From this one must conclude that endogenous growth through public capital means the rejection of any industrial-policy intervention, because the latter causes distortions and diverts regions from their optimal growth paths.

To conclude this section, it is worth noting that recent developments in the theory of endogenous growth support the view that EC structural intervention is compatible with the goal of stable and lasting economic development. What remains to be done is to measure empirically the expected impact of structural intervention.

4. The results of macroeconomic assessment

This section presents the results of the assessment of the potential impact of the Structural Funds in Objective 1 countries or regions where the macroeconomic scale of transfers was great enough to warrant a modelled approach. The models chosen range from neo-Keynesian econometric models to computable general equilibrium models, and from input-output models to dynamic general equilibrium models with endogenous growth. This rather eclectic approach is due to the fact that there is no single model capable of carrying out the required assessments. All the models used have strengths and weaknesses which vary according to time-horizon, degree of aggregation and available data. The measurement of expected macroeconomic impact is generally based on a simulation of economic growth without the Structural Funds in relation to a central projection including the complete Community Support Framework.

The following conclusions were reached. Thanks to the demand effects, the Structural Funds should make it possible for all the Objective 1 areas (Greece, Ireland, Portugal, the Mezzogiorno of Italy and the Objective 1 regions of Spain) to grow during 1989-93 at a faster rate than the Community average (i.e. 3% as opposed to 2.7%; without the Funds these areas' growth rate would have been no more than 2.6%). The demand effects should be particularly marked in Portugal and Spain, whose growth rates remain considerably higher than the EC average despite their strict budgetary policies, and in Greece, where the Funds play an important anticyclical role, helping that country to avoid a severe recession as it undergoes a difficult adjustment process. As for the labour market, the Funds should enable the creation of 350,000 jobs in Objective 1 regions.

At the sectoral level, the Funds should contribute to the strengthening of certain key activities in the regions concerned. Studies based on an input-output model show that, in addition to the building sector, which is directly linked to infrastructure projects, rather strong growth should be evident in agro-food and metal-working industries and in mechanical engineering. Market services should also receive a stimulus, particularly services to firms, which should bring about a sustained process of modernisation and rationalisation of the production apparatus. Last but not least, in those regions with great historic or scenic attributes, tourism should grow considerably.

As far as supply effects are concerned, different calculations were made for Ireland, Italy and Portugal. In the Irish case, the results of microeconomic analysis in the major sectors of agriculture, market services and industry, together with the labour market, were introduced into the neo-Keynesian macroeconometric model *HERMES*. Certain effects of the Structural Funds were found to be significant: it was estimated that by the year 2000 the cumulative effects on the supply side would be of the same order as the demand effects for GDP and even higher for GNP (+1.2% and 1.7% respectively). In addition, different types of intervention would give rise to different effects on growth.

Another study, using a computable general equilibrium model, was carried out in the Mezzogiorno. This showed that the Structural Funds should lastingly modify the terms of trade between the Mezzogiorno and the centre-north of Italy by reinforcing the former's productive capacity and the efficiency of its economic system. Thanks to Community intervention the Mezzogiorno should be capable of producing at a lower level of costs and prices. However, in view of the expected gains in productivity relatively few extra jobs would be created.

In the case of Portugal, a dynamic general equilibrium model was used to assess the overall efficiency of the Structural Funds over a long period. This assessment, incorporating increasing returns on public capital, predicted cumulative GDP growth of 5% to the year 2000 if the Funds were maintained at their 1993 level as a percentage of GDP in the 1994-2000 period. The acceleration of the growth rate due to the Structural Funds would be between 0.4 and 0.5% over an extended period. Private investment would increase by 1-1.5% of GDP per year, and public investment by 3.9-4.4%. Finally, assuming an annual long-term growth rate of 2.6% in the Community, per capita GDP in

Portugal would increase from 56% today to 63.7% in 2006, as against an increase to 57% without the Structural Funds.

Beyond these significant effects on both the demand and supply sides, the results of these macroeconomic investigations show the lessons to be drawn from the theoretical discussion earlier in this chapter: while expenditure on infrastructure and human capital appears relatively effective from all the studies, one cannot reach a definite conclusion on aid to industry.

5. The results of microeconomic assessment

These can be dealt with more briefly, not because they are any less important but because there is less systematic information on the microeconomic impact of EC structural intervention.

Three main aspects should nevertheless be noted. First, all the assessments of the reform mechanisms and their application, both in Objective 1 areas and in all the others concerned by the Funds, come to very favourable conclusions about the new approach. The effect of economic planning and multi-year budgeting has led to the selection of a set of coherent actions which seek to respond effectively to the regions' needs. Similarly, the policy of partnership, bringing together Community, national and regional authorities in the monitoring committees, allows for Community structural intervention to be adapted to the realities encountered whenever projects are set up.

Second, all financial indicators show that after three years of the reform, the funds available more or less match the sums budgeted for and that, more significant still - because they are linked to the state of progress on the ground - the sums actually paid out have reached 70% of the funds committed for Objective 1 regions and nearly 80% for Objective 3 and 4 regions.

Third, and by contrast with the above, the collection of microeconomic data, essential for a solid assessment of the efficiency of the Community's structural policies, has definitely fallen behind. The Commission services have developed indicators to measure the effects of structural policies. These range from physical indicators (infrastructure set up, numbers of people trained, etc.) to "intermediate" indicators (e.g. reduced transport costs following the building of a motorway with Community funds), and socio-economic indicators (evolution of per capita GDP in assisted regions, unemployment rates, evolution of production structures, numbers of firms set up, etc.). However, some technical difficulties remain in the measurement of these criteria.

6. Conclusion

Because of a lack of information, particularly at the microeconomic level, only tentative conclusions can be reached about the efficiency of the Structural Funds.

First, recent developments in economic growth theory suggest that the means adopted suit the objectives chosen. The Funds make a significant contribution in areas thought to be the potential sources of increasing returns. They may therefore constitute a determining factor in a cumulative process of growth which will help the less-developed regions to move towards the Community average.

Second, beyond a certain level of Fund involvement, their macroeconomic impact is significant. From the point of view of business-cycle (i.e. short-term) developments, the Funds enable growth rates to increase and external pressures to be partially eased, while excessive inflationary tendencies are avoided. The results of the assessments also show that the Structural Funds have a high *potential* efficiency (i.e. over longer periods), and that if this is exploited, the regions' catch-up rate will be increased.

Third, available microeconomic data are still insufficient, making it impossible to say whether there is a gap between the Funds' real and potential impact, or how large that gap might be.

Fourth, the reform of the Funds has helped very significantly to improve the efficiency of their planning, management and financing procedures. These improvements are substantial and signify considerable progress over the situation prevailing before the reform.

These conclusions should nevertheless be seen in a broader context. One must take account of the relationship between the Community's cohesion and convergence policies; of the compatibility between strict budgetary policy and the fulfilment of member-state commitments in terms of additionality and support for the growth process in the regions concerned; and, finally, of the possible need for accompanying industrial measures to enhance the overall efficiency of Community actions on the structural level. This raises three issues which bear directly or indirectly on the efficiency of the Structural Funds.

i) Should the goal of cohesion be subject to that of convergence, or vice versa? The answer may considerably influence the choice of macroeconomic policy and lead economies down different paths in search of growth.

ii) In the same connection, there is the question of additionality and support for public investment in countries which are, or will be, forced to adopt strict budgetary policies. There could be a conflict between budgetary discipline and respect for additionality. If the former is given priority, there will be positive effects on interest rates and consequently on private investment, but the effects of the Structural Funds will be reduced because they will simply replace investment which the state would have made in less stringent budgetary circumstances. In this event, the overall effect will be that the Structural Funds help to *support* growth, but not to increase it; and the same goes for supply effects. If, on the other hand, additionality is given priority, the Structural Funds will have a positive effect on growth and growth rates, but the lack of budgetary discipline and the non-fulfilment of political commitments could discourage private and foreign investors.

Part of the solution to this dilemma, as far as the Community is concerned, lies in the constitution of the Cohesion Fund provided for in the Maastricht Treaty. This should allow national economic policy-makers to adopt strict budgetary policies without being forced to weaken or reduce state development policies.

iii) As noted earlier, where returns are increasing overall, national rates of growth tend to be highest in the most developed countries, which have the highest levels of human capital, infrastructure and advanced production technology. The Structural Funds alone cannot reverse this trend. One might therefore ask whether accompanying industrial measures could not play a role in reinforcing and modernising production structures in ailing or less-developed regions.

This they could do by encouraging the quicker spread of technological progress and the establishment of industrial networks in expanding markets; by turning the most dynamic firms towards external markets and the diversification of their products in high-tech and higher-value-added market segments, and by enabling them to adopt new methods of management and industrial organisation; in a word, by supporting all these activities, which are particularly weak in the regions targeted by the Structural Funds, and ensuring that these regions effectively make up the economic ground between themselves and the rest of the Community.

All these problems must be solved before measures can be adopted which will permanently strengthen economic and social cohesion in the Community.

NOTES

1. The opinions expressed here are those of the authors and should not be attributed to the Commission of the European Communities. This chapter was translated from French by Peter Lomas.

References

Abraham-Frois, G. (1991), *Dynamique Economique*, Paris: Dalloz.

Aschauer, D. A. (1989), "Is public expenditure productive?", *Journal of Monetary Economics* 23 (2), March.

Barro, R. J. (1989), "Economic growth in a cross-section of countries", *NBER Working Paper* 3120.

- (1990), "Government spending in a simple model of endogenous growth", *Journal of Political Economy* 98 (5).

- (1991), "Economic growth in a cross-section of countries", *Quarterly Journal of Economics* 106.

Bertoldi, M. and P. Goybet (1992), "Politiques structurelles communautaires et croissance économique: quelques réflexions à la lumière de recherches récentes", mimeo.

Bradley, J., J. Fitz Gerald and I. Kearney (1992), *The Role of the Structural Funds: Analysis of Consequences for Ireland in the Context of 1992*, Policy Research Series No. 13, Dublin: Economic and Social Research Institute.

Bradley, J. and K. Whelan (1992), "Econometric modelling and technological change: a review of issues", in *MONITOR-SPEAR: The Quantitative Evaluation of the Impact of R&D Programmes*, Brussels: Commission of the European Communities.

Burmeister, E. and A. R. Dolbell (1970), *Mathematical Theories of Economic Growth*, London: Macmillan.

Commission of the European Communities (1989), *Guide to the Reform of the Community's Structural Funds*, Luxembourg: Office for Official Publications of the European Communities.

- (1991), *Annual Report on the Implementation of the Reform of the Structural Funds: 1989*, Luxembourg: Office for Official Publications of the European Communities.

- (1992), *Second Annual Report on the Implementation of the Reform of the Structural Funds: 1990*, Luxembourg: Office for Official Publications of the European Communities.

D'Antonio, M., R. Colaizzo and G. Leonello (1991), "An interregional CGE model, Mezzogiorno/Centre-North, for the Italian economy", mimeo, Final Report for Commission of the European Communities.

Ford and Poret (1991), "Infrastructures et productivité du secteur privé", *Revue Economique de l'OCDE*, automne.

Grossman, G. and E. Helpman (1989), "Growth and welfare in a small open economy", *NBER Working Paper* 2970.

- (1990), "Trade, innovation and growth", *American Economic Review* 80 (2).

Krugman, P. (1987), "Economic integration in Europe: some conceptual issues" in T. Padoa-Schioppa (ed.), *Efficiency, Stability and Equity*, Oxford: Oxford University Press.

- (1991), "Increasing returns and economic geography", *Journal of Political Economy* 99 (3).

Lordon, F. (1991), "Théories de la croissance: quelques développements récents", *Observations et Diagnostics Economiques* 36 & 37.

Lucas, R. E. (1988), "On the mechanics of economic development", *Journal of Monetary Economics* 22.

- (1990), "Why doesn't capital flow from rich to poor countries?", *American Economic Review* 80 (2).

Munnell, G. (1991), "Why has productivity growth declined? Productivity and public investment", *New England Economic Review*.

Pereira, A. M. (1991), "A dynamic general equilibrium analysis of EC Structural Funds (with application to Portugal)", mimeo, Final Report for Commission of the European Communities.

Rivera-Batiz, L. and Romer, P. M. (1991), "Economic integration and endogenous growth", *Quarterly Journal of Economics* 106 (2).

Romer, P. M. (1986), "Increasing returns and long-run growth", *Journal of Political Economy* 94 (5).

- (1990a), "Endogenous technological change", *Journal of Political Economy* 98 (5).

- (1990b), "Are non-convexities important for understanding growth?", *American Economic Review* 80 (2).

Shaw, G. K. (1992), "Policy implications of endogenous growth theory", *Economic Journal* 102, May.

Solow, R. M. (1956), "A contribution to the theory of economic growth", *Quarterly Journal of Economics* 71.

15 The role of the European Investment Bank

Eugenio Greppi

1. Introduction

The European Investment Bank contributes to the promotion of Community structural policies - in the first place cohesion policy, but also environment, transport, energy and industry policies. The financing which the EIB provides is long-term, generally between 8 and 12 years for industrial and service ventures and up to 20 years or more for infrastructure. Terms are flexible and can be tailored to borrowers' needs; rates can be fixed, with or without a revision date, or variable; grace periods on capital repayments can be modulated; and there is a range of alternatives as to the choice of currency.

The EIB has always financed its operations in the EC primarily by raising funds on international capital markets and without imposing any burden on the Community budget. It has a "triple-A" credit rating which enables it to raise funds on the best terms, and the cost advantages derived from its high international credit standing are passed on to borrowers. This can be an important advantage to business in less-developed regions, and to small and medium-sized enterprises in particular, as these are less likely to have access to funds on the best terms on the international market.

The level of Bank activity has been rising significantly in recent years. It reached about 15.3bn Ecu in 1991. Most lending is for operations within the Community, which grew at an average annual rate of 12.5% in real terms between 1987 and 1991, reaching about 14.4bn Ecu in 1991.

2. The Bank's role in regional development

The EIB supports investment in lagging regions as long as it meets quality criteria, basically designed to select the most appropriate projects. Investment financed by the EIB should also be compatible with other Community policies, particularly those in the environmental and competition spheres. Compromising on these matters would ultimately slow down the full participation of those regions in the single European market.

2.1 Quantitative aspects

Financing the economic growth of the less-developed areas of the Community has been the EIB's dominant objective throughout its existence. In 1991, signed loans in assisted regions accounted for 63% of aggregate financing, or 8.5bn Ecu. Since the reform of the Structural Funds in 1989, 23bn Ecu has been made available for financing projects in regional development areas, representing a capital investment of the order of 78bn Ecu.

The Bank is a co-financing institution which is permitted to lend only a fraction of the cost of each project. In 1991 it co-financed about 5.6% of investment in the Community, reaching a significantly higher share in less-developed areas such as Greece, Portugal (23% of gross capital formation), some regions of Spain and the Mezzogiorno of Italy. Since gross capital formation statistics include sectors such as housing and social infrastructure which are not eligible for EIB funding, these figures understate the Bank's contribution to investment in eligible sectors.

The traditional breakdown of the Bank's activity is between infrastructure and productive investment, the latter often being identified with the private sector. This distinction is becoming somewhat artificial owing to increasing private involvement in infrastructure financing. In 1991, the private sector accounted for about 52% of investment financed within the Community. In the energy and infrastructure fields, 30% of projects financed were within the private sector, whereas only a few years ago funding in these fields centred almost exclusively on public-sector projects. Similarly, 88% of financing for projects in industry and services, and all investment covered by so called global loans, fell within the private sector.

2.2 Qualitative aspects: infrastructure to complement productive activity

The scope of Bank action has extended over the years from basic infrastructure such as road and rail links and the supply of energy and water to more advanced areas such as telecommunications. Whatever the type of infrastructure to be financed, however, the Bank has always been careful to ensure that requirements of technical viability and economic interest are met. Infrastructure investment financed by the Bank must respond to existing or projected demand conditions, be they for waste treatment, telecommunications or road transport. Careful demand analysis is needed to ensure that infrastructural provision actually plays a complementary role to business activity and helps productive investment in lagging regions.

In 1991 EIB financing of infrastructure for regional development amounted to 4.4bn Ecu,[1] or 52% of all such projects in the Community. Between 1987 and 1991 infrastructure financed by the Bank in less-favoured regions amounted to 16.4bn Ecu,[2] out of a total of 31.8bn.

2.3 Qualitative aspects: the enterprise sector

The Bank's lending to the enterprise sector was 32% of total lending in the less-developed regions, or about 2.7bn Ecu in 1991. This lending helped to finance some 8.1bn worth of private investment. Bank loans are made available to firms either directly - for large-scale initiatives - or indirectly, through financial intermediaries, for smaller ventures mainly promoted by small and medium-sized enterprises. The benefits of Bank lending in less-favoured regions are therefore widely spread. They address both large firms, which are more likely to bring lagging regions into contact with high-technology and international markets, and the network of small and medium-sized enterprises, thereby supporting local entrepreneurial resources. About 52% of lending to industry and services in lagging regions, or 1.4bn Ecu, has gone to over 4,000 small and medium-sized enterprises. Tourism has been the main beneficiary in the service sector, reflecting the importance the EIB attaches to the development of tourist resources in many of the less-developed regions.

2.4 Co-operation with the Structural Funds

The EIB has always co-operated with the Commission in furthering Community policies inside and outside the Community. In 1988, the Single Act established a framework for the EIB and the Structural Funds to work together. This framework was later made explicit in detailed EC Regulations. In line with this, the Bank has worked in close co-operation with the Commission to ensure that the European Regional Development Fund and itself are used as complementary instruments to pursue regional-policy objectives.

Operating guidelines have been developed to combine loans and grants in an appropriate way. The underlying principle is that the loan/subsidy combination should be modulated according to the income-generating capacity of each project and the gravity of particular regional problems. Thus subsidies should be concentrated on low-revenue infrastructure in more seriously-lagging regions, and loans on industry, services and revenue-producing infrastructure or on regions suffering from less acute problems.

In order to guarantee optimal co-operation, the EIB was associated with the Commission in the establishment of the Community Support Frameworks. Since the reform of the Structural Funds, out of the 23bn Ecu of investment for regional development, 20bn was financed in regions eligible for the Structural Funds, of which 53% in Objective 1 regions. Almost two-thirds of loans financed in Objective 1, 2 and 5b regions were consistent with the Community Support Frameworks' priorities (86% in Objective 1 regions). Of these, one-third were supplemented by ERDF grants. Since the presentation of the "Delors-II" package, the Commission and the EIB have been examining how to improve their co-ordination and the loan/grant combination, as well as activities under the Cohesion Fund provided for in the Maastricht Treaty.

3. Operating procedures and the Bank's catalytic role

The EIB can be easily approached at a relatively early stage in a project. Promoters often contact the Bank for a preliminary view of a project's eligibility for EIB financing.

International tendering is always expected in sectors where this is required by Community regulations and strongly encouraged in sectors where international procurement is not compulsory. The effect of this is to keep costs low, help in diffusing up-to-date production technology and contribute to the integration of the international market. The EIB's purpose, which sets it somewhat apart from a commercial institution, is to see that projects are successfully carried out, not just that loans are repaid. Projects are therefore monitored after the approval of loans, to make sure that work is completed on schedule and - as far as possible - that their potential is fulfilled.

Last but not least, the reputation that the EIB has acquired over the years in assessing project risks and rewards, together with its financial strength, have encouraged other lenders to provide financial resources to support certain operations. The Bank has therefore acted not just as a provider of funds but also as a catalyst for other resources - not always purely financial. This role could be reinforced by the establishment of an equity facility in favour of SMEs, mainly in assisted regions, an idea now under consideration.

4. Conclusion

Severe regional imbalances persist in the Community, and economic change almost invariably brings with it the need to adjust local economies that are affected by structural changes. Therefore much work remains to be done to give the people of the less-favoured areas economic opportunities similar to those available in more wealthy regions of the Community.

The obstacles on the way to achieving this objective should not be underestimated. They include inadequate planning and implementation capacities among public administrations in lagging regions, the lack of an internationally-minded entrepreneurial class and the weakness of local financial systems. All these factors combine to make returns on investment lower and riskier. This risk can be reduced by the complementary activities of the Structural Funds and the EIB.

Because of the EIB's diversified lending experience and its institutional position, the combination of services it can provide is somewhat unique. Its most valuable asset is its expertise. Over more than thirty years of activity, the Bank has financed investment across the entire Community and in a very broad spectrum of sectors. It has accumulated a stock of experience which is extremely useful when assessing new projects. Secondly, as a Community institution, the Bank can put to use its familiarity with the making of Community policy and its extensive network of contacts. Thirdly, as a financial institution, it can rely on the network of European banking organisations, to many of which it is bound by long-lasting co-operative relationships. Finally, as a provider of long-term funds, it can rely on the experience gained in years of contacts with a unique customer base. This includes central and local government authorities as well as several major public and private enterprises, some of them at the leading edge of technological development.

In an increasingly-open European economy and with increased structural Community resources targeted on lagging regions, potential funding sources are numerous. A great deal of points of entry into this complex system of financial options and resources are now open to public and private promoters in lagging regions.

The task of regional development is a challenge to Community institutions and to European governments. The involvement of private capital is also essential to the building of a more cohesive European economy. The Maastricht Treaty on European Union strengthened the EIB's role in economic cohesion "for the benefit of the poorer regions". Together with other policy objectives such as European networks, the environment, and the increased competitiveness of European industry, the development of the Union calls for significant investment. Through its diversified experience and its privileged institutional position, the EIB can provide an essential contribution to the attainment of these objectives.

NOTES

1. Excluding energy.

2. Excluding energy.

Index

Index

Index